Horse Trading in the Age of Cars

Gender Relations in the American Experience
Joan E. Cashin and Ronald G. Walters, Series Editors

Somewhere West of Laramie

SOMEWHERE west of Laramie there's a broncho-busting, steer-roping girl who knows what I'm talking about.

She can tell what a sassy pony, that's a cross between greased lightning and the place where it hits, can do with eleven hundred pounds of steel and action when he's going high, wide and handsome.

The truth is—the Playboy was built for her.

Built for the lass whose face is brown with the sun when the day is done of revel and romp and race.

She loves the cross of the wild and the tame.

There's a savor of links about that car—of laughter and lilt and light—a hint of old loves—and saddle and quirt. It's a brawny thing—yet a graceful thing for the sweep o' the Avenue.

Step into the Playboy when the hour grows dull with things gone dead and stale.

Then start for the land of real living with the spirit of the lass who rides, lean and rangy, into the red horizon of a Wyoming twilight.

JORDAN

JORDAN MOTOR CAR COMPANY, Inc., Cleveland, Ohio

Horse Trading in the Age of Cars

Men in the Marketplace

Steven M. Gelber

The Johns Hopkins University Press
Baltimore

The Johns Hopkins University Press
2715 North Charles Street
Baltimore, Maryland 21218-4363
www.press.jhu.edu

Library of Congress Cataloging-in-Publication Data

Horse trading in the age of cars : men in the marketplace / Steven M. Gelber.
    p.   cm. — (Gender relations in the American experience)
    Includes bibliographical references and index.
    ISBN-13: 978-0-8018-8997-4 (hardcover : alk. paper)
    ISBN-10: 0-8018-8997-9 (hardcover : alk. paper)
    1. Automobiles—Purchasing.   I. Title.
    TL162.G45 2008
    381'.45629222—dc22   2008021238

A catalog record for this book is available from the British Library.

Frontispiece: Ned Jordan's "broncho-busting, steer-roping girl" may
have raced her own car across the Wyoming prairie in 1923, but it is
likely a man assisted her in buying it. "Somewhere West of Laramie,"
Saturday Evening Post, 23 June 1923, 129.

Special discounts are available for bulk purchases of this book.
For more information, please contact Special Sales at
410-516-6936 or specialsales@press.jhu.edu.

The Johns Hopkins University Press uses environmentally friendly
book materials, including recycled text paper that is composed of at
least 30 percent post-consumer waste, whenever possible. All of our
book papers are acid-free, and our jackets and covers are printed on
paper with recycled content.

In loving memory of Catherine Bell,
my wife, my companion, my colleague

Contents

Preface xi

Introduction: The Cowboy and the Flapper 1

1   Horse Trading: Duping the Buyer 4
    *Horses as Masculine Symbols / The Manly Art of Horse Trading / The
    Reputation of Horse Traders / The Horse Trading Business / Horse Trading
    as a Game / The Rules of the Game / Hiding Faults / Warranties*

2   Retailing: Satisfying the Buyer 25
    *Manufactured Transportation: Carriages and Bicycles / Negotiated
    (Discriminatory) Prices / Single (Democratic) Prices / Satisfaction
    Guaranteed or Your Money Cheerfully Refunded*

3   Cars: Joining the New Marketplace 41
    *Coachmen to Chauffeurs: The Male Lineage / Cars in Stores / One Posted
    Price to All / One-Price by Law / Advertising List Prices*

4   Used Cars: Undermining the New Marketplace 63
    *Origins / Trade-In Allowances and Over-Allowances / Controlling
    Over-Allowances / Cheating: "Buyers Are Liars"—And So Are Sellers*

5   The Triumph of the Price Pack: Selling the Deal 88
    *Price Padding with the Pack / After-Sales Packing / The 1950s: ". . . for
    Thieves to Sell to Mental Defectives" / Advertising and Blitz Marketing /
    Posting a Price / The Great Warranty War*

6   Bad Guys 115
    *The Car Seller's Career: Nasty, Brutish, and Short / The Sales Game:
    Tactics / The Sales Game: Strategy / Car Dealers' Reputation and
    Character*

7   Bargaining and Gender 138
     *"The Great American Sport of Bargaining" / Brokers / Cars and
     Masculinity / Women as Buyers and Sellers*

     Epilogue: Still Horse Trading in the Internet Age 164
     The Dealer's Cost / Make Me an Offer!

     Notes 175
     Index 219

     Illustrations follow page 114

Preface

My work on this project benefited from the contributions numerous friends, colleagues, and students who both supported and challenged me. More than one thought it odd that I should be exploring the ways in which culture constrained economics when so much of my previous work had focused on the ways that economics constructed culture. My only response to their eyebrows cocked in curiosity is that "I call them as I see them." I started with the problem, why do we buy cars in such an anachronistic, anomalous, and annoying way? The answer emerged from the data, and the fact that it does not fit the patterns I have described in previous historical analyses is just one more piece of evidence that while history may not treat our preconceived notions kindly, it is always interesting. I hope that is as true for the reader as it has been for me.

The thesis may be different, but my indebtedness to libraries and their staffs remains constant. I know that my school's library, despite the fact that it was recently demolished to make way for an "information commons," will continue to house the kinds of professionals who have worked with me on this book. Special thanks are in order for Cindy Bradley, Carolee Bird, and Helene Lafrance for their assistance in finding obscure material both real and virtual. I also wish to thank the staff of the Henry Ford Museum and Greenfield Village Research Center, now the Benson Ford Research Center, whose knowledge of the holdings of the Ford archives and whose helpful cooperation make doing work in Dearborn a researcher's delight. In addition, I am grateful to Marc Stertz, publisher of *AutoExec* magazine and the National Automobile Dealers Association for allowing me access to their library. Though parts of this book may be critical of the retail car industry, their cooperation ensured that any criticism was tempered by a much clearer appreciation of the dealers' problems and perspectives.

My faculty colleagues Nancy Unger and Bill Sundstrom were kind enough to read versions of the manuscript. Their comments and suggestions made the final product better than it would have been, especially when they did not agree with my conclusions. Finally, I wish to acknowledge the support of Don Dodson, Vice-Provost for Academic Affairs at Santa Clara University, for his continuing support for faculty scholarship, always a challenge in an environment focused on undergraduate education.

A note on gendered language: This is a study about the role of gender in the marketplace. As a scholar of sex roles, I am acutely aware of the exclusionary implications of inclusionary masculine terminology. Prior to 1980, women were essentially nonexistent in automobile sales positions and only slightly more common as car buyers. As I discuss in chapter 6, after 1980 the percentage of women car sales staff grew, but even then it was from virtually zero to only somewhere between 3 and 8 percent. At the same time, however, the number of female car owners did increase significantly. Nevertheless, when women went to buy a car they often took men along to help them. For these reasons I have used male pronouns and variations of the word "salesman" when referring to car sellers and buyers prior to 1980. I have tried to use gender-neutral language when referring to the post-eighties time period. I hope that any discomfort that many modern readers will find with the gendered vocabulary of the earlier era will serve the purpose of reminding them how masculinized the selling and buying of personal transportation has been.

Horse Trading in the Age of Cars

The Cowboy and the Flapper

In 1923 American magazines ran an advertisement for the Jordan "Playboy" that featured a woman driving an open two-seat automobile style known as a roadster. A few years later the indomitable Nancy Drew and her chums would scoot about their detective business in a roadster that followed in the tire tracks of the spirited young woman driving the Playboy as she sped across the prairie "somewhere west of Laramie." A cowboy on horseback raced alongside but slightly behind the car. The modern woman was driving into the twentieth century, leaving the horse-riding man of the nineteenth century in her dust. The image was a powerful one, and the copy, composed by the company's president, Ned Jordan, is considered the best early example of advertising based on promoting a lifestyle rather than the product itself. In this case, the female driver was described in freewheeling prose as a spontaneous sportswoman who was perfectly at home driving a car model named the Playboy. A blend of fin-de-siècle Gibson Girl and 1920s flapper, she was a symbol of the contemporary woman who was willing not only to take on male roles but to take on men themselves. (See frontispiece.)

When the ad appeared, the horse was already history. Yet riding unseen in the passenger seat (or maybe hidden back in the rumble seat) was the spirit of the cowboy, and it would emerge when the prospective buyer entered a new-car showroom. Behind the wheel she may have been the very embodiment of the new woman, but when she (or more likely her father or male friend) went to purchase an automobile, she would step back into a retail arena that would in all respects be more familiar to her cowboy road mate than to her college room-mate. Rather than buying her car in a retail store for an advertised price the way she bought her cloche hat, she or her surrogate would have to haggle over the trade-in allowance on her superannuated Playboy and quite possibly bargain over the price of the fresh new mechanical boyfriend she was buying to replace it.

The persistence of wrangling over car prices is an example of a gender-oriented practice that had become so deeply embedded in economic relation-ships that it was able to defy the historical forces that changed everything around it. While the meaning and methods of most retail sales shifted in the second half of the nineteenth century to a female-centered, nondiscriminatory, rationally modern form, auto retailing would take a different road. Car dealing continued the lead of the preindustrial marketplace haggling that characterized almost all retailing but that had been refined into a dark art by the men who engaged in horse trading.

Both buyers and sellers grumbled about the lack of a one-price system in au-tomotive retailing where neither the buyer nor the seller could know what a car would cost until they had negotiated an agreement. The bargaining often in-volved not only the price of the new car and the value of the buyer's old car (the trade-in), but also the cost of financing the new car and other options, fees, and services. While negotiating is not in and of itself an irrational way to establish a price, within the context of contemporary consumer society it is an anomaly that has irritated consumers who are unfamiliar and uncomfortable with bargaining and has made car dealers and their sales staffs both angry and self-conscious at being the butt of constant jokes. Nevertheless, the system—technically rational but culturally exotic—has survived with no end in sight.

Automotive exceptionalism began because men wanted to own an auto with the latest innovations and needed to trade in their current cars to offset the high cost of new ones. Dealers, under pressure from the factories, indirectly cut the manufacturer's suggested retail price (MSRP) by offering to buy back trade-ins for more than they were worth on the resale market (over-allowances). The pro-cess of swapping an old ride for a new one and making up the difference in their values with a cash payment was an established practice in horse trading. Car buyers demanded that car sellers continue that tradition by accepting their old vehicles as partial payment for new ones. When the dealers acquiesced, they ensured that a form of retailing that had disappeared from almost every other product would continue with cars.

Peter Stearns has recently adopted the label "behavioral" for historians who seek to explain contemporary beliefs and actions as artifacts of past conditions.[1] Stearns's approach complements the earlier work of economist Paul A. David, who coined the term "path dependence." Path dependence suggests that some irrational economic choices are not based on psychology (as behavioral economists would have it), but occur because initial technological decisions (such as the width of railroad tracks) become standards that no single participant can change.[2] This is not to say that present decisions are slaves to the past. Behavior is affected as much or more by current conditions as by history. Nevertheless, in some cases, such as the retailing of automobiles, patterns set generations ago for reasons that may have made more sense then than they seem to now continue to shape conduct in ways that appear to defy common sense. The way men bought and sold horses became the model for the way people (mostly men) bought and sold cars—despite a multitude of reasons why it would have been more rational for cars to be retailed in the same fashion as other manufactured goods.

The history of car buying is not a history of inertia. It is rather the history of a complex set of interactions between cultural and economic forces that actively worked against the express desire of both the public and the industry to have automotive retailing conform to general retail standards. Historians confronted with long-term continuity have to respond like ethnographic field workers who are told: "We do it this way because this is the way it has always been done." They have to try to determine if this is in fact "the way it has always been done," and if so, to explain why it did not change. Buyers are not doomed in perpetuity to haggle over the price of cars. Powerful external forces can and do change even deeply ingrained behavior. Yet the pattern of men bargaining over the things they rode on survived the transition to the things they rode in, and it prevailed through shortages and surpluses, wars, depressions, two major bouts of government regulation, the growth of a female customer base, and most recently, online sales. Change may yet come, but the external force will have to be greater than the old century's never-ending complaints—and even a new century's Internet.

CHAPTER ONE

Horse Trading

Duping the Buyer

It may be useful to think of the cultural history of the buying and selling of personal transportation as a meander in the river of retail history. At some time in the distant past, for reasons that are not altogether clear, men developed a pattern of playful hard bargaining when they dealt in horses. Before the mid-nineteenth century, buyers and sellers, both male and female, haggled over the prices of all marketplace goods, but male horse trading became something of a game. For many it was bit of fun in which each party sought not a fair exchange but an unfair advantage. The continuation of horse-trading forms in car retailing is a meander in the otherwise smooth flow of retailing mainstream (rather than a cutoff oxbow lake) because automobiles are such a large component in the modern family's budget. The cost is what makes bargaining over personal transportation more than a quaint reminder of bygone behavior like hunting trips or quilting bees. Buying the family's most expensive manufactured product is a retail transaction that still bears the marks of the gendered performance that was horse trading.

Horses as Masculine Symbols

When horses were the primary means of personal transportation, men judged other men by every aspect of horse ownership. If a man could not exercise his ownership responsibilities in a masculine way, then maybe he did not really own the horse, mused the *New York Times* in 1889—maybe the horse owned him: "The man who has bought a horse which he is afraid to ride lest he should fall off, afraid not to ride lest he should be called a coward, and afraid to sell lest he should be a loser, is literally a slave and not the master of the beast."[1] Men wanted their horses to project a public image of themselves as powerful, knowledgeable, and shrewd. "Everybody considers a compliment to his horse as fully equivalent to one to himself," noted a Boston lawyer in 1861.[2]

Being a respected horseman was a multifaceted role that included understanding horses well enough to at least talk a good game. "I think I have never met a man who didn't feel it necessary to his reputation to pretend, on occasion, that he knew something of horses," noted Charles Dickens, who understood that men judged men by how well they judged horses.[3] The idlers along Broadway would eye the rigs driving by and scorn the man who could not "'keep it up' in proper style."[4] Since this particular observation came from the *National Police Gazette*, a favorite of pool hall and barbershop loiterers, the double entendre may well have been intentional. It followed that a man who had a good eye for horseflesh was also a man who had a good eye for the fair sex, and nineteenth-century bystanders assumed that a man driving a fast trotter was apt to have a "pretty bit of muliebrity" sitting by his side.[5]

Nineteenth-century men of all classes understood the symbolic parallel meanings of horses and women. A fine horse, like a fine wife, was a public representation of male wealth and power, and as sociologist Thorstein Veblen recognized, both could be forms of conspicuous consumption. Writing in 1899, just a couple of years too early to include automobiles in his commentary on upperclass wastefulness, Veblen argued that horses were more than an expression of wealth—they were also an extension of the man himself. A man's horse, he wrote, was a means to "express his own dominating individuality," especially when it gratified "the owner's sense of aggression and dominance" by "outstripping his neighbor's" horse in a race.[6]

Veblen's characterization of horses conflates their masculine and feminine meanings. The feminine horse was a possession under the control its male owner, who could relate to it as he would to a female companion. For example, in 1868, reminiscing about his favorite horse named Vix (as in vixen), an army colonel remembered how "with an immense excitement" she fancy-stepped down Fifth Avenue so prettily that "few people allowed us to pass without admiring notice." He recalled that their relationship "went on for three years, always together," that they had their differences from time to time when "she was pettish and I was harsh," but that they always made up to be close friends again.[7] The colonel's commentary was unusual only in the fact that he acknowledged his horse's biological sex as well as its gendered cultural meaning. Horsemen admired their fellows who were brave or foolish enough to ride stallions rather than mares or geldings, but they usually ignored the sex of their own horses and focused on the animal's performance. That way fast female horses could have masculine meaning. In 1923, after cars had replaced horses, Alfred Stieglitz sardonically titled a photograph of a castrated horse "Spiritual America." Before the turn of the century, however, both male and female horses could act as culturally gendered female status symbols and culturally gendered male ego extensions. In either sense, the horse was more than a means to get from here to there; it was a reflection of its owner.

The Manly Art of Horse Trading

Decisions about self-representation involve complex social and psychological variables that make it very difficult to act rationally and very easy to respond emotionally. Because horses were status symbols and ego extensions, the process of buying and selling them also took on special meaning in an environment that admired bargaining skills. Competitive interpersonal commerce of all kinds struck foreigners as peculiarly American. Commenting on his two-year sojourn in the United States, Englishman Frederick Marryat noted with some surprise that he had actually seen American *girls* swapping hats on a riverboat. By recounting a backwoods joke about a man who boasted that his two sons were so clever at bartering that if he locked them in a room without a cent in their pockets an hour later they both would have made two dollars, Marryat made it clear that bartering was "the ruling passion of the country" in 1839.[8]

Pride in bartering, or "swapping," as Americans called it, had a special place in male culture. Boys at a horse fair in western Georgia in 1925 would swap coats or hats just so they would "be a-doin'" like their fathers. For these boys swapping was an introduction to the methods and mores of the market system.

For their fathers it was an exercise in the principles of masculine economics. Every man who traded wanted to believe that he had gotten the better of the deal. A visitor reported, "No matter how badly he may have been beaten, pride would not permit him to acknowledge it."[9] Thus, for men it was not merely what they rode but how they obtained what they rode that contributed to their sense of pride. It was not enough to receive fair value; each side in the deal wanted to come out ahead. There was a bragging winner and a shamed loser.

According to an 1855 account, a man who had unknowingly bought a horse with "heaves" (a severe and noisy pulmonary disorder) became the laughing stock of his town, with word of his poor choice spreading faster than the winded nag could move. "I was so much ashamed," the buyer related, that in order to avoid the neighbors, "I took a roundabout road to the stable . . . and dismounted with a chastened spirit." He finally decided to sell the sickly beast after a "colored person" stopped to help him when the horse broke down and announced, "I heerd about you, and you hos. Dats de hos dats got de heaves so bad."[10]

The only thing as damaging to a white man's ego as being laughed at by a "colored" man would be being laughed at by a woman, especially over a horse trade. Prior to the twentieth century, men believed that women knew as little about horses as they would later believe they knew about cars. Women who rode or drove horses were considered slightly daring, and women who bought horses committed an act alien to their sex. Dealers, it was said, hated female buyers because they did not know what to look for in a purchase and were invariably unhappy with the lack of perfection in any horse they chose. They would then badmouth the dealer unless he returned their money, and when he did, he would find that the female buyer had ruined the horse so that it was no longer saleable to a knowledgeable horseman.[11]

Horse trading with a woman was a classic double bind; if you cheated her, you were not a gentleman; if you were cheated by her, you were not a man.[12] The man in one unusual account of misleading a woman when selling a horse was overwhelmed with remorse and got his just deserts when the woman was unexpectedly able to control the unruly beast.[13] The gender-affirming nature of horse trading is illustrated by the comment of a "rascally" dealer who "resolves to 'take in' the next greenhorn of a man-milliner" who came his way.[14] By combining the naïve "greenhorn" with the homosexual "man-milliner," the dealer manages to convey both his contempt for the novice untutored in the art of horse trading and his assumption that a male so unskilled was not fully masculine.

The Reputation of Horse Traders

The man who bought a horse from a trader in the nineteenth century felt exactly like the man who bought automobile from a used-car dealer in the twentieth. He proudly but anxiously took his family out for a drive, fearing that first sign of trouble that would mark him as a sucker. Even though being "done" in a horse trade was "the most common of misfortunes," explained an industry observer in 1895, it still carried with it "a measure of disgrace."[15] Ordinary men knew they were no match for professional dealers because horse traders, like lawyers, were "as a class, great rogues"—but what choice did they have when it came time to buy?[16] They could only take the advice that Cicero gave his friend Trebatius Testa, who was going abroad: "Look out in Britain that you are not cheated by the charioteers [horse traders]."[17]

The seamy reputation of horse traders permeated the equestrian economy. William Henry Herbert, an observer of the New York demimonde in the Gilded Age, said, "There cannot be conceived a race of more arrant cheats and swindlers than the whole set of jockeys, grooms and horse dealers." Herbert, who also wrote as "Frank Forester," warned that horse dealers not only cheated but also positively reveled in their cheating. Wall Street brokers and steamboat commodores also defrauded their business associates, he noted, and delighted in their wrongdoing, but at least each had the common decency to do so in his "own secret soul." Men who engaged in horse trading bragged about their dishonesty, however, and expected to "gain éclat or good report by its publicity."[18]

At best, horse traders were viewed as clever scamps or wise rogues from whom one could learn some expensive lessons about life and the marketplace. At worst, they were such conscienceless scoundrels that the term "horse trader" was a universally understood synonym for moral reprobate. For example, in 1863 when the Democratic Party wanted to depict Republican President Abraham Lincoln as both a buffoon and untrustworthy, they produced a bogus election circular in the form of a "public announcement." The notice informed the residents of Springfield that Lincoln would soon be leaving Washington and returning home, where he would once again be available to swap jokes and horses.[19] A horse-swapping man was assumed to be dishonest until shown otherwise.[20] In fact, there was a widely held and only half-joking belief that engaging in horse trading would turn a saint into a sinner. Even members of the notably honest Quaker commercial community engaged in dissimulation when they traded horses. A stranger who stopped by a Quaker's farm in 1894 said he had heard the man wanted to sell a horse and was able to strike a bargain with the farmer. The buyer soon returned, complaining that he had bought the horse as a draft animal, but it would not pull as the Quaker had promised. The farmer said that he had promised no such thing and explained that what he had said was, "Pull! I wish thee could see him pull."[21]

Nobody—not your closest neighbor, your best friend, your church brethren, not even the minister himself—could be trusted in a horse trade.[22] The very term "jockey" (which prior to the twentieth century meant professional dealer as well as professional rider) was also a verb that meant to cheat, and horse traders were represented as the incarnation of all that was corrupt in society.[23] Boosters of Penn Yan, Pennsylvania, admitted that their town had not always been a salubrious place to live. Not too many years prior to 1855, they acknowledged, Penn Yan had been the location of gambling, drinking, horse trading, "and the other proclivities which go to make up an evil reputation."[24] In other words, the real Penn Yan was like the fictional town in an 1870 children's story where instead of going to church on Sunday, the men "got drunk, or played cards for money, or swapped horses,—those who had any horses to swap and those who had none lounged round to see the others swap, and help do the swearing."[25] If there was a murder in a town and the police needed to round up some suspects, an itinerant horse trader was a good bet.[26] If a novelist wanted to depict a lowlife who would starve his own family rather than work, he would make the man a horse swapper, and if the village wiseacres wanted to play a joke by running a useless fool for a meaningless office, they would nominate the town horse dealer.[27]

In an age when popular opinion about a man's moral values and consequent standing in the eyes of God was taken seriously, horse trading was an almost sure sign of depravity and damnation. Evangelists preached against whiskey drinking and horse trading as they poured "hot shot" into camp meetings.[28] A family man who gave up cursing and drinking nevertheless despaired of salvation because, as he explained to the minister, "I cannot trade horses and be honest and I won't make a profession unless I can live up to it."[29] Because it was "next door to impossible" to sell a horse without cheating and lying, there was no doubt about the ultimate fate of a horse trader's soul "unless indeed Providence has arranged for him a special dispensation."[30] Providence was disinclined to hand out such dispensations, according to a 1911 anecdote in which Saint Peter welcomed an honest circulation manager to heaven by observing that their one horse swapper had been there for twenty years and was becoming conceited.[31]

The public's generally poor regard for horse dealers was reinforced in the second half of the nineteenth century by the close association between Gypsies and horse trading.[32] The vernacular term "gyp" (cheat), used both as a noun and a verb, is a truncation of Gypsy and continued to be applied to shady car dealers long after its ethno-occupational origins had faded. Americans generally recognized two distinct cultural subgroups, both of which they called Gypsies (a name that derives from the Roma's putative origin in Egypt). One group was made up of the more traditional Roma, the dark-skinned central Europeans of Indo-Asian origin who lived a nomadic lifestyle and engaged in small-time trading, crafts, fortune telling, and, according to popular belief, petty crime. The members of the second group were ethnically Irish and referred to themselves as Travelers, although outsiders called them Gypsies. They followed a lifestyle very similar to the Roma. Because both groups were nomadic, handy with horses, spoke a distinct argot, and lived both literally and legally on the margins of society, the mainstream public often failed to distinguish between them.[33] Almost any itinerant horse trader might be called a Gypsy, and by extrapolation all small-scale dealers were tarred by the quasi-ethnic prejudice that linked Gypsies and horse trading.

The Horse Trading Business

The tar brush of dishonesty did not mark every professional horse trader, however. The most trustworthy horse marketers were the large-scale dealers who sold to mines, drayage companies, the military, and other mass consumers of horseflesh. They tended to operate like most other business suppliers filling big orders with specialized products. They signed contracts specifying quantity, quality, and price, and delivered the goods at the designated time with the understanding that the terms of the contract were enforceable in court. The same generally held true for the field agents who bought horses for these large dealers from farmers and breeders.[34] These, however, were not the men who captured the public imagination.

The popular culture of horse trading was constructed from the tall tales, humor, and war stories about two men and a horse or two. Smaller scale dealers fell into two broad categories generally called "road traders" and "barn traders." Road traders were sometimes the storied Yankee peddlers who sold light manufactured goods farm-to-farm in the eighteenth and early nineteenth centuries, stocking a few extra horses along with their clocks and pots.[35] Others were exclusively horse traders who went out on a circuit with a string of animals, continually swapping for new ones, collecting small cash differences on each trade, selling when they could, buying when they had to, and living from day to day by their wit and wile. Given their propensity for trickery, road traders tended to avoid returning to particular farms and towns—at least until their previous customers had time to cool off.

Barn traders, on the other hand, worked out of a fixed location, usually a livery stable, which was an all-purpose horse and carriage repair shop, public garage, and rental agency. Some village barn traders might refrain from taking gross advantage of their customers because they were dealing with members of their own communities. "Po Boy" Jenkins, a Georgia barn trader in the 1920s, explained: "I wanted to leave my customers satisfied and make a profit. I wasn't like a gypsy." The Irish Gypsies would "cheat the hell out of a farmer" and be gone, but "I was here permanent," he said, and would make good if anything were wrong.[36] Jenkins's willingness to stand behind his sales was an admirable but not widely shared trait. Most barn traders reasoned that the men who bought horses from them "ought to know what they are doing; and if they do not, they should be taught through severe lessons."[37]

Urban small-scale traders tended to cluster in horse market neighborhoods. Some of them may have been trustworthy, established businessmen, but many were fly-by-night swindlers who would rent space for a few days. These semi-itinerant dealers would advertise horses for sale by "recent widows" or a "gentleman going abroad" and sell poor-quality horses to men who thought they were getting a great bargain. Any warranties they provided meant nothing when they moved on.[38] In New York City, the area around Bull's Head Tavern at Twenty-fourth Street and Third Avenue was a particularly well-known example of this kind of market. Working on commission, "cappers" roamed through the crowds, looking for likely buyers and steering them toward particular dealers.[39] Brooklyn had its version of the Bull's Head market on Halsey Street, where even more disreputable dealers sold animals so far gone they could hardly stand on their remaining three legs.[40]

Horse Trading as a Game

Like saloons and pool halls, horse trading settings were venues for the display of male culture. Men were buying and selling equine representations of themselves on a one-to-one basis in a way that they understood to be a contest. The game element in horse trading took on particular importance in liminal spaces. Men who met casually to deal in horses tended to view the occasion as entertainment as much as economics. Militia muster days, court days, national holidays, public hangings, and even Sundays, provided an opportunity for men to swap horses.[41] Prior to 1900, said one observer, women used the time between church services to gossip; young people went off to the graveyard to talk of "things not in the sermon"; and men took the time to swap horses, even though it was the Sabbath.[42] Horse swapping, like whiskey drinking, was sinful, and a sure way of denigrating a rival minister was to accuse him of doing both.[43]

Whiskey played a central role in fueling the playful side of the horse-trading business. The inebriated participants at a typical first-Tuesday-of-the-month horse swapping in Georgia hurled good-natured insults at each other and traded horses for pocketknives, watches, and, in one case, a cow that the buyer subsequently saddled up and drunkenly rode home.[44] Trading with a drunk could have its pitfalls, however, since there is a least one documented case where an inebriated trader was able to collect damages because the jury sympathized with his impaired ability to judge the horse he was buying.[45] Southerners in particular had a reputation for trading under the influence, and when they were not drunk and trading horses, they were drunk and trading horse-trading stories. One member of a group of antebellum southern reprobates gathered around a hotel bar boasted that he had sold a half-dead horse as "a perfect paragon of horseflesh; a real Arab; nimble as a cricket; sounder than a nut; gentler than a cooing dove, and faster than a tornado."[46]

Nothing was more likely to drive away women than men expostulating over their horse trading triumphs.[47] When the Abingdon County, Virginia, court convened to do business on the fourth Monday of each month, local farmers came into town to drink and swap horses. Their wives were furious because the men wasted time and money only to wind up with useless animals. The men, however, viewed the monthly "jockey lot" as a place to show off their bargaining skills and prove they could put one over on their neighbors. Such exchanges supposedly taught quick thinking and self-reliance because every trader knew that every other trader was lying about his stock.[48] So, for instance, a Yankee sold a horse that would not pull to a Kentuckian, but the Kentuckian traded the Yankee a horse that would not move. When the Yankee complained, the Kentuckian explained that you had to "warm him up"—by kindling a fire under him.[49]

Not appearing to be a fool or a loser in the eyes of the male community was of paramount importance, so the losers either lied or hid.[50] A man bought a mare he believed was pregnant by a champion Tennessee walking horse. When the foal was born however, it was a mule (meaning the sire had been a donkey). The unfortunate buyer was so ashamed of having been "snookered" that he took to his bed to recuperate and to "avoid his peers for as long as possible."[51]

Buying a champion walking horse in utero and getting a mule instead was a typical horse story punch line. As often as not, tales of horse trades were not about getting the better horse (in the sense of coming out of the deal with a useful animal) but about *not* getting the worse horse (in the sense that the horse traded away was even more useless than the useless horse gotten in return). This equine equivalent of lowball poker (in which the worst hand wins) had more to do with being cleverer than the next fellow than it did with personal transportation.

The most imaginative of such transactions involved horses that could not carry anybody anywhere but ensured that the reputation of the winner would travel everywhere. In 1849, for example, a couple of Massachusetts jockeys met in a tavern, and to determine which was the sharper trader, they agreed to exchange horses, with the one who got the *worst* horse buying a round of drinks for the house. The first jockey brought out a horse that was blind, lame, infected with glanders, and prone to both biting and kicking. Then the second jockey fetched his horse, which in comparison looked pretty good. However, before the first trader could claim his prize, the second jockey removed first one false ear and then the other. He then plucked a glass eye out of the horse's head and proceeded to remove its artificial mane and tail. Those were just the trimmings, he announced proudly. He had "manufactured" this horse especially for such a trade, and now he would begin to unscrew the poor beast's major body parts, starting with a wooden leg. At that point, the first jockey pulled out his money and ordered the drinks.[52]

Abraham Lincoln, a famously sharp horse trader, was reputed to have lost a similar wager; but like all good Lincoln stories, the tale was self-deprecating and an example of the future president's wit. Lincoln and a local judge entered into the swap, agreeing that the one with the worse animal would get not only the other person's horse but also $25. The judge showed up with an unbelievably broken-down wreck of a horse, but Lincoln returned with a sawhorse. The crowd applauded, but Lincoln took one look at the judge's animal and promptly handed over both the wooden horse and the $25.[53]

In more serious horse-for-horse trades, the cash payment was not a wager but a way to cover the difference in perceived value between the two animals. The cash was referred to as "boot," and that word is still used when sellers try to close a sale by saying they will throw in something extra "to boot." As this residual usage suggests, boot could be something other than money. So in a horse trade it might be cash, but it might also be a blanket, saddle, tack, or a bottle of whiskey, whatever it took to consummate the deal. When Thomas Jefferson made an even swap of his black horse for John Hylton's five-year-old sorrel mare in 1774, he promised to pay an additional three pounds if the mare turned out to be pregnant. A couple of days later Hylton had second thoughts, so Jefferson noted in his journal that he sent the unhappy seller forty shillings "to boot."[54]

Traders often considered boot the profit in a deal, especially if it was cash. Serious traders frequently told unhappy customers that they would trade back but keep the boot (or sometimes buy back the horse at a discount, which amounted to the same thing).[55] Nevertheless, there was no automatic expectation that a deal could be undone. Given the tradition of exaggeration in horse trading, there were bound to be a large number of unhappy customers, and boot made it easy to trade back at a profit without any additional money changing hands.

Because trade-backs and refunds were never the norm, traders considered it a major concession to reconsider a deal at all and usually expected to earn something for their trouble. Some dealers figured out how to turn this apparent act of beneficence into a moneymaking swindle. They stocked attractive horses with easily hidden faults or, in extreme cases, would teach a horse a vice that would not be immediately obvious.[56] The dealer would take a trade plus boot for the good-looking animal. As soon as the new owner discovered the problem, he would come back to complain that the horse would turn only left, bite fellow animals, break down after an hour of work, or had some such deficiency. The trader would then magnanimously agree to reverse the trade less the boot. The buyer usually considered that a fair price to pay to be rid of the problem, and then of course the dealer could trade the horse to the next unsuspecting victim. Such a horse, known as a "snide," was worth more to a dealer than a sound, well-mannered horse, because it could be repeatedly sold, generating a profit each time it was returned.[57] Knowing this ruse, canny buyers would occasionally confound the con artist by refusing to the return the horse as expected but instead hold it for ransom, forcing the dealer to buy it back at a premium if he wanted to continue the con.[58] Whether these double-crosses actually occurred or were simply part of the folk legends of horse trading, they emphasize the gamesmanship that lay at the heart of much small-time horse trading. Getting a good deal in a horse trade was rewarding, but turning the tables on somebody who was trying to take unfair advantage was even more satisfying.

The "snide" double-cross illustrates how a participant could win the horse-trading game without getting a usable horse. For the symbolic victory to be more important than the value of the commodity, the winner had to feel that he had come out ahead both psychologically and sociologically. Unlike a regular game, where the score determined the winner, the horse-trade game had to be won twice. First the individual (it could be either the buyer or the seller) himself had to believe that he had won, then he had to convince other members of his community that he had won. In fact, many horse trade stories turned on this two-stage process. One of the parties would be set up to boast of the good deal he had gotten and then be shamed in the eyes of his peers when the real winner demonstrated that he had tricked the would-be trickster.

The Rules of the Game

The morality—or more precisely, the immorality—of horse trading derived from the way it operated as a game. Games have their own rules: nobody is punished for stealing second base in baseball or stealing a pass in basketball. To the extent that it was a game, horse trading was exempt from broader principles of behavior. Horse traders expected to be judged by the ethics of the game, not the ethics of the larger commercial world. They carved out a unique business space that balanced the competing demands of law, morality, and game playing. As late as 1977, an old Appalachian horse trader who admitted to half a dozen different ways of hiding a horse's faults could claim, "I didn't play any tricks." As far as he was concerned, what he had done was part of the accepted game conduct, and he said he dismissed threats of legal action, knowing that a jury of his peers would not find his actions out of bounds.[59] The fraternity of horse swappers created a precedent of retail exceptionalism that would become its legacy to automobile dealing.

The horse-trading game had rules, but because it was an informal sport, the rules were not codified and they varied over time and geography. Ultimately, the players viewed their transaction as a contest in which a game-like victory was more desirable than a business-like equal exchange of value. At stake on the one side was the buyer's perceived ability to judge the quality of a horse without depending on the word of the seller. On the other side was the ability of the seller to obscure his animal's faults without actually lying about them. "Honest" horse traders tried to avoid the sin of commission—that is, deliberately not telling the truth—but celebrated the sin of omission in which the fault lay with the horse not the trader.[60]

In the purest form of the horse-trading game, the seller actually acknowledged or even volunteered his horses' shortcomings. The buyer, however, was so convinced that everything the seller said was a lie that he fooled himself into not believing the truth. In his commentaries on Jacksonian Georgia, Augustus Longstreet wrote of a couple of horse swappers who expatiated at such length about their respective horses' faults that neither side would believe the other, even though both were telling the truth.[61] The mule trader "Po Boy" Jenkins, who prided himself on not lying, remembered a somewhat similar situation, also in Georgia but about a century later, when a buyer would not let him open his mouth, saying, "I wouldn't believe nothing no horse trader ever said about a mule [because] I'm my own judge." In front of a dozen laughing witnesses, Jenkins kept his counsel, asked for $150, accepted $125, and later remarked that if the buyer had not been such a know-it-all, he would have told him the truth about the balky mule and let it go for fifty bucks.[62]

Traders could not count on buyers refusing to hear about a horse's faults or disbelieving the truth when they did. More commonly, the seller avoided a direct answer when asked about the horse or, in the standard horse-tale trope, gave an honest answer that was nevertheless misleading.[63] Sellers would say that a blind horse "don't look so good" or that one suitable only for dog food was "fit to go to any hounds." They might describe a kicking horse as "lifting the feet well up," and if it had a fractured leg, it was "well broke for a gig or a saddle."[64] Nuncupative misdirection was at the heart of horse trading game. While outright lies transgressed the conventionally established boundaries, clever rhetorical feints were accepted and admired. A particularly nasty bit of verbal byplay combined the two forms so that the seller would warn the buyer about a nonexistent fault to distract him from the real one. Thus early in the twentieth century a North Carolina trader told a buyer he did not want to hear any complaints if one of the horse's legs fell off. The buyer could the see horse's legs were perfectly sound but was so busy examining them that he neglected to notice that the beast was blind.[65]

The fact that the seller did not tell a direct lie did not immunize him from general opprobrium, which is why horse dealing had such an awful reputation. Almost by definition, a good horse trader was a bad citizen. The moral ambiguity rose to the surface when horse trading mixed with religion. Religiously motivated men who were also honest horse traders warranted special mention: a Quaker, for example, who would not bargain and would not lie about his horse, or a Dunkard (another pietistic sect) who refused to take extra payment for a horse sold to the army during the Civil War.[66] Much more commonly, horse trading stories emphasized the ways in which religious scruples gave way to shady trading ethics. Thus a typical trader's elaborate praise of his animals' assets and apparent blindness to their faults led an early nineteenth-century humorist to muse that the horse dealer must be a true Christian because he "would not disparage the character of even a brute" and "sees only virtue" while gazing at vice.[67]

Religion or the lack thereof provided a steady subtext to the world of horse trading. Like drinking and gambling, with which it was often linked, competitive horse swapping was a pastime that violated the moral tenets of American Protestantism. Despite this—or perhaps because of it—most of the religious commentary about horse trading was subversive, acknowledging the underlying civic principle of honesty but excusing dishonesty in swapping as unavoidable or at worst merely a venial sin. Underhanded church deacons were stock characters in horse-swapping tales, although real churchmen were not amused.[68] In 1901 a Methodist bishop told a New Jersey conference that no one ought to read the wildly popular horse-trading novel *David Harum* because the story hinged on a minister trying to fool the protagonist but being tricked himself instead. The unsympathetic newspaper account of the bishop's speech noted, "Everyone knows that there are few things which a Methodist minister likes better than a horse trade."[69]

In the 1870s, Uncle Ike Barlow, a Michigan horse swapper, explained the true relationship of horse trading and religion. When he was *buying* a horse, said Barlow, he was a pretty good member of the church. When he was *selling*, he would do penance by skipping a prayer meeting or two, but when he was *swapping*, he would stop going to church for a month or until he knew the victim would not bring a lawsuit.[70] Uncle Ike's prayer hiatus while he waited to see whether he was going to be sued reflects the fact that the rules of the horse-trading game were not merely informal but sometimes illegal. Horse traders had to be constantly aware that if push came to shove in swapping, the legal code outranked the rules of the game. Most game players accepted the outcome of trade, win or lose. As one trader said, "I never goes to law to mend my bargains."[71] However, the traders had to juggle the expectations of those who knew they were playing a game with the expectations of customers who might not know that there was a game, or if they did, how to play it. This second class of customers was less likely to be amused by sharp dealing and more likely to denounce the trader as immoral or criminal.

There were unhappy buyers who sought judicial relief and found it. In 1888 the victims of a Brooklyn "gyp" dealer sued over the sale of a snide named Josiah. Josiah looked so good but was so bad that he had been sold 380 times in a single year. The dealer had warranted the horse in writing, using classic trader doublespeak in which every guaranty had a hidden meaning. For example, the dealer affirmed that "he works equally well in single or double harness," meaning he would not pull either way, and that he "feeds good and takes his rest well," meaning nothing at all except that the horse ate and slept. The courtroom rocked with laughter as the defense explained what each of the clauses in the warranty *really* meant, but the dealer's verbal legerdemain did not amuse the judge, who sent the defendant to jail.[72]

The judge in this Brooklyn case may have ordered the stiff sentence because the defendant was a well-known professional conman. The judge in a different Brooklyn suit awarded the plaintiff six cents in damages, a judicial acknowledgement that he had been technically wronged but should have known better.[73] In fact, the historical record is replete with stories of judges and jurors who refused to convict or who awarded only pro forma damages for behavior that would have been more severely punished in any other business transaction. In such cases the courts concluded that the plaintiffs should have known that horse-trade ethics were more malleable than those that governed other commercial transactions. There was, as the fictional horse trader David Harum observed, a difference between the "gospel truth" and a "good enough jury truth."[74]

The frequency with which these stories appear and their lack of specificity raise doubts about their authenticity but nonetheless attests to a male folk culture that was bent on warning losers not to be crybabies and go running to the courts. Deane C. Davis, an ex-governor of Vermont, approvingly recounted the trial of a local jockey who sold a badly winded horse. The trader denied that he had misrepresented the animal. He testified that he told the buyer that the horse did not kick or bite, that the horse was not lame and was free from various other specific faults. However, when he was asked if the horse had the heaves, he replied, "If this horse has got the heaves, I got the heaves," and, he explained to the jury in his breathy, asthmatic voice, "Gentlemen, I got the heaves."[75] The plaintiff in a similar case explained that when asked if a team pulled well, the seller replied, "You'll be surprised to see them work." When the judge found out the complainant had been horse trading since he was seven years old, he dismissed the case with the clear implication that he was finding the plaintiff guilty of stupidity.[76]

Hiding Faults

Some judges seemed inclined to excuse incidents of verbal misdirection because the perpetrators had obeyed the rules of the horse-trading game. When it came to false advertising, however, the record is clearer—if less amusing. As natural commodities, every horse was different, and horse advertisements were more analogous to the later used-car ads than to brand-oriented new-car advertising. Like each used car, each horse had to be sold on its own merits. Surprisingly, horse advertisements almost never identified breeds, but they were not modest in their application of complimentary adjectives, invariably describing the animals as fast, strong, elegant, and sound.[77]

As would be the case later with used-car ads, the public was repeatedly advised to read all horse ads with a jaundiced eye.[78] In fact, the most hackneyed cliché of used-car dealing, "This car was only driven to church on Sundays by an old lady," had its origins in horse advertising. While some men believed women used horses poorly and ruined their training, others thought women used their horses sparingly, so sellers falsely advertised female ownership as a way of indicating that a horse had not been pushed beyond its limits.[79] By the same token, horse buyers were warned to avoid any horse advertised as being sold by "a poor widow in order to raise money to pay the rent" or some similarly distressed elderly woman who might not know its value.[80]

Rather than lie about the animal in advertising, traders could alter the animal so that it lied about itself. These alterations sought to hide diseases, injuries, physical shortcomings, age, and behavioral problems (referred to as vices). There was no shortage of issues to obscure. One legal encyclopedia listed more than eighty different problems that rendered a horse unsound. Alphabetically, they ranged from "abrasions" to "wind sucking," and bodily, from "nasal gleet" in the top front to "thick urine" in the bottom back.[81] Horse buyers were advised to have a veterinarian check over the animal before they paid for it, which they seem to have done as infrequently as secondhand auto buyers take prospective purchases to a mechanic.[82]

The most storied form of hiding a fault was to rework the appearance of a horse's teeth to make it look younger. Sellers monkeyed with horse teeth as frequently as used-car dealers reset the odometer. The proverbial advice about not looking a gift horse in the mouth derives from the fact that a horse's age can be roughly judged by the condition of its teeth—at least until the age of eight. That is why, explained one expert, "no one has a horse more than eight years old for sale!"[83] Very occasionally a dealer would pull or pound milk teeth to make a horse look more mature, but much more frequently they doctored older teeth to make the horse appear younger.[84] The dental rejuvenation process was often referred to as "bishoping" (the etymology of the term is disputed) and consisted of restoring the ground-away cusps in the incisors by filing and burning them with a hot iron. Horse buyers who wanted to learn how to check teeth could consult detailed descriptions of natural and artificial changes in horse dentition, some of which read suspiciously like how-to-do-it instructions even though the practice required a great deal of skill and was seldom engaged in by amateurs.[85] (See fig. 1.)

Besides cosmetic dentistry, sellers used a variety of other devices to obscure the telltale signs of a horse's age. Older horses develop hollows above their eyes, which traders could temporarily hide by blowing air into them through a quill or straw—Botox for the aging horse.[86] Not only do horses' teeth yellow, gums recede, and faces collapse, but they also go gray as they get older, a fact that made hair dye as popular among owners of old horses as it was among old horse owners.[87] The beautician's talents could be used to enhance a horse's aesthetic value as well as to disguise its age. A horse with scars, droopy ears, or a thin mane or tail might otherwise be a perfectly functional animal, but the blemishes would make it undesirable for public use. A little bit of strategically applied coloring, some carefully hidden wire ear props, or a fall of extra hair woven into the mane or tail could transform a light work horse into a personal carriage or riding horse.

The horse-trading community may have frowned on purely cosmetic alterations, but it generally accepted them with good humor. Bishoping drew harsher criticism, perhaps because the process was more difficult and therefore more likely to be the work of a professional scoundrel. Whatever its true appearance, however, at least the person who bought a horse that had been given a superficial makeover still got an animal that could do the job, although perhaps for fewer years than the buyer bargained for. Serious health defects or behavioral vices were another matter altogether. A sick, disabled, or badly behaved horse could be anything from a nuisance to a useless waste of feed and barn space. Even if the disability were temporary, the buyer was still not getting a horse that could do the job for which it was being purchased, and hiding that fact violated even the permissive ethical code of horse trading.

Making a horse appear sound when it was not crossed the line into criminal activity. Soundness, that is, being free of serious disability or vice, was a key principle in the contentious world of horse warranties. Hiding unsoundness was widely condemned and almost as widely practiced. Amateurs seem to have avoided tampering with a horse's basic physiognomy either because the techniques were more arcane or because there was a sense that it violated horse-swapping principles. Professional traders who did not expect to do repeat business were willing to do whatever it took to make a sale. Like the amateurs, the professionals would verbally dissemble and misdirect, but they did not limit themselves to polishing up their animals to look better; they would also take steps to hide more serious shortcomings.

The most notorious "copers" (unscrupulous dealers) were reputed to go so far as to hide glanders, a highly contagious and debilitating disease that rendered a horse useless. Glandered horses were supposed to be quarantined and euthanized, not sold after having their telltale nasal discharge hidden by inducing sneezing and then plugging the nostrils with tow.[88] Copers could temporarily suppress heaves, the pulmonary disorder, by wetting the horse's feed.[89] If a symptom could not be hidden, its chronic source could be disguised by inflicting a visible and obviously superficial wound on the disabled horse.[90] Shady traders made old, tired horses act young and frisky by feeding them nitroglycerin or inserting an irritant (ginger and red pepper were popular) into the horse's anus.[91] Sometimes they augmented the animating suppositories by putting pebbles in the horse's ears, causing it to toss its head in a lively manner. On the other hand, a horse that was so frisky as to be unmanageable could be calmed down with a variety of opiates.[92] Occasionally an unprincipled buyer, usually a barn dealer who was boarding a horse, would use the dealers' black arts to make it look sick, rather than vice versa. By inducing symptoms of heaves or glanders, the dealer could buy the horse for pennies on the dollar. The horse would recover as soon as the dealer withdrew the aggravating agent and could then be sold for a fine profit.[93]

Warranties

Traders who obscured the truth about their horses walked (and frequently crossed over) the fine line between acceptable praise and polish on one side, and illegal lying and fraud on the other. Just when they crossed that line was hard to determine because the equine branch of contract law was a specialty unto itself. The tradition of obscurantism in horse trading is the contentious nexus between folkways and legal procedures. Folkways allowed for obfuscation, while the law wanted specificity. In the larger commercial realm, contract law recognized that sellers were given to exaggerating the positive qualities of their products, and as long as they did so in general terms, the law did not consider sellers bound to the literal meaning of their terms. This sort of sales language, known as "puffery," was assumed to be part of all commercial culture.[94]

When applying this rule to horse trading, the courts held that general statements such as "This is exactly the horse you want" were no more than "badinage" or "allowable chaffer," not a promise of performance.[95] Indeed, one of the English judges in the case that laid the foundation for warranty law used horse sales as an example even though the lawsuit itself involved a goat: "Every one in selling his wares will affirm that they are good, or that the horse which he sells is sound."[96] Well into the nineteenth century a court could find that the statement that a horse was "sound as a bell of brass and quiet as a lamb" was not intended to be a warranty.[97]

Warranties themselves were subject to a variety of restrictions, most commonly a time limit. Some sellers would warrantee a horse for only a couple of days, while others might extend that to a week or a month or even to several months.[98] Experts, however, warned sellers against extended warranties because even the most honest and best-intentioned dealer could not know what troubles might be incubating inside a horse or what injuries or diseases it might sustain after it left his control.[99] Buyers understood the unpredictability of living creatures and generally considered themselves fortunate if the seller was willing to give any warranty at all, no matter for how short a time.

Sellers often wrote these time-limited warranties in general terms, broadly warranting the horse "sound." But what did it mean for a horse to be sound? A lawyer's idea of soundness would probably be very different from that of a veterinarian, and those, in turn, would differ from that of a buyer or a seller.[100] An 1847 treatise on equine law listed over one hundred "diseases, defects or alternations in structure, and bad habits" that would render a horse legally unsound.[101] Minimalists (usually sellers) said soundness meant only that the horse suffered from no permanent physical disability. Maximalists (usually buyers) argued that soundness included temporary disabilities such as transitory diseases or minor injuries as well as vices or personality traits that they found objection-able. Needless to say, the interpretation of warranties constituted a large per-centage of horse trade cases that showed up in court; and as noted earlier, judges and juries tended to apply looser interpretations to horse warranties than they might to assurances about other goods. When a buyer was able to extract a specific warranty from a seller, and especially if he could get it in writing, the buyer could expect judges and juries to hold the seller accountable. The more general principle was that if the buyer told the seller what he wanted to use the horse for, and if the seller knew that the horse would be unsuitable for that pur-pose, for example, to pull a plow or to be ridden by a lady, then the seller was vi-olating an implied warranty.[102]

To avoid legal liability for unsoundness sellers often played a version of the verbal misdirection game. In essence, they issued a limited warranty that cov-ered only a few issues and served to steer the buyer away from recognizing a more serious fault. For example, one seller warranted that a horse was "quiet to ride." The buyer soon discovered that while it was indeed quiet to ride, it also refused to turn left, which meant the rider had to circle right to go left. Never-theless, the buyer did not consider this fault a breach of the warranty.[103] A trader in Boston before the Civil War warranted a horse "perfectly sound and kind" and even let the buyer take it on trial for a week. It was more than a week later and after he had paid that the buyer discovered that this very fine saddle horse would not pull a carriage. Players of the trading game would normally have chalked that one up in the loss column and moved on, but this buyer was a lawyer. He sued to get back his $250. Lawyer versus horse trader; it was a battle of pariahs. When the jury awarded the buyer only $125, he admitted that it was "probably upon the idea that a lawyer ought not to recover more than half that he is cheated out of."[104]

The male culture of competitive horse trading evolved in an environment in which the prices of all goods were determined by bargaining. Before the mid-nineteenth century, buying a horse may have been different in degree from buy-buying a teapot, but it was not different in kind. The process of negotiated give and take that marked horse dealing was essentially similar to the dickering over prices that every man or woman did when buying anything. The absence of women in the horse-trading business distinguished it from more general acts of consumption, and that, combined with the contestational nature of the bargaining, gave horse trading an air of raffish masculinity. Thus, horse trading was typical of retailing in general but was distinguished by its somewhat playful environment. The differences between horse trading and the broader retailing world would increase dramatically after 1850 as female-centered single-price selling replaced price haggling in almost all retail commerce other than the sale of personal transportation.

CHAPTER TWO

Retailing

Satisfying the Buyer

As the retail marketplace became dominated by women buying manufactured goods, haggling in horse trading hung on because men bought horses—and horses were made by horses, not factory workers. The variability of individual horses made it difficult for them to be sold like mass-produced goods, but both natural and manufactured goods were exchanged in a retail transaction predicated on the idea that an object should serve the purpose for which it was bought—or in the language of horse trading, it should "suit." This common-law principle was incorporated into civil codes as "implied warranty," meaning that the buyer could assume both that the item would work in the way all such items are conventionally understood to work (merchantability), and that it would perform any specific task affirmed by the seller (fitness).

Implied warranty was one of three elements of a new retail world that evolved at the end of the nineteenth and the beginning of the twentieth century; the other two were single-price (sometimes called "fixed-price" and often referred to by stores as "one-price") and refundability. Unlike implied warranty, which was a legal principle and therefore enforceable in court, single-price and refundability were commercial conventions with no force of law. Together they made up an emerging "culture of satisfaction," which was a consumer-oriented marketplace environment that could be summed up in the credo "The customer is always right." The culture of satisfaction gave rise to the promise Susan Strasser uses as the title to her history of American mass markets: "Satisfaction guaranteed."

In a retail culture of satisfaction, customers could not only assume that anything they bought would work as expected, but they could also assume that if they did not like their purchase for any reason at all they would be able to return it for a full refund. Furthermore, they could assume that the price they paid was the same price paid by everybody else who bought the same item at the same time and place. None of these three principles ever applied to horses, and only the first one, implied warranty, would apply to automobiles. No auto dealers or manufacturers have ever had a standard policy of refunding the purchase price of a car to an unhappy buyer, nor did car buyers ever know the net cost of the same vehicle purchased by another person, even when bought at the same place and time. The retail haggling over the price of every sale and the refusal of car dealers to embrace the conventional retail return policy have left cars as a twenty-first-century manifestation of a commercial world that disappeared for other manufactured products more than a hundred years ago.

From the early sixteenth to the end of the nineteenth century, the fundamental legal principle in horse trading was that the buyer assumed all the risk in a sale unless the seller had deliberately disguised a fault (fraud) or had promised in writing that the horse did have particular qualities or did not have particular flaws (warranty).[1] There was, in other words, no *implied* warranty when it came to horses. Many of the disagreements that arose among horse traders, however, did not involve outright fraud or the violation of an express warranty but were the result of buyer's remorse: the horse bought was not the horse expected. These were the situations in which the common-law principle of caveat emptor (let the buyer beware) usually superseded the civil-law concept of implied warranty.[2]

To a significant degree, the history of caveat emptor is the history of horse trading. The locus classicus of the concept was a 1534 English decision that stated that as long as a horse was tame and could be ridden all else was caveat emptor.[3] Seventy years later the courts reinforced this view in a non-horse decision holding that the seller bore no liability absent an express warranty.[4] Subsequent development in English case law frequently involved horse sales and the question of what statements constituted a legal promise of performance.[5] Early on, the courts determined that it was the buyer's responsibility to examine the animal before he bought it. The judicial system also assumed that the buyer was competent to judge the quality of a horse; therefore, if the horse had some patent shortcoming that would be obvious to a reasonably knowledgeable buyer, it was not covered even by a general warranty of soundness.[6] Furthermore, the courts assumed that the seller could not be held responsible for flaws (such as a disease) that had not revealed themselves. In other words, once you bought it, it was yours.

Despite its Latin appellation and sixteenth-century origins, the doctrine of caveat emptor was not an "ancient maxim." As legal scholar Walton Hamilton spelled out in mordantly sarcastic detail in 1931, caveat emptor did not become a broad legal principle until the eighteenth century.[7] More recently, legal historian Morton Horwitz has discussed the rise of caveat emptor as an essential part of "the transformation of American law" in the antebellum period. The works of Hamilton and Horwitz emphasize that the idea of buyer responsibility emerged in tandem with laissez faire economic thought and served to free producers, distributors, and merchants from the burdens of just price and other traditional constraints on free-market capitalism. Instead of assuming that a contract (sale/purchase) should in some abstract sense be a fair exchange, the new model assumed only that each party had freely agreed to the exchange. A contract was now no more than the representation of a convergence of wills.[8]

The older paradigm had taken for granted an equivalence between a just price and a just contract. In theory this meant that the price of an object was an indication of its quality. A cheap product could be assumed to be of poor quality, and an expensive one, of good quality. Therefore a high price for a poor product was unjust. In other words, price was an implicit warranty of quality. The rise of free-market ideas created a legal separation between price and value, and a thing became worth whatever somebody was willing to pay for it.[9] However, even as it was gaining wider judicial application, the principle of caveat emptor was being eroded by the civil law of merchantability and fitness, which said that a buyer could assume an item would do what it was sold to do.[10] Merchantability and fitness were not the same as a fair or just price because there was no assumption of equivalence between price and value. Nevertheless, the concept did assume that an item would perform as expected—whatever the price. Implied warranty was also not the same thing as fair price, but neither did it require the buyer to be an expert judge of every product on the market.

The argument for merchantability was particularly strong as it applied to manufactured and processed goods because they were essentially different from natural products. While nobody could see inside a horse, the manufacturer (and by extension, the distributor and merchant) could and therefore should know exactly what was inside a factory-made product. The consumer could not be expected to have the same knowledge.[11] In other words, in place of the presumption of equal ignorance in a caveat emptor world, there was a presumption of unequal knowledge, with the seller having the advantage.

The consequence of this new relationship between buyer and seller was the growth of the principle of implied warranty. This meant not only that a product would do what its seller (manufacturer or merchant) said it would—that is, truthful advertising—but that it would do so for a reasonable period. Ultimately, the concept of implied warranty grew so ubiquitous that it became normative. Consumers began to assume that a guaranty of merchantability and fitness covered any new manufactured product they bought unless there was a specific disclaimer to the contrary. From a situation in which the burden of product suitability lay with the buyer, the new model, the one that still obtains, placed the burden of suitability on the manufacturer and, in one form or another, on the distributors and merchants of those products.

This new world of warranted goods was the backdrop for a cultural phenomenon that fixed the image of the horse trader in the public imagination even as horse traders were being replaced by car dealers. At the turn of the nineteenth century, when the doctrine of caveat emptor was under full assault from Progressive Era reformers demanding more seller accountability, Americans embraced one horse trader as a popular hero when Edward Noyes Westcott's 1898 book *David Harum* became the best-selling American novel of its time. The fictional David Harum was not a scoundrel; he was not a Gypsy road trader or New York Bull's Head dealer with a stable full of broken-down plugs. Rather, Harum was small-town businessman in upstate New York with a passion for horse trading. The novel was quickly adapted for the Broadway stage. The play was followed by two screen versions, a silent movie in 1915 and a 1934 sound version featuring Will Rogers, and a long-running radio serial.[12] For readers who were buying their goods anonymously at urban department stores, David Harum was a nostalgic look back at a rapidly disappearing world. He embodied the humanizing person-to-person interaction of the traditional marketplace, while reminding readers that not every negotiator was goodhearted. His cracker-barrel philosophy and heavy local dialect made him the perfect representation of a way of life already doomed to become a fond memory by the recently invented automobile.

Manufactured Transportation: Carriages and Bicycles

All the horse-trading folklore, tall tales, jokes, stories, and reminiscences were about men like David Harum who exchanged horses for horses and money. Carriages are conspicuously absent from the historical record. Most people who traveled by horse power did not travel on horseback but were pulled in carriages, and yet carriages almost never played a role in the horse-trading game. Every once in a while a carriage might be part of a larger deal involving horses, but the carriages themselves did not become the objects of negotiation.

The reasons for this marketplace disassociation between the puller and pulled may derive from the cultural differences between them. First, unlike horses, carriages appear to have been relatively non-gendered objects. And second, as a manufactured product the quality of a carriage was under the control of its maker, so the courts would have given more credence to the principle of implied warranty in a dispute between seller and buyer. By the 1890s the carriage manufacturing business had matured into an industry that foreshadowed the production of automobiles. Teams of semiskilled workers not very different from the men who would staff Henry Ford's plants built many of the most popular horse-drawn vehicles from standardized parts in large factories. Specialized use and luxury carriages were still custom made, but the average carriage customer could see a neighbor's vehicle, or a picture in a newspaper advertisement, or Sears Roebuck catalog and know that he or she could get an identical one for a standard price.[13]

Considering that almost a million horse-drawn passenger vehicles and more than half a million farm and business wagons were produced in 1899 (the earliest year for which there are production figures) and that the carriage industry had the tenth-largest capitalization of all American manufacturers, there is surprisingly little contemporary commentary on how they were bought and sold.[14] Automobiles and motor trucks did not reach that same volume until 1915, by which time there was an extensive literature on their sale and purchase.[15] It is not clear why such a major industry received so little attention from the people who bought its products, but one reason may be that few of the shenanigans that accompanied horse trading spilled over into their associated vehicles.

All indications are that the sale of carriages and wagons was relatively straightforward. There were, of course, unscrupulous dealers and manufacturers who would use inferior materials and cover up their shortcuts with paint and decoration. To prevent auction frauds, New York State found it necessary to prohibit false nameplates on carriages in 1877.[16] However, there is no indication that duplicity was more frequent in the carriage industry than in any other branch of trade. There is certainly no evidence that dealers, manufacturers, or person-to-person sales were steeped in the kind of behavior that marked horse trading. Carriage ads for both new and used vehicles carry no indications that there was a tradition of aggressive negotiation over prices. To the contrary, once mass production had been achieved after 1871, many carriages, including those displayed in showrooms and those available by mail, were sold via catalogs at published prices. Buyers could customize their carriages, but the cost of extras such as special colors, upholstery, or lamps was also standard and listed in the catalogs.[17]

Driving a carriage, like riding a horse, was primarily a male activity. A woman could drive a horse the same way a woman could ride one: it was done, but it was suspect. The blond driving her own "canary-coloured brougham with a pair of black cobs" in Edith Wharton's *The Age of Innocence* got it as a gift from a man who was not her husband.[18] Women who had the temerity to drive, despite its unladylike implications, could expect to be criticized for their lack of skill. Like their early-twentieth-century car-driving sisters, female carriage drivers had a reputation for being unequal to so masculine a task. "The husband, father, or other male relative" who turns loose a woman "on the highways and byways without a groom or other thoroughly competent companion," warned a proudly male horseman, "does a wicked and reprehensible thing." He claimed that women drivers lacked the necessary strength of arm, hand, and grip; they lacked the skill with reins and the presence of mind to control a single horse safely, much less a team. "No horse," he declared, was "safe for a woman to drive," no matter what the lying horse trader promised.[19]

They may not have driven carriages as a matter of course, but women placed great store in having a nice carriage to impress their peers. Before the Civil War, carriages were standard symbols of foolish female pride. When storywriters wanted to make the point that it was best to live within one's means, they would depict a shallow wife tearfully begging her husband either to buy a fine carriage or not to sell the one they had. Unfamiliar with the economic realities of commercial life, fictional wives regularly ruined their husband's credit by flaunting rigs that the local business community knew they could not afford.[20]

The sale of carriages generally remained separate from the masculine culture of horse trading, as did that of bicycles, an alternative form of personal transportation whose popularity peaked just as automobiles were beginning to appear on the roads. Like carriages, bicycles were factory-made items, and their retailers made a heroic effort to sell them like other manufactured goods for a single price. However, rather than providing a model for standard selling practices, bicycle retailing eventually joined the trading game in a minor way, and instead of opening up a new historical path for auto retailing, bicycle sales left the situation ambiguous.

Bicycles paved the way for cars—quite literally. Bicycle enthusiasts of the 1890s were a major force in getting municipalities to increase the number of surfaced roads, roads that automobiles would soon take over. Bicycles also created a cohort of engineers, machinists, inventors, manufactures, and retailers who produced and sold the first generation of automobiles (with a significant assist from the firearms, sewing machine, and carriage industries). Ultimately, the very vehicles conjured up by the bicycle industry left it in the dust (if not the dustbin) of history. However, for a period of about twenty years, from 1885 to roughly 1905, bicycles were a major alternative to horses as a means of individual transportation. They could take their riders to places that railroads did not go in a way that was much cheaper and more convenient than old-fashioned horse power—assuming, of course, that where they wanted to go was not too far away and could be reached via a paved road, and that it was not too cold, too hot, raining, or snowing.

Before 1884 riding a bicycle was a male-only undertaking because of the strength necessary to propel the machines. A Frenchman named Pierre Lallement had solved the problem of transforming human power into mechanical locomotion around 1855, but his velocipede was a hard-to-drive 150–pound contraption with steel tires on wooden wheels driven by pedals attached directly to the front hub.[21] The English and the French improved the velocipede by increasing the size of the front wheel, decreasing the size of the rear wheel and encasing both in rubber tires. Larger front wheels, however, lifted the bicycle seat high off the ground so that mounting and dismounting became a daunting feat in itself that effectively excluded women from riding. The craze for these ungainly vehicles died out after peaking in 1870, and when an epidemic of distemper emptied New York City streets of horse-powered vehicles in 1873, young men chose to walk rather than ride the already-passé velocipedes.[22]

Public rejection of two-wheeled transportation reversed after 1884 when the first chain-driven bicycles appeared in England. With equal-sized wheels, the new "safety" bicycle (thus rendering the older high-wheeler the "ordinary") brought the rider back down to earth, and improved metal pipe technology allowed manufacturers to cut the weight by more than two-thirds. With increased accessibility and affordability, the market for bicycles exploded in the late 1880s as bicycling became an option for people other than athletic young men. Now women and middle-aged people could take to the roads under their own power.[23]

The demand for bicycles sparked continuing innovation and led to the idea of an annual model change. Manufacturers announced new models early each spring in preparation for the summer riding season.[24] Riders who wanted to take advantage of the improvements had to buy a new "bike" (an abbreviation dating to the mid-1880s). The rapid pace of technological innovation in the decade after 1884 meant that bicycles got "old" much faster than horses. A horse might remain good for twenty years; a bicycle was obsolete in a year. Replacing a bicycle, however, was an expensive proposition. At a hundred dollars, bicycles cost about the same as a good light carriage from Sears. Bike riders found themselves in much the same position as horse riders who wanted a new mount. The cost could be reduced substantially if the seller would take the rider's existing mount (and "mount" was often used to refer to bikes as well as horses in the 1890s). Sellers, however, did not intend to fall into the trading trap. As long as the demand for bicycles exceeded the supply, retailers resisted the pressure to buy back (trade) used machines. Instead, they chose to treat bicycles like other branded manufactured goods.

Selling a bicycle like a sewing machine made additional sense not only because many of them were made by sewing machine companies but also because the great safety-bicycle craze drew much of its strength from female participation.[25] When the bicycle seat descended from the ordinary's dangerous altitude, women quickly adopted the new machine. On the one hand, female bike riding fit a growing pattern of women's participation in sports that included archery, tennis, basketball, and volleyball—the last two invented at the height of the bicycle craze. On the other hand, however, it violated a widely held late-Victorian disapproval of women riding anything (including horses) astride. Women's sidesaddle riding outfits did not work for bike pedaling, so female cyclists had to violate both behavior and dress codes to take up the new sport. This, in addition to the older established position of the bicycle as a male machine, the physical exertion necessary to ride these single-speed bikes, and the high cost of buying one in an era when few women earned their own money, should have presented an insurmountable (so to speak) barrier to women's bicycling, but it did not.[26]

Various sources estimate that once the safety bicycle became the norm as many as a quarter of all bike riders were women. For the most part, men welcomed women into what had previously been the "fraternity of wheelmen," and bicycle riding became one of the symbols of the increasing liberation of turn-of-the-century women from the strictures of the Victorian era. This generation was used to shopping in single-price department stores, so it made sense that bicycle store owners would sell to women the same way. In fact, department stores sold bicycles alongside other consumer products. Similarly, Montgomery Ward and Sears Roebuck sold bicycles through their mail-order catalogs.[27] Since neither department stores nor catalog stores had any history of trade-ins for used items, bicycles seemed to be on their way to shifting the retail paradigm for personal transportation.

For a brief period, bicycles demonstrated that a change in the nature of the object (from the organic horse to the mechanical bike) could substantially alter the way it was sold. Economic forces, however, conspired to bring the no-trade era of bicycle selling to a close. There were too many small firms making too many bicycles that were too expensive. By 1896 the supply had begun to exceed demand, and prices started coming down, although the desire for a good deal could still bring out bike buyers in droves. When a rumor swept the New York metropolitan area in 1896 that $100 bicycles were going on sale for ten dollars at a store on Sixth Avenue, reportedly *forty thousand* people, one-third of them women, were on hand waiting for the doors to open, and a minor riot ensued when the shoppers surged inside.[28] The existing bicycle industry, however, could not hope to make money selling bikes for ten dollars, and the lower prices began driving more expensive and less efficient manufacturers and retailers out of business.[29]

To keep people buying, those retailers who stayed in the business began to take used bicycles in trade on new ones. There had been a market in used machines even before the arrival of the safety bicycle in 1885. Stores in New York and Massachusetts advertised that they bought as well as sold bicycles. Although there is no indication that they took trade-ins as a matter of course, it is hard to imagine that trades were not in fact occurring.[30] Certainly, by 1892 trade-ins were common enough that used bicycles "taken in trade" had become a standard industry category.[31] The bicycle bubble finally burst in the summer of 1897. Marginal firms disappeared, and those that remained sold their much-cheaper bicycles more or less as commodities. Nevertheless, as late as 1912 stores were still selling secondhand bicycles "taken in trade."[32]

Negotiated (Discriminatory) Prices

Bicycles were sold by independent shops that might give the buyer an allowance on a trade-in, but they were also sold by department stores and mail-order catalog companies that did not buy back used products or negotiate over the prices of new ones. By 1900 the retail system used by department stores had become the rule for the sale of all consumer products except cars. Before the 1860s all goods were sold the way cars still are: the price of each item was determined at the time of sale by negotiation. That pattern began to shift toward a single-price model in the decade before the Civil War and was firmly established at the time of the bicycle craze in the 1890s.

In the preindustrial world, markets were local and people were assumed to be knowledgeable about the things they bought. Ceteris paribus, in such a world face-to-face negotiation was a reasonable way to determine the value of goods and services. However, ceteris are seldom paribus, which is why Quaker founder George Fox famously bid his shopkeeper followers to charge all their customers the same price so that even children could safely buy goods.[33] If Fox's countrymen were willing to "cozen and cheat" inexpert buyers, then the presumption that bargaining resulted in a fair price was false. Buyers and sellers were not equally knowledgeable, and it was the seller who usually held the whip hand.

Price negotiations took place in an environment defined by legal constraints that went beyond the strictures against outright fraud but not so far as to preclude cajolery, flattery, transparent puffery, and similar inducements to buy. However, vendors who used these tactics to excess or who shaded over the fine line from puffery to false claims developed poor reputations, and consumers learned to be wary of individuals or categories of sellers who had a reputation as slick bargainers.

The quintessential American example of the slick salesman was the Yankee peddler, an itinerant trader who traveled through the rural back country bringing light manufactured goods such as tinware, clocks, and brushes to the front doors of isolated farmsteads. Contemporaries were both welcoming and wary when the peddlers showed up. The peddlers, who tended not to duplicate each others' territories, provided a service that saved the farm family a long trip to a store, which itself might not have been much more than a shed with limited inventory. Peddlers' customers, however, were often both poor and self-sufficient; so while they may not have had much of a choice from whom to buy, they could more easily "do without" than their less isolated contemporaries. Furthermore, farmers were suspicious of these traveling storekeepers because they were reputed to deal in fraudulent goods such as wooden nutmegs, brown paper sausages, and stationary barometers—and because they were inveterate horse swappers.[34]

A willingness to swap horses was a sure sign that a peddler was not merely a negotiator, but an underhanded one. Peddlers engaged in many of the same kinds of false promises and verbal misdirection for all their goods that members of the horse-trading brotherhood used for their stock, warranting, for example, that a certain clock would not vary one minute over six months, which was true only because it would not run at all.[35] The southern expletive "damn Yankee" originated long before the Civil War to refer to these fast-talking and none-too-honest traders who became the subjects of a folktale tradition that paralleled that of horse swappers. One example tells of a sheriff who bought a knife from a peddler so he could arrest him for not having a license. The peddler, however, produced the requisite permit, and the sheriff, stung by his own sting, offered to sell the unwanted knife back at half price. The peddler accepted and then charged the sheriff with unlicensed peddling.[36]

The tradition of bargaining over the prices of retail items was not limited to transactions with backcountry peddlers. Farm families that patronized local general stores and urban citizens who shopped in city retail districts also engaged in price negotiation. The custom in both village and city was for customers to indicate what they wanted and then to ask the clerk, who was often the proprietor, for the price. Shoppers usually had an idea of what staples cost but had to take the proprietor's word on the precise rate or try to negotiate a lower one.[37] Evidence indicates that both rural and urban shopkeepers set prices according to their best guess of what the customer might agree to: "That is the rich Mrs. Cotton," whispered one fictional dry goods clerk to another in an 1840 story. "Be sure you put an extra shilling on every yard."[38] If the customer balked, the seller would steadily lower the price rather than let the shopper walk out empty-handed. In an atmosphere that would be familiar to any contemporary car buyer, sales staff hounded shoppers to buy, and if one clerk failed to make a sale, he would turn customers over to a second. "Just browsing" was not an option.[39]

The pressure-to-buy atmosphere in retail stores mellowed considerably after the Civil War, but discriminatory pricing has hung on in isolated pockets. Antiques, collectibles, art, crafts, and other unique goods have maintained a tradition of flexible pricing. In addition to the prices of one-of-a-kind and second-hand items, which are rendered unique by the vicissitudes of history, the cost of even some brand-new, mass-produced goods can be bargained down. How-to articles and books appear regularly with instructions about where, how, and over what goods to ask for a price reduction. Almost all of the items covered are expensive, with generous profit margins that can be cut, especially if demand is slack. However, the advice givers make it clear that most shoppers do not ask for, nor do they expect to get, a discount off the posted price; single-price is the norm and has been for more than a hundred years.[40]

Like single prices, posted prices, whether or not they were subject to negotiation, were also a Gilded Age phenomenon linked to two revolutionary changes in the consumer environment. The first was the rise of brand-name manufactured goods and their associated advertising. The second was the emergence of women as the prime family consumers. Evidence is scarce, but indications are that before the arrival of brand-name products, shopping itself was not a particularly gendered behavior but was an extension of the gendered division of life in general. Men bought items they used, and women bought things that they used. Yankee peddlers, for example, made a particular effort to aim their sales pitch at women, who felt more comfortable shopping at home than at the local store, which could be less congenial.[41] In many small towns the general store was a center for casual male socializing. Men gathered on porch benches in the summer and around the stove in the winter to smoke, spit tobacco, drink, talk politics and business, and swap horse-trading and hunting stories.[42] When a store was an informal masculine hangout and a locus of ritual male bonding, it was unattractive to most women.

Single (Democratic) Prices

The role of women in retailing underwent a dramatic transformation in the second half of the nineteenth century. As men's work moved away from home, the house became increasingly dominated by women, and shopping for the house and its occupants became a female task. David Monod points out that the very words used to describe the process changed in a way that acknowledged the differing mindsets of male and female buyers. Mostly male "consumers," who used up what they bought, became mostly female "shoppers," whose emphasis was on the process itself. Likewise, "stores," warehouses for goods, became "shops," where the shopper carried out her activity.[43] Historians, including

Lloyd Wendt, William Leach, and Elaine Abelson, have demonstrated how shopping became women's activity and how shopping venues, especially department stores, became women's places.[44] Even Mark Swiencicki, who has manfully sought to restore some balance to the picture of an almost-all female retail world, only succeeds in reinforcing the utter dominance of women in the purchasing of manufactured goods in the Gilded Age and after. Men, it seems, did a lot of buying, but their purchases were usually limited to exclusively men's items, like sports equipment or services in male-dominated locations such as theaters and saloons.[45] The department store, with its one-price-to-all and satisfaction-guaranteed policies was predominantly, but not exclusively, female territory.

Isolated examples of mostly Quaker one-price retailing predated department stores by a good two hundred years, but the norm changed only when shopping became feminized, and the change took some getting used to. A longtime salesman at Wanamaker's, one of the earliest large department stores to use what it called the "one-price system," recalled the first day the new policy went into effect. A customer came in for a suit, tried it on, liked it, and asked the price. Told it was $22, he smiled and replied, "That's your asking price; what's your selling price?" Refusing to believe the price was fixed, he tried several bargaining ploys to get the cost down. Eventually, convinced that one-price meant the same price to all, he bought the suit and pronounced himself a convert to the new system.[46]

Wanamaker's reveled in its somewhat exaggerated reputation as the store that reformed retailing in America. When founder John Wanamaker died in 1923, one obituary inaccurately hailed his store as the first in America to adopt a one-price policy. His honesty and candor, said the article, replaced "the selling tactics of the horse-trader which preceded him" and "did away with the policy of 'Let the buyer beware!'"[47] In fact, a number of high-profile merchants had adhered to a one-price policy before Wanamaker, including abolitionists Arthur and Lewis Tappan and New York retail magnate Alexander T. Stewart.[48] Furthermore, there are indications that even some small rural stores posted prices in the antebellum period.[49] Following the lead of Bon Marché in Paris, which had created the genre, other European department stores had begun to use price tags on their goods in the 1850s.[50] As early as 1854, a Macy's advertisement promised, "Lowest Prices always named First." It is unclear whether those prices were being "named" by the clerks or actually posted. Whichever it was, Macy's was not shy about publicizing its policy and backing up its "lowest price" boasts by quoting some of them in its advertising.[51]

The retailers who embraced the one-price policy around the time of the Civil War liked to claim that they did so because of its democratic nature. By democratic they meant that every customer was treated the same and that certain categories of people were not charged more because they appeared to be more vulnerable. This equalitarian premise had been the basis for the historic one-price policy of the Quakers and was the reason African Americans preferred to shop at single-price department stores.[52] In the case of African Americans, the economic term "discriminatory pricing" had an equivalent cultural meaning.[53]

On the other hand, people who lived in poor urban neighborhoods with large immigrant communities continued the non-gendered tradition of retail haggling. Betty Smith's autobiographical novel *A Tree Grows in Brooklyn* has a scene set in 1916 in which two Irish-American children and their mother engage in a heated set of negotiations with a female Jewish shopkeeper for a new hat. Through aggressive bargaining, the threesome manages to whittle down the price of the hat from ten dollars to $2.50. Reeling from the battle, the son says, "No wonder Mama waits five years to buy a new hat if it's all that trouble." His sister, trained in the art of retail combat, responds, "Trouble? Why, that's fun!"[54] Such stores and such women were common in large cities until the mid-twentieth century. These shops catered to their customers' traditional marketplace mentalities, giving them not only the products they wanted but also the sense that they were able to get them at a special price. They provided the comfort of the familiar in other ways as well by stocking culturally unique products and providing ethnically specific services (especially the ability to speak the buyer's native language). Ethnic shops, with the exclusionary effect of their foreign-language-speaking staffs and signs, served to highlight the inclusionary democratic nature of the mainstream stores.[55]

A single posted price for new items would have been meaningless, of course, if shopkeepers had undermined it by giving trade-in allowances, but they never did. From time to time stores would advertise that they took trade-ins of sewing machines, typewriters, radios, and other household appliances, but this practice was more of an advertising stunt than a real trading situation.[56] The stores would promise a certain amount for the old item, and everybody who turned one in would get the same allowance. While that might amount to a discount for current owners but not for first-time buyers, there was still no negotiation involved, and both sides still knew the net cost in advance. The market for secondhand manufactured items other than cars was always distinct from new-product sales.

Satisfaction Guaranteed or Your Money Cheerfully Refunded

Along with charging the same price to all customers, postbellum stores were increasingly willing to refund buyers' money if they were dissatisfied for any reason. In this, as in so many areas of modern retailing, Aristide Boucicaut, the founder of Bon Marché, led the way with his "money-back guaranty."[57] Department store magnates Potter Palmer in Chicago and R. H. Macy in New York both introduced the return privilege in the 1850s, although Macy's did not formally adopt it as store policy until 1875, when it gave its customers one week to return anything for any reason.[58]

As with single-price, the increasingly liberal refund policies were a response to market pressures, not legal obligation. Commercial law required only that goods not be misrepresented (fraud) or manifestly unfit for their intended purpose (implied warranty). Before the mid-nineteenth century, local market pressures, including the desire for repeat business, may have prompted merchants to exchange unsatisfactory items, but only when there was some inherent defect in the goods, and then only for an equivalent item, not for cash. No laws required a store to take back an item because it did not satisfy the buyer as the new return policy did. The dissatisfied buyer did not have to demonstrate some failing in the goods; the retailer would refund the purchase price of any item if it proved unsatisfactory for any reason, even if that reason were merely that the buyer had simply changed his or her mind. From the beginning there were customers who abused this policy by buying and using an item (especially clothing) for a single event and then returning it.[59] Nevertheless, the policy was sufficiently popular that retailers were under tremendous market pressure to adopt it, and by the 1870s not only did stores advertise that they accepted returns, but those that did not felt compelled to warn their customers that all sales were final.[60] Like the one-price policy, the money-back guaranty gave all customers, not just a favored few, the right to be fickle and furthered the democratic ambiance of the urban shopping experience.

The liberal return policies coincided with the rise of manufactured and highly processed brand-name consumer goods. Because they were usually packaged, processed foods and toiletries could neither be examined before purchase nor judged until consumed. Manufacturers (as opposed to retailers) thus began to issue guaranties that would allow consumers to return unsatisfactory items as a way to reassure them it was safe to buy something based on its advertising and packaging, and consumers began to assume that they had a "right" to return products.[61] Advertising that touted and guaranteed a product's qualities was the handmaiden of branding. A standardized item sold at a standardized price could be promoted in a standardized way. As historian Ellen Gruber Garvey has shown, the magazine advertising of brand-name products played a major role in the gendering of consumer culture at the turn of the century. Women became a particular target of manufacturer advertising, which in turn encouraged gender-focused publications and gender-focused retail outlets.[62]

Stores took advantage of the emergence of brand-name manufactured goods by coordinating their own advertising with the manufacturers' national product advertisements. The producers could call attention to the unique qualities of their goods, while the retailers could sell at an advertised price that would be the same to every customer. Brands competed against each other, and stores competed against each other, but individual merchants did not compete against individual buyers in this new consumer marketplace. The implicit adversarial relationship between the retailer and the consumer dissolved in favor of one that emphasized price and service. Once the buyer could compare sellers' advertised or posted prices and any sale could be undone by a return, the sellers had to concentrate on volume to ensure profit. This new way of retailing may not have been economically more rational than bargaining, but within the social context, it did even the playing field for all buyers. From the perspective of the average shopper, one price with the option of a refund meant that the consumer could make each purchase with both forethought and hindsight. Rather than the high-pressure caveat emptor world of the traditional marketplace epitomized by horse trading, the modern consumer could be a coldly calculating buyer of the best product at the lowest price. To buy any other way now seemed irrational.

The department store was the archetype of the new retail paradigm, and it retains its iconic status to the present. Important as they were, however, department stores did not sell everything. As a general rule, the stores did not stock goods with relatively short shelf lives or that required extensive attention, which excluded fresh food and live animals (sometimes overlapping categories). They also shied away from items that were too large to conveniently stock in a multistory urban setting. Thus, neither horses nor carriages ever appeared on the sales floors of Macy's or Wanamaker's.

CHAPTER THREE

Cars

Joining the New Marketplace

Early bicycle boosters predicted that the new machines would seriously reduce dependence on horses. There is some evidence that they did have a slight impact, but it was much less than forecast.[1] Motorcars, not bicycles, replaced horses as the primary means of individual transportation.

In the first third of the twentieth century, the new automobile industry tried very hard to become part of the new one-price retail marketplace. By World War I, automobiles were being sold in well-appointed stores at advertised prices. Car manufacturers and retailers tried to appeal to women as well as men, and they repeatedly denounced price haggling when it broke through this façade of modern marketing. Bargaining, however, could not be suppressed. All too often, published auto prices were not selling prices, and from a retail perspective cars would turn out to be not horseless carriages but horseless horses. The auto industry sought to retain the appearance of modern retailing by advertising new car prices through the late 1930s and even sought laws to mandate manufacturer-set retail prices, but bargaining persisted and became the acknowledged norm after World War II. Even when General Motors' Saturn line finally broke the pattern of negotiated new car prices in 1990, it was unable to bring along the rest of the industry.

Despite its significance for household and national economics, the dealer-customer relationship has remained almost invisible in automobile scholarship. The perennial conflict between factory and dealer has been the focus of most academic research on automobile retailing. In his study of automobile sales James Rubenstein mentions customers only briefly in conjunction with his discussion of early cars as luxury items. Similarly, Walter Friedman omits the interactions between sales staff and customers in his history of salesmanship as a profession.[2] Their very useful studies do, however, help flesh out the ways in which manufacturers used dealers to market their products through a series of stages, usefully classified by Richard Tedlow as fragmentation, unification, and segmentation. Tedlow shows how the marketing of automobiles, like that of many new consumer categories (personal computers are a good recent example), passed through each of the three stages. Initially, in the *fragmentation* phase, large numbers of manufacturers competed in a virgin market until the public reached a consensus on what it expected. Fragmentation was followed by *unification*, which took place as marginal makers dropped out of the competition and public taste consolidated behind one particularly successful example—in the case of the automobile, the Ford Model T. However, once the mass demand for the new standard was satisfied, firms sought to expand their market through *segmentation*, a stage in which manufacturers diversified products to appeal to a variety of niche markets. In the automobile industry, General Motors took this step under Alfred Sloan when it marketed "a car for every purse and purpose."[3]

Marketing, however, is not selling. If industrial histories tell the story of cars from the top down, and social histories relate it from the bottom up, then selling is the interface where the trajectories meet—perhaps collide would be more accurate.[4] In modern department stores and supermarkets the sale, that is, the decision to buy a product, occurs seamlessly when the consumer plucks it off the shelf. The product and store advertising have done their job, and little if any input from a sales staffer is needed. This is the rational, democratic process that remains so conspicuously absent when a customer decides to buy an automobile.

Coachmen to Chauffeurs: The Male Lineage

Early car dealers did not want to be saddled with the shady reputation that clung to horse traders and made every effort to create an industry structured according to the newer single-price retail model, but history and economics ambushed them at every turn. The gendered aspects of personal transportation helped atavistic patterns survive, not because they were more economically rational, but because they were deeply ingrained and the reasons to change were weaker than the momentum to continue. An early example was the continuity between horse workers and car workers. Wealthy urban horse owners (and most urban horse owners were wealthy) employed grooms and coachmen to look after their personal transportation. As cars began to replace carriages ("car" is a linguistic variant of cart or carriage), coachmen made the transition by learning to drive and attend to the needs of automobiles. Classified advertisements during the first decade of the twentieth century featured men who had skills in handling both horses and cars, and automobile schools advertised instruction in driving and car care for coachmen who wanted to become chauffeurs.[5]

Horse owners had often given their equine-care staff the responsibility of buying new animals. Not surprisingly, given the general moral tone of horse trading, many grooms and coachmen saw this as an opportunity to make some extra money. Horse dealers cultivated grooms by paying them a commission on sales to their masters, but at the same time they complained bitterly about coachmen who extorted them by demanding kickbacks for recommending their horses.[6] This pattern of collusion between sellers and buyers' agents was easy to continue in the purchase of cars. A large number of the first generation of car owners were not car drivers and assumed there was no reason to learn to drive or maintain their vehicles.[7] They were used to being driven around by others, and looking after the well-being of an automobile was only marginally less unpleasant than looking after a horse. Just as horse buyers were advised to rely on the expert advice of their grooms, car buyers were warned that unless they were master mechanics, they would be wise to take along a "disinterested professional chauffeur" if they were planning to buy a used car.[8] Early cost comparisons of horses and cars usually factored in the coachman's wages in the former and the chauffeur's wages in the latter.[9]

The writer who advised taking along a chauffeur when looking at used cars was recommending that the car be examined by a professional, but trusting a professional chauffeur was as risky as trusting a professional coachman. In 1908 the Times Square Automobile Company sought to assure its customers that it was an honest outfit by announcing, "We pay no commissions to chauffeurs."[10] Historian Stephen McIntyre has found that chauffeurs were extorting commissions from auto repairmen as well during the same period.[11] Thus, the first of many seeds of impropriety were planted at the start of the automobile era. The widespread use of chauffeurs was, to be sure, a temporary phenomenon that disappeared quickly, especially after the introduction of the self-starting ignition in 1912. It is doubtful that the stain of this original sin would have been enough to taint the whole history of retail automobile sales, but it surely did not set a propitious precedent.

Cars in Stores

The basic question of just who would sell automobiles and how they would do so took about twenty years to sort out. Early manufacturers, who were mostly small, poorly capitalized, and essentially experimental, were not in any position to dictate how their products would be retailed. They wholesaled autos however and to whomever they could. The standard mode was to find a man willing to act as an agent, supply him with a sample car, and have him take orders and deposits. These early agents came from a variety of backgrounds. Some were simply salesmen who saw cars as a product to peddle. Most, however, had some relationship to the field of personal transportation. They were often bicycle shop or livery stable owners who had the space or the technical experience to take on a product as large, as new, as complicated, and as unreliable as the automobile.[12]

The size and cost of automobiles, as well as the attention they required, militated against selling them in department stores. Nevertheless, there was a brief experiment in doing just that. John Wanamaker was a car buff and a man who was proud that customers could buy almost anything in his stores, which carried low-cost items like handkerchiefs, stickpins, and stockings as well as expensive ones like diamonds, sideboards, and sable robes. Furthermore, boasted a store ad in 1900, they carried unusual items like banjos, rowboats, and automobiles, which, like all the store's goods were sold "at fair prices and with the Wanamaker guaranty of quality."[13] Wanamaker's stopped carrying cars in 1905, apparently because of their size and the staff needed to maintain them.[14]

Sears Roebuck was the one other mass retailer that attempted to use the standard retail model to sell cars. Sears already had experience selling light carriages and carts through its catalog when automobiles made their appearance at the turn of the century. However, the mail-order store waited until 1909 to decide that the automobile was here to stay and introduce its "Sears Motor Buggy." It would ship the motor buggy, complete with driving instructions, for prices starting at $370. Complete, but not ready to drive; the car came partially knocked down, and the purchaser had to have sufficient mechanical skill (and tools, also available from Sears) to finish the assembly at home. Sears stopped selling its unprofitable car three years later, driven out of the market by other brands that gave drivers more car for their money. The Sears car was cheap, but it was also little more than the motorized buggy its name implied. And even on the farm in 1912, car drivers were demanding at least the modicum of style provided by Ford.[15]

Universally acknowledged as the perfect combination of product design and production engineering, the Ford Model T was introduced in 1908, and the assembly line was first used to make it in 1913. Ford's mass manufacturing of a light, cheap car demonstrated that the sales strategy used for small household consumer products like soap and breakfast cereal could be applied to large ones as well. A company could make a lot of money by turning a luxury into a commodity and by selling more cheap items rather than fewer expensive ones. The Model T was no beauty in its day, but at least it was an improvement over the Sears Motor Buggy. It cost about the same, and with its numerous options and superior reliability, it quickly dominated the market. Henry Ford did not invent the design or manufacturing concepts he used, but he did combine them in a way that turned him and his company into the embodiment of modern practicality.

Selling Ford's paragon of automotive efficiency presented an entirely different problem. The cost-effectiveness of centralized factory production did not transfer easily to the automotive retail sphere, as the isolated experience at Wanamaker's showed. Like almost all automobile manufacturers, Ford started in 1903 with independent agents who could collect deposits and handle the details of final preparation and delivery. For three years, from 1907 to 1910, the company experimented with direct factory-owned outlets in six large cities; these were abandoned in favor of a return to a network of independent agents who could act as buffers against the seasonal swings in customer demand. To even out production schedules over the course of the year, Ford required its dealers to purchase their annual orders in equal monthly allotments, an inconvenience to the dealers who had to stock up in the slow winter months to meet the spring demand. In return, the dealers were given exclusive sales territories, and the factory stores were closed so that the company would not be competing with its own retailers.[16]

These early agents were often combination storeowners, salesmen, mechanics, and driving instructors. Most Ford owners were not the kind of people who would hire chauffeurs, so they needed to learn to drive their new cars for themselves (though, on doctor's orders, my own grandfather hired a chauffeur to drive his Model T). Dealers discovered that often the only way to make a sale was to give driving lessons to the new owner. Doctors who made house calls were a prime market segment, and John Eagal, a Ford dealer in Iowa, found that he frequently had to teach them to drive by going with them on their patient rounds. Eagal remembered that the absent-minded doctors complained that driving a car demanded too much attention; they were used to their horses navigating the routes by memory while they attended to deeper thoughts.[17]

After they taught their customers to drive, the dealers had to be there to repair what they sold. Every year after about 1900, the car press published encomiums to the progress that had been made in automobile reliability, each one an unintentional affirmation of how bad cars had been in previous years. While there is no doubt that automotive quality did improve significantly over time, there is equally no doubt that a good mechanic was a vital dealer accessory. The first generation of drivers, or their chauffeurs, expected to do a lot of minor repairs and adjustments themselves, and magazines said that the man who could not learn to do so in a month's time "ought to push a perambulator" rather than drive.[18] Cars may have become more reliable as the years passed, but they also became more complex, which meant that there were more parts to fail and it took greater skill and more specialized tools to set them right.[19] Having a properly equipped and staffed maintenance department was one of the standard requirements for holding a retail franchise. Dealers and manufacturers frequently cited well-equipped service departments as the reason why showrooms were not just another retail outlet.[20]

The first generation of manufacturers sold their cars through mail-order catalogs, traveling salesmen, consignment agents, franchise dealers, and factory-owned stores.[21] Many of the agents sold cars as a sideline to another business and sometimes handled competing brands. Bicycle store owners, who had experience with selling and servicing mechanical transportation, were good prospects as car dealers, as were livery stable owners who had large buildings and experience selling personal transportation to men. For example, Clarence Vallery, who opened a livery stable in southern Ohio in 1900, added cars to his inventory fourteen years later by dividing his stable down the middle, horses on one side, Fords on the other.[22]

The businesses that sold cars to the public might refer to themselves as agencies, dealerships, or branches, with the actual contractual relationship between the factory and retailer varying considerably.[23] After World War I, however, a pattern crystallized that remained the industry standard for the next thirty years. Retail automobile outlets, with very few exceptions, became franchises with exclusive geographic territories. In return, they sold only one company's cars under conditions set forth in contracts that generally gave the manufacturers undisputed authority to terminate the agreement if they did not approve of the way the dealer was operating.[24] Some unauthorized gray-market dealers sold diverse brands in the 1950s, and in 1957 a group of dealers near San Francisco combined their sales floors, but each brand was sold by a different business.[25] By the 1980s, several other forms of multiple brand dealers emerged, but none of these was akin to a standard retail store because buyers did not have an opportunity to compare similar models from different manufacturers, nor did they have a posted one-price policy.[26]

Although sometimes challenged on the state level, closed territories and fixed prices (wholesale and retail) generally remained intact until 1949, when the Justice Department warned manufacturers that "territorial security" provisions in franchises were probably a violation of federal antitrust policy. To the regret of a majority of the dealers, territorial protection subsequently disappeared from franchise agreements as all three branches of the federal government continued to weaken the factories' iron grip on their dealers.[27] Nevertheless, and despite sporadic attempts to encourage more competition among dealers, the fundamental relationship between factories and dealers remained intact until the 1950s, when federal and state franchise laws began to make it harder for manufacturers to cancel retail agreements.[28]

The retailer existed in what an observer during the Depression called "comfortless independence," almost like a factory worker in his obligation to obey the rules of the manufacturer if he wanted to earn a living.[29] The aspect of this one-sided power relationship that dealers found most onerous was the maker's expectation (sometimes a virtual requirement) that they sell a minimum number of cars if they wanted to maintain their franchise, a tactic that the manufacturers could not have used if they owned the dealerships themselves.[30] The factory wholesaled cars to every dealer at the same price but varied the quotas according to its estimate of how many cars each should sell.[31] These factory quotas put the retailers under tremendous pressure to move cars by cutting their profits during slow times, but published retail prices and limited production capacity gave them no way to expand their sales in good times.[32]

An anonymous Ford dealer complained publicly about these problems in 1927, describing how he had agreed to sell twenty cars a month but World War

I had interrupted the supply. Buyers were willing to pay a premium, but his franchise agreement bound him to sell at the retail price set by the manufacturer. This allowed customers in effect to buy at a discount. He found that they would take delivery of a new car, "drive around the corner, and sell it for fifty dollars profit." Unwilling to let the "bootleggers" make all the profit, he added phantom names to his waiting list and sold those cars sub rosa for an additional markup. The Ford factory representative got word of the scheme and demanded an end to the practice. When, however, demand diminished in the slump of 1920, the factory said it expected him to sell thirty cars a month, which it shipped like clockwork even when his unsold inventory exceeded 140 vehicles. One month the factory, anxious to reduce its own surpluses, told him that he had to accept fifteen cars above his already inflated quota if he wanted to stay in the automobile business.[33]

One Posted Price to All

The mythical narrative that auto industry affiliates repeat to each other contends that prior to some original sin, there was an era when the car business was a clean, upstanding profession in which owners and their sales staffs were admired members of the community who sold their high-prestige product at the same fair retail price to all customers.[34] "There was a time (back prior to 1955)," said a speaker at the 1960 National Automobile Dealers Association (NADA) convention, "when I (and others in my [non-auto] industry) looked upon automobile retailing with respect and envy. You fellows knew how to sell value and features . . . service and satisfaction over price."[35] Observers variously date the fall from grace as 1909 (when the first wave of consumer demand was satisfied), 1925 (when used cars were identified as a "problem"), 1930 (when the Great Depression decimated discretionary income), 1947 (when pent-up wartime demand created a peacetime black market), or, as in this case, 1955 (when the marketing sins of the late 1940s became the standard culture of auto retailing).

Each of these events did in fact have a discernible impact on the way cars were bought and sold, but the real original sin predated the car: it was horse trading. As soon as car dealers and car buyers tapped into the culture of horse trading, any paradise was lost. Tales of a Golden Age of auto retailing circulate within the business because dealers know they sell mass-produced consumer goods differently from any other industry and are as uncomfortable with the process as are their customers. The idea that there was a era when car salesmen conducted themselves in the standard retail fashion implies that there is no insurmountable obstacle to once again selling cars at one price, if only the retailers could figure out how to recapture the elements that once upon a time made it possible. Was there ever such a prelapsarian age when conservatively dressed, soft-spoken salesmen filled their clients' needs with just the right car, which the clients bought at the advertised price the way they would have purchased a new suit? The answer seems to be yes, but it was a fleeting Eden, lasting less than a decade, from 1900 to 1908.

For five or six years after their first appearance in 1895, automobiles were handmade and more experimental than practical. The people who made them and the people who bought them were mostly adult males intrigued by the machinery, the power, the danger, and the reputation of being on the cutting edge of a new technology that promised to combine the speed of the railroad with the flexibility of the horse. Despite automobiles' obvious shortcomings (unreliability and high price prominent among them), society seemed to grasp almost immediately that cars were the future. Their superiority as personal transportation was so evident that after 1900 it is difficult to find a contemporary who thought there was any long-term future for horses. Between 1900 and roughly 1908, the nation's cities were in the grip of an automania very similar to that which had marked the bicycle business a decade earlier. There were more buyers than sellers, innovations came on almost a daily basis, and early adopters were advocates as much as they were customers. Buying a car in these circumstances was not a typical consumer purchase. It was a financial transaction between members of a fraternity of adventurous pioneers, none of whom could be sure that either their company or their car would be operating a year hence.

Despite the product's unproved reliability, manufacturers and their agents had no trouble selling cars at published list prices as was required by the terms of most franchise agreements.[36] As standardized products, manufacturers could market automobiles as a uniform commodity, and prices, which held steady at high levels for almost a decade, appeared in advertisements.[37] Because there was no need to adjust prices to reflect the peculiarities of the individual vehicle, retail sales could take place in an environment more like a store than a stable. Historical materials from this period make little reference to negotiation, bargaining, trading, or otherwise dickering over the price of the car, other than an occasional reference to buyers paying premiums of as much as 25 percent to avoid having to wait months for delivery. It was a true sellers' market, and the sellers were not shy about taking advantage of it.[38]

There is some evidence from this pre-1909 period that a few auto retailers lured customers by promising to sell at less than list price. However, price flexibility on the showroom floor could not be a significant selling point as long as demand outstripped supply.[39] The balance shifted some time between 1908 and 1911 when, to attract reluctant buyers, a number of dealers began to offer discounts off the manufacturer's list price. A small advertisement for the Times Square Automobile Company at the end of the 1908 season promised half-off list price on certain unnamed "popular makes" bought from "overstocked" manufacturers.[40] Four years later Elliott Ranney, a Hudson dealer in New York City, felt obliged to warn car buyers about "the fallacy of buying a 'discount' automobile." Ranney explained that there were two kinds of discounts, those deducted from an artificially inflated list price, and those taken off a legitimate list price by cutting dealer profit. With the former, Ranney said, the discount varied with each sale so that the buyer never knew the real value of the car being bought. The latter, he said, was an unmistakable sign of a failing dealership that would soon be out of business.[41]

The Ford Motor Company fought a continuing battle to keep its dealers toeing the price line in the years before World War I. The company, which aggressively marketed its cars' low prices, started its war on price-cutting early on, when it found that some distributors had circumvented the company's strict list-price policy by giving dealer discounts to individuals.[42] Then in 1911 and again in 1913, the factory had to send warning letters to all branches to stop underpricing so-called demonstrators that had not in fact been used to demonstrate rides to customers.[43] Any dealer who sold a Ford below list did not deserve to be called a businessman because he was "nothing but a short-sighted bungler," a "fraud," and a "disorganizer in the business," charged the management in Dearborn. Name-calling was followed by threats as the company reminded dealers that "the provision of the Ford contract regarding price cutting will be enforced to the dot of an i. Better read the contract and see what will happen if you cut prices on Fords." Finally, the company appealed to the dealer's ethical sense by insisting that a price-cut to any one customer "is manifestly unfair to those who pay the full price in good faith."[44]

Invoking the still-common male experience of horse swapping, Ford management reminded the dealers that when shopping at their stores "The Buyer Doesn't Have to Beware or have his eye-teeth cut to horse-trades when dealing with us."[45] No trading also meant no boot: Would a customer ask a railroad to throw in a meal or a sleeper car when he bought a ticket to the Falls? asked the factory. Of course not. "It is just as much of a joke to throw in chains and gas tanks."[46] "In six cases out of seven when a prospect tries to make his price your price—*he is merely testing your nerve as a salesman.*" And not only that, warned the factory, he will tell what happened "to every other prospect in your community."[47] No salesman wanted to get a reputation as a pushover. Any concession was the first step down a slippery slope that would take the cars out of the one-price world of manufactured goods and back into the horse-trading arena with its flexible prices and equally flexible ethical standards.

Even as Ford management was railing against price-cutters, the company offered the industry's first manufacturer's rebate, a factory-sponsored version of the retail discount. In the spirit of its new five-dollars-a-day factory wage, Ford called its customer rebate program "profit sharing." The company announced that if it increased its sales from August 1914 to August 1915 by 20 percent, it would give between forty and sixty dollars back to every one of the 300,000 or more people who bought a new Ford "at full list price."[48] The program worked, and each of the 308,000 people who had registered their new Ford with the company received a fifty dollar check. Ford's rebate program was a one-time event that constituted a 10 percent discount. No other firm followed Ford's lead until 1960, when American Motors tried a similar but much more modest program.[49] Other manufacturers offered rebates to their dealers during the 1960s as a way to encourage them to cut prices to their customers, but it was not until 1975 that the factories started giving rebates directly to the buyers.[50] The customer rebates started in the 1970s were de facto admissions that buyers did not trust dealers to pass on price cuts.[51] Factory rebates had to function independently of the sales staff because both the manufacturers and the buyers knew that otherwise salesmen would try to pocket the rebate.

One-Price by Law

The Ford anti-price-cutting campaign that ended with the company-sponsored price-cutting rebate is just one of many indicators that list prices were subject to negotiated discounts before World War I. Something was starting to go wrong in the automobile market. Traditional horse-trading tactics were threatening to displace newer department store methods. Ford tried to nip this self-destructive behavior in the bud but failed. It kept pleading and threatening, and the dealers kept giving discounts. So in 1915, as they would again in the 1930s, car manufacturers looked to the government to save them from themselves. This took the form of a demand for what the American business community cleverly, if somewhat misleadingly, called "fair trade" laws. Neutral observers labeled the law "resale price maintenance," and critics referred to it as "price-fixing." Fair trade laws would permit contracts that required all retailers to sell their products at the price established by the manufacturer. There would still be price competition among manufacturers of similar products, but not among retailers of identical brands. Legally enforceable list prices were popular among small retailers, who feared competition from bigger and more efficient department and chain stores. Manufacturers generally supported price-maintenance because they thought discounted list prices undermined the public's confidence in their brands and because they did not want to alienate their many smaller retailers in favor of their few larger ones.[52]

Oblivious to the inconsistency of their position, the advocates of fair trade laws borrowed the logic that an earlier generation of department stores had used to promote their one-price policies. The department stores had prided themselves on posting prices and not dickering over them with each customer. Now the same kinds of small-store merchants who had clung to discriminatory pricing as department stores abandoned it wanted mandated prices to protect them from the department stores. What had been touted as "fair to all" and "democratic" when practiced within a single department store now became a way of ensuring that prices were not discriminatory among different stores. "It is clear that if certain hats are advertised to patrons all over the country at five dollars," explained a price-maintenance proponent in 1914, "the makers should be allowed to enforce the sale of their product at that price." To do otherwise was to be "guilty of discrimination" because the salesman would be free to adjust the price according to his estimate of the customer's ability to pay.[53]

Not only would fixed prices be more democratic, said advocates, but they would also promote other reforms popular in the Progressive Era. Supporters argued that by maintaining a set price competition would take place on quality, rather than be determined by cost, which had resulted in "unsanitary conditions, overwork and underpay, [and] employment of children." In the absence of such legal protection, they warned, "either manufacturers and publishers would have to cease advertising any price, or the price advertised would no longer mean anything because it was not the actual selling one."[54] They warned, in other words, about an end to the single-price marketplace and the return of universal haggling, which is exactly what would happen in the automobile business.

Representatives of both Ford and Packard testified before Congress that price maintenance was "the only moral and truthful method of doing business," because unfair competition was just as bad as unfair monopoly.[55] Ford briefly attempted to finesse court prohibitions on price maintenance in this period by once more setting up its retail outlets as company agencies but preferred to have independent dealers—as long as they were not independent enough to set their own prices. Small business champion and progressive reformer Louis D. Brandeis, soon to be appointed to the Supreme Court, argued in 1915 that a federal law guaranteeing the legality of price maintenance contracts would put all business on an equal footing. Brandeis pointed out that large businesses like Ford could open factory agencies to sell their products at a standard price, but smaller manufacturers lacked the same opportunity, allowing corporate money to buy unfair protection from the pressures of the marketplace. Brandeis wanted that protection from price competition guaranteed to all businesses.[56]

Neither the courts nor Congress were convinced that resale price maintenance was good for the economy, and American retailers remained free to set their own prices until the 1930s. Denied a specific legal basis for price maintenance, the auto industry maintained the quasi-fiction of manufacturers' suggested retail prices through the 1920s. "The principle of one-price to all has been generally accepted as fundamental in modern merchandising," explained an auto sales manual in 1919, turning a blind eye to numerous violations in the auto business. A rare pre-Depression academic study of the auto industry also accepted the generalization that list prices were firm, claiming that the informal norms of car selling "have led to a system of price maintenance equaled in few other industries."[57]

There is no way to judge precisely how many dealers adhered to the suggested list price, but there is no question that a significant number were willing to bend the legally unenforceable rules. "The dealer who begins to cut prices to a few of his customers is likely to find that within a short time everybody knows about it and everybody expects to be given the cut price," warned a dealer's manual in 1919.[58] "Do not make concessions. You have one price—stick to it," ordered (or begged) the marketing experts at Ford.[59] Price-cutting continued through the decade, and in 1929 one General Motors executive despaired, "Selling-buying relationships in business during the past few years have been pretty much on a plane of horse-trading," during which the seller would "make allowances and discounts and preferential terms until his fair price could no longer be recognized."[60] As late as 1930, Chevrolet was officially instructing its salesman to respond to customer requests for free extras (boot) by saying it was the same thing as asking for a price cut: "If you were to offer me $740 for a $765 car, naturally you would not expect me to accept."[61] That, however, is exactly what many customers had come to expect.

Then the Great Depression dealt a severe blow to the already shaky tradition of selling at list. With money hard to come by and buyers scarce, dealers had to fight for every sale, and discounting the factory price was an obvious way to lure customers. "It takes very little effort to get from $75.00 to $100.00 reduction on either Chevrolet or Plymouth," complained a top Chicago area Ford salesman in 1935.[62] By 1937 members of the industry were routinely referring to dealers who competed on retail price as "chiselers." Such a man, said the National Automobile Dealers Association (NADA), is engaging in "unfair and underhanded methods to compete in business. Lacking business ethics and ability, the only weapon that the 'chiseler' can use is price advantage."[63] The last three stanzas in a parody of the "Ten Little Indians" nursery rhyme in NADA's newsletter sum up industry antipathy to price competition and customer bargaining:

> THREE little chiselers, didn't know what to do;
> One met a low price, now there's only two.
> TWO little chiselers, a-cuttin' by gum;
> One cut the other's throat, now we have one.
> ONE little chiseler, left without a penny;
> He can't cut no more, so now we haven't any![64]

The vociferous criticism of "chiselers" in the 1930s makes two things clear: first, price-cutting was common enough to warrant both a specific appellation and a concerted attack from industry spokesmen; and second, even in the Depression era, there was a sense that cars should be sold at list price, despite a thirty-year tradition of negotiating discounts.

The vituperation of 1937 was the backlash to the end of an experiment in legally sanctioned price-fixing. For two years, from 1933 to 1935, the auto industry had operated under a set of price regulations put into effect by the National Recovery Administration (NRA), Franklin Roosevelt's experiment with centralized business self-regulation. While the industry-wide codes established under the NRA did set minimum prices, they were usually much lower than the retailers desired.[65] However, for the automobile merchants the NRA did something even more important; it established a list of maximum prices that could be paid for used cars traded in as part of the purchase of new cars. This issue will be dealt with more completely in chapter 4 on the "used-car problem." Suffice it to say here that dealers liked this experiment in regulating the market. Twenty years later, a NADA spokesman told Congress that trade-in allowances made legally established prices impractical in the retail automobile business, forgetting how dealers had welcomed them during the Depression.[66] When the Supreme Court declared the NRA unconstitutional in 1935, NADA, along with other small businesses groups, looked for ways to bring back the benefits of an unfree market. They managed to secure two pieces of federal legislation that made half-hearted attempts to limit price discrimination, but neither would have a major impact on the retail auto business.

The two laws, the Robinson-Patman Act of 1936 and the Miller-Tydings Act of 1937, appeared to hold out some possibility of "price stabilization," as proponents sometimes called it. Congress passed both laws despite continuing judicial disapproval and a distinct lack of enthusiasm from the executive branch.[67] The first law defined the circumstances under which manufactures could give larger discounts to some distributors and retailers than to others. The second permitted manufacturers to require resale price maintenance agreements from their customers in states where it was legal.[68] NADA backed the passage of both laws and threw its support behind the necessary state legislation that would allow manufacturers to prohibit competitive price-cutting.[69] By 1939, forty-four of the forty-eight states had passed such laws.[70] Wisconsin, a perennial pioneer in neo-Jeffersonian progressivism, led the way with a state "Recovery Act" that gave the governor the power to impose industry codes prohibiting unfair business practices. One such rule forbade companies from selling below cost, which the auto dealers interpreted to mean that over-allowances were illegal.[71] In 1940, NADA hired ex-NRA administrator Donald Richberg to represent it before the Federal Trade Commission, whose rulings on the application of the two federal laws did not always work to the advantage of the dealers.[72] Pulled between the mutually exclusive interests of the consumers and the merchants, the FTC, along with Congress and the executive branch, sometimes leaned one way and sometimes the other.

The post-NRA experiments with fair trade legislation never gained much traction. As business historian Jonathan Bean explains, they were undercut by changing state laws, judicial interpretations, consumer antipathy, and ultimately by an inability to enforce them in either letter or spirit. Chain stores and cut-price stores flourished in spite of them, and fewer and fewer manufacturers insisted on price maintenance contracts after the end of the Depression. The number of states with fair trade laws had fallen from a high of forty-four before

World War II to eleven in 1975 when Congress finally repealed the Miller-Tydings Act, ostensibly as an anti-inflation measure, although in 2007 the Supreme Court muddied the waters once more when it declared that manufacturer-set retail prices might be permissible under some (unspecified) circumstances.[73]

The automobile industry was not a major player in the fair trade law endgame because its circumstances had changed dramatically and list price discounting had ceased to be the focus of industry concern. From the beginning of World War II to the early 1950s, the issue facing the industry was not charging too little but charging too much—not price cutting but price gouging. After the war started in Europe in 1939, American production rebounded, and auto retailers quickly reverted to the established practice of pushing for every last dollar. Harlow Curtice, the president of General Motors, recalled that when he was head of the Buick division in 1939, he tried to publicize Buick retail prices, but he ran into stiff opposition from dealers who complained that national price advertising reduced their opportunities to jack up local prices with dealer add-ons.[74]

Once America entered the war in 1941, the list price issue was moot since no new cars were produced, but after the transition to a peacetime economy had been officially ratified with the lifting of wartime price restrictions in 1946, market forces came into play again. What emerged was a gray market in which speculators, including some dealers, used a variety of subterfuges to acquire new cars and then resell them at a premium. The public was furious. The manufacturers were worried about their reputations. The dealers were frustrated at not being able to take open advantage of the opportunity, and the whole situation gave rise to a mentality that ushered in what could be called the "definitive" (in the sense that it defined the business) period of American automobile dealing. The excess that characterized the automotive retailing environment between the end of the war and 1958 were so extreme that they will be detailed in their own chapter.

Advertising List Prices

Both manufacturers and retailers knew what was wrong with the automobile business, and both knew how to fix it: post list prices and stick to them. Every time a factory executive or a car salesman bought a new suit, the difference between his and other industries was obvious. Like the car salesman, the clothing salesman did not just collect money; he "sold" the suits. He assured the customer that the suit fit perfectly and looked great on him. He praised his product's quality and style, and promised the customer that wearing it would enhance his prestige. He noted that such a high quality suit at such a remarkably low price would not last long on the rack, and if the buyer wanted it, he had best buy immediately. Finally, the suit salesman, like the car salesman, collected a commission on the sale. The clothing salesman did everything the car salesman did except bargain over the price. The lesson was not lost on the car industry. As George Romney, the president of American Motors, observed in 1956, "After all, John Wanamaker built a great business by having one price." Harlow Curtice, the president of General Motors, agreed.[75]

From the local retailer's perspective, the major change that took place in the dozen years after the end of World War II was the virtual disappearance of manufacturers' retail prices from both national and local advertising. Car ads with prices had begun in 1901 with the curved dash Olds, America's first mass-produced car, which was regularly advertised at the factory price of $650.[76] Ford, too, was prominently advertising prices in 1904, well before the Model T appeared.[77] The pattern of prices in manufacturers' ads before 1920 indicates that both the factory and the retailer expected that the cars would be sold to the public at a single price, although consumers could sometimes get discounts if they tried.

List prices remained the advertising norm through the 1920s and 1930s, although the advertised figures were often misleadingly low because they did not include shipping costs and frequently excluded essential "accessories" such as bumpers and spare tires. During an investigation of industry practices in the late 1930s, the Federal Trade Commission found that the manufacturers' national advertisements were deceptive and that the prices the customers actually paid were "packed" with a variety of additional fees.[78] The prices may have been minimized, but they were there. Between 1924 and 1940 approximately half of the automobile advertisements in national magazines contained a list price, and in some months almost 90 percent did. During the same years, prices also appeared in about half the car advertisements in local newspapers. After World War II, however, selling prices were nowhere to be found. Fewer than 5 percent of national ads and only about 10 percent of local advertisements told the public what the car was supposed to sell for. Car stores would offer "low prices," "great deals," "$372 savings," and similar promises, but no actual prices.[79] The carmakers still issued retail price schedules to dealers as the basis for dealer wholesale discounts, but they were not used for price advertising.[80]

There were no formal announcements about this change in advertising pol-

icy. Manufacturers' suggested list prices just faded away over a fifteen-year period of retail price turmoil that started with the price controls of the NRA in
1933 and proceeded through the post-NRA period of fair trade laws, the wartime Office of Price Administration and black markets, and the postwar gray
markets. Dealers told customers that the factories prohibited them from giving
over-allowances because they amounted to slashing the list price, but they refused to disclose that list price.[81] The case of the disappearing list price came to
an end in 1958 when Congress mandated the manufacturer's suggested retail
price (MSRP) window sticker beginning with the 1959 model year (dealt with in
more detail in chapter 5). The legally ordered price tag was intended to force car
sales to adhere more closely to the standard conventions of the retail marketplace. The disappearance of posted prices had been a de facto acknowledgement
that cars were still being sold in a preindustrial style, and the new law was an attempt to force car sales into closer compliance with the standard retail model.

The desire to attract customers, not legislative mandates, had given rise to
the original retail culture of satisfaction in department stores, and a law that
only obligated posted prices was not enough to change the traditions of sales-
floor negotiation in car dealerships. The sticker requirement did, however, add
an unprecedented element of honesty to the process. Around 1979, in a moment
that deserves an award for car-market candor, automobile sellers began to include a price sticker labeled "ADM" or "additional dealer markup" on high-
demand cars. If customers wanted a car badly enough, they were going to have
to pay more than list price for it—up front and above board. *Forbes*, a conserva-
tive business publication, referred to the practice as "baldly labeled additional
dealer profit."[82] It was "bald" only because the law required car price tags to cat-
egorize the charges. Free market advocates pointed out that hiking the price of
desirable cars was merely the flip side of discounting dogs. Buyers, however,
complained that it was unfair dealer gouging, even as they bragged about haggling down the dealer's asking price.[83]

Isolated examples of dealers advertising and posting non-negotiable prices
popped up from time to time after the war. In 1957 a Philadelphia Pontiac
dealer let customers browse alone through his inventory. The owner said the
salesmen were just there to take orders: "Customers pay the price painted on the
windshield. No haggling."[84] Every couple of years another dealer would get the
bright idea to embrace the one-price system. He would generate a flurry of publicity when he announced that at last automobiles would be sold like all other
consumer goods—by helpful sales personnel at posted prices.[85] A California

Buick dealer, self-proclaimed as "the only honest guy in the business," tried selling at a flat $150 over invoice beginning in 1973. He abandoned the cost-plus scheme three years later but continued to sell at a firm posted price and refused to bargain over trade-in allowances. In a move that emphasized his deviation from the masculine practice of price negotiation, he fired his salesmen and hired four "girls" who greeted the customers, showed them around, and directed them to the office when they were ready to buy.[86]

Usually the one-price dealer would claim that profits were up sharply and that both customers and sales staff were happier in the new non-adversarial environment. A General Motors dealer in Michigan who sold cars for $49 over wholesale in 1983 said he thought there were about fifteen other dealers in the country doing the same thing. Other GM dealers were reportedly furious with him for poaching their customers, but he liked the program because there was "no trickery, no dickering, no lowballs." He contrasted his method of selling with that of his father, for whom he had worked as a sales manager. When it came time to sign the final papers and turn the car over to the customer, it had been his job to "discover" that the salesman had made a mistake and then bump up the price.[87]

There is no indication that any of these posted-price experiments lasted more than a couple of years. A solitary one-price seller might make some sales to people who hated to haggle, but other customers would use his posted price to bargain down competitors' prices, forcing him to cut prices further or lose sales. Single-pricing would be much easier if prospective buyers could not go to another dealer for a competitive quote, which is what General Motors accomplished when it introduced its Saturn in 1990. For the first time since the days of the Model T, a manufacturer was able to make a single posted price stick— for almost twenty years thus far. But Saturn has remained an exception. Its no-dicker sales policy did not chart a new course that other auto retailers followed. Instead, Saturn found a market among people (especially women), who did not want to haggle.[88] By the mid 1980s, the women's movement had changed the retail car culture sufficiently that a significant number of women were buying cars by themselves for themselves. Saturn's sales pattern vindicated the assumption that women disliked the hardball negotiation process and wanted to be able to buy a car the same way they had been buying everything else for a hundred years, off the shelf for a standard price. In the mid-1990s Saturn had a higher percentage of female sales staff, almost a quarter, and a higher percentage of female buyers, almost two-thirds, than any other brand.[89]

Saturn is an aberration in the history of retail car sales because of the longevity of its one-price policy. It managed to survive because the manufacturer was able to control the way the retailers sold the car by limiting the number of franchises.[90] Each of these relatively scarce dealers could attract enough negotiation-averse customers to stay in business and, for the first decade at least, make higher per-unit profits than other brands while enjoying unprecedented customer satisfaction with its sales system.[91] Yet even for Saturn buyers, car shopping was a one-price experience only if they did not have a trade-in. A Saturn manager told a would-be salesman that his store was a great place to work because "when you work here you won't have to lie" about the price of the new car. On second thought, he added, "Actually, it depends on your definition of lying." He explained that if the used-car manager said a trade-in was worth $4,500, it was perfectly okay to offer the buyer four thousand, thus adding $500 profit to the deal. "But," he concluded, in a telling commentary on sales staff ethics, "we won't ask you to do anything that conflicts with your core beliefs."[92]

The Saturn experiment was the first real opportunity to turn the 1959 window sticker price into a new-car market standard. Purveyors of other brands understood this and responded to it with something they called "value-pricing," which turned out to be a negotiable non-negotiable price. This new system offered a handful of selected models with a large number of optional accessories at a posted price that was much less than a similarly equipped car would normally cost. However, the "value-price" was limited to certain models that were excluded from rebates being offered at the same time on most other models. And the amount of the rebate just happened to be the amount the value-priced car buyers would save. If all of this seems confusing, it was supposed to. Although Ford officials (who originated the concept) conceded that "without exception, consumers have told us there's too much hassle buying an automobile," at the same time they asserted, "There's a psychology in the market that says you barter for a car." The value-pricing plan seemed to reduce the hassle but still left room for bartering (i.e., negotiating) if the dealer were tempted and the customer insistent.[93]

Saturn and "value pricing" prompted a boomlet in what dealers called "no-dicker sticker" prices. The dealers who switched said they were pleased because they were able to reduce the size of their sales force and attract larger numbers of women and minorities, two groups particularly suspicious of high-pressure sales. The general manager of the Chevrolet division of General Motors said he had seen marketing fads come and go, "but this one has staying power." At the same time, however, the sales manager of a no-dicker local dealership admitted that if a customer offered \$9,900 for a \$10,000 car, "I'd have a hard time not taking the deal."[94] Both the factory and the retail executives were right. The new system did have staying power for some. These dealers believed that their customers felt good—not because they had gotten the lowest possible price but because they knew nobody else had gotten a lower one.[95] At the same time, however, most dealers had a hard time not accepting a customer's final offer that was a few dollars shy of the "no-haggle" price.[96]

Dealers said they were pleased to abandon the "lies and games" that characterized their predatory sales techniques.[97] Yet even as some dealers were praising the new "soft sell" pricing strategies, others were complaining, especially about value-pricing.[98] They worried that by advertising a low package price, the factory made it impossible for them to squeeze maximum profits from unsophisticated customers, and since some customers still insisted on bargaining, overall profits were likely to decrease.[99] In 1994 an industry insider said that dealers were so "predatory that they can't stand losing the possibility of a person walking in and paying full sticker."[100] Over half the dealers surveyed by NADA in 1993 opposed value-pricing by manufacturers, and about half opposed one-price selling as well. Perhaps because per vehicle profits dropped to an all-time low in 1993–94, the one-price concept could not grow beyond a small retail niche.[101] Salespeople still dreamed of hitting the "home run" of a full price sale, and buyers worried that paying the sticker price meant they were not getting the best deal.[102] Estimates of the number of one-price dealers varied from 1 to 5 percent of the country's 23,000 dealers at their peak in 1992 and fell by half four years later.[103]

In an attempt to rein in price competition and customer exploitation, in 1999 both Ford and General Motors experimented with a technique that recalled the early days of the century by purchasing substantial shares in some regional dealerships as a way to impose a consistent standard of retailing that included no-haggle pricing.[104] A growth in factory-owned, one-price dealerships might have changed the face of car retailing, but it was a feint not a strategy, because the big changes were expected, not from the revival of an old system, but from the arrival of a new one—the Internet. Many dealers' initially feared they would have to abandon their forty-five-year tradition of bargaining down from the sticker price and simply post their non-negotiable price on the Web, where their customers could do comparison shopping. At long last, cars would be sold like washing machines.[105] The Internet will be discussed in more detail in the epilogue, but suffice it to say that it took only about three years for the ever-evanescent promise of normal retail pricing to evaporate as the retail car market learned how to incorporate the Internet into the time-honored tradition of individual negotiation over each and every sale.

The dealer's desire to maximize profit on the sale of a new car and the customer's desire to minimize it are the reasons usually cited for the failure of posted one-price selling to become the car industry norm. That is an accurate but incomplete explanation because it deals with only half of most car transactions. In addition to buying a new car, the vast majority of customers are selling a used one. The easiest customer to sell the used car to is the dealer from whom they are buying the new car. These trade-ins have always been the flies in the ointment of modern auto retailing. Used cars are what forced automobile retailers to be car *dealers*. The "deal" in car dealer was the equivalent of the "trade" in horse trader. Even if the custom of one-price sales had taken hold in car stores, the "used-car problem" had to be confronted. The manufacturer might suggest or even insist on a retail price for the new car, but nobody could suggest a price for a used car because each secondhand car, like each horse, was different.

CHAPTER FOUR

Used Cars

Undermining the New Marketplace

People referred to early automobiles as horseless carriages because that is what they resembled physically, but culturally and economically they functioned more like horses than carriages. The ongoing rhetorical trope that compares used-car dealers to horse traders, which is employed by everybody from Nobel laureates to folklorists, expresses a cultural memory based on a historical reality: for the first forty years of the twentieth century, used cars functioned as horseless horses in the male community.[1] The sale of used cars to and by new-car dealers prevented the full integration of new cars into the standard single-price marketplace. The flexible pricing that used-car trade-ins in effect imposed on new-car sales emerged in tandem with the commercial production of automobiles and continued unabated into the age of the Internet. All attempts to make posted prices the real prices that cars sold for foundered on the horse-trading culture that characterized used-car sales.

A 1910 cartoonist showed two farmers on the main street of a small northern town swapping cars the same way they would have traded horses a couple of years earlier. One is offering to trade his car and to throw in a hardly used plow to boot. Meanwhile, the usual gaggle of men and boys assembles to enjoy the show.[2] It is obvious that neither of the men in the cartoon is a car dealer and that neither car is new. By removing the scene from the retail environment, the cartoonist was able to emphasize the horse/car parallel, still unexpected enough in 1910 to be considered funny. The humor in equating cars with horses persisted until the World War II era because there continued to be a population of men who were familiar with horses and horse-trading culture. (See fig. 2.)

In 1939 a Kansas City Ford dealer ran a large advertisement with a picture of a horse and the bold headline, "Big 'Hoss' Swappin'!" The text urged readers to "bring in your old 'nag' and swap for one of these registered thoroughbreds."[3] By putting "nag" in quotes, the dealer was signaling that the whole offer was a marketing metaphor. Until just about the date of that ad, however, horse-trading language had not been merely metaphorical. As soon as they were widely available, cars became another commodity to be exchanged in the informal world of rural men's swapping, while horses became barter that could be traded for cars and tractors.[4] In rural areas, horse trade-ins were so common until World War II that farm equipment dealers often became both swap centers and sales barns for the animals they took in trade.[5] The expectation that dealers would accept horses as partial payment for motor vehicles, and the willingness of dealers to accede to that demand, established a basis in reality for calling car price negotiations "horse trading," making it more than a linguistic anachronism like "dialing" a push-button telephone.

If we think of used-car sellers using horse-trader categories, there was (and continues to be) a reasonable parallel among three groups. First, new-car dealers who resell used cars they took in trade were similar to the barn traders who, as established businesses, were under a certain amount of social pressure to conduct themselves in an ethical manner. Second, independent used-car dealers unaffiliated with a factory franchise were analogous to the road traders of the horse world. Their inventory was of poorer quality, and their business standards were more flexible than those of larger dealers. Finally, there were the private person-to-person sellers of used cars. From a broad retail perspective, new-car dealers were the most unusual category of used-car sellers because they incorporated elements of bargaining into the sale of new manufactured goods. They did this both by reluctantly bargaining over the price of new cars and by more enthusiastically haggling over the price of the trade-in. Before World War II, when most dealers and buyers at least paid lip service to the advertised list price, new-car discounts were often given in the form of "over-allowances," in which the dealer paid more for the used car than he could sell it for.

A dealer who gave an over-allowance might not have to sell it for less than he paid because there was always the possibility that he might turn a profit on both ends of the deal. Except for a brief period near the end of World War II, when the government established used-car prices, dealers were free to put any price they wanted on used cars—or to post no price at all. Long before they were doing it on new cars, dealers were plastering huge signs, advertising "Cheap," or "Reduced," or "Great Deal" on their used car without giving any indication of the asking price, although a special code would tell the salesman what the car had cost the dealer. The sign boldly announcing the amount of dollars down and dollars per month to drive off in this or that beauty would conveniently omit the number of months required, which would be varied to accommodate the customer's bargaining skill.[6] Since used-car customers often had used cars of their own to trade, the economic dynamics of secondhand car transactions could closely resemble those of classic horse trades.

If the purchase of used cars from their current owners or their resale to new owners could have been handled as distinct transactions, the cars could have been sold at fixed prices. Some dealers tried. In 1916 the Willys-Overland outlet in New York advertised that each of its used cars was tagged with a price "that will be the first and only price that car will have." You did not need the "bargaining sense of [the fictional horse trader] David Harum," promised the ad, to get the best price.[7] The idea did not catch on. A dozen years later another dealer claimed that he sold used cars on a one-price-to-all basis. He wrote a book and supplied sample copy for a newspaper advertisement emphasizing that the tag price was the price everybody paid, with the added benefit of a five-day return privilege.[8] There may have been other non-negotiating used-car dealers during the first three-quarters of a century of car dealing, but they too would have been isolated cases.

Attempts to sell used cars at nonnegotiable prices remained rare until 1971, when the Hertz and Avis car rental firms opened outlets that sold automobiles with reasonably low mileage and documented mechanical care at an advertised price. The companies offered warranties, arranged financing, and refused to take trade-ins. In other words, Hertz and Avis sold used cars the way most retailers sold new goods, and they had that small niche market entirely to themselves for two decades.[9] Then the siren song that Saturn sang in the 1990s was heard by several entrepreneurs who thought they could do for used cars what Saturn was doing for new cars and the rental companies were doing for their own used rental fleets. That is, they thought they could create used-car supermarkets where they would sell cars for posted prices with guaranties. Unlike Hertz and Avis, these used-car supermarkets also bought used cars, either as trade-ins or as "straight sales" (sales without a trade-in). However, the price they offered for each used car was the only price they would pay. They bought the same way they sold.[10]

CarMax, owned by electronics retailer Circuit City, began the one-price used-car business in 1993. Starting in Richmond, Virginia, and then expanding into several other southern cities, CarMax stores stocked a thousand vehicles that the customer could preview on a showroom computer and then buy by scanning a barcode. Just as chain stores had driven out mom and pop retailers in the 1920s and 1930s, observers predicted that the new used-car chains would mark the end of the pennant-bedecked neighborhood used-car lot and its fast-talking horse-trading owner. Like Wal-Mart and Home Depot, these new stores would be "category killers," not so much because they were cheaper, but because they sold their products straightforwardly. In the words of a *Wall Street Journal* headline, "Cars Are Sold Like Stereos by Circuit City."[11]

CarMax was followed by AutoNation, a venture underwritten by H. Wayne Huizenga, a Florida tycoon and sports team owner. It was to be Huizenga's AutoNation versus Honest Harry's Used Cars, or Huizenga's Miami Dolphins versus the Smallville junior varsity. It was to be, in the optimistic words of a news magazine headline, "Goodbye to Haggling."[12] In February 1996, "nine of the nation's biggest and most powerful automobile dealership owners" got together in Dearborn, Michigan, to meet the superstore challenge by setting up their own Driver's Mart. They promised that they too would sell used cars at non-negotiable prices and with the same kind of return privileges and guaranties offered by the two industry leaders.[13] They need not have bothered. Driver's Mart was destined to an early demise because it was under-capitalized in two vital areas. It lacked sufficient funds to establish itself on a solid nationwide basis, and it broke the cardinal rule of retail startups for the twenty-first century—its name did not contain an internal capital letter. AutoNation, a firm with proper cyber-era orthography, bought it out two years later.[14]

The consolidation of used-car superstores continued. The flash and glitter of these roaring-nineties startups turned out to be no match for Honest Harry and his hard-sell peers. Threats and promises to use modern marketing methods, computers, and the Internet to revolutionize the sale of used cars fizzled out even as the popular press was announcing that the Internet was making the traditional hand-to-hand combat in the used-car lot obsolete. Sales at the superstores were below the level needed to turn a profit, either because Huizenga and his ilk underestimated the market or because used-car buyers became angry and walked off when they found they could not bargain on the posted prices.[15] It certainly did not help that the posted prices were often many hundreds of dollars more than negotiated prices at traditional dealers.[16] AutoNation ceased operation in 1999, while CarMax hung on, catering to a niche market that was willing to pay a premium for an off-the-shelf used-car-buying experience.[17]

Despite the Saturn and CarMax business models, despite their savvy use of the Internet, and despite the increasing number of women car owners, historical inertia once more forestalled the impetus to change. The twenty-first-century sale of used cars began much the same as the twentieth—that is, with the promise of a new approach but with those hopes quickly dashed as the horse-trading tradition barreled on.

Origins

The failure of the one-price used-car outlet assured the continuation of negotiated prices for *new* cars because of the trade-in allowance. There is some disagreement among industry observers as to when used cars first became a concern to new-car dealers. They variously set the key date at about 1910 or about 1920. Almost everybody agrees that by the mid-twenties, the auto industry had a "used-car problem," and that problem became a crisis during the economic depression of the following decade. A good argument can be made for either of the initial dates. Which of the two one chooses depends on the definition of "problem." Dealers first articulated their concern about used cars in 1910 but did not confront it systematically until after the First World War.

The high price of the earliest new cars meant that there was an immediate market for cheaper used cars. Prices in New York dealer catalogs in the first five years of the century ranged from $750 to $3,000 and averaged about $2,000 for domestic brands; European imports could cost more than $15,000.[18] To put that in perspective, for an unskilled worker in 1903 the $750 car would be the equivalent of a $72,000 car in 2004, and a car that light and cheap was dismissed by industry experts, who suggested spending more than twice as much ($1,750) for a minimally acceptable vehicle.[19] The high cost of the new car could be offset by its strong resale value. The purchaser of that $1,750 car, for example, was told that if he maintained it well, he could get $1,100 for it on the used-car market after two years.[20]

As with horses, carriages, bicycles, pianos, and other relatively expensive items, secondhand autos were regularly sold through classified advertisements. As early as 1901, New York newspapers were running ads for used cars.[21] Between then and 1910, automobile owners looking to buy newer and better cars regularly tried to sell their current vehicles through private newspaper advertisements. In an era when telephones were still a luxury, classified ads meant publishing the seller's address and meeting strangers at the front door. There was, however, an alternative solution. The bicycle business had established a precedent by accepting used vehicles as trade-ins. If bike riders could get their dealers to buy back $100 machines, then could new-car owners who had paid two thousand dollars more expect less? In 1903 the Ansonia Motor Car Company on the Broadway auto row claimed it was the only "exclusive used-car dealer in New York."[22] If that claim of exclusivity was accurate, it means that other dealers who sold used cars also sold new ones. Indeed, just a year earlier *Scientific American* had asserted that the "disposition of second-hand vehicles has become a most important part of the business of every dealer."[23]

Just how "every dealer" was disposing of the secondhand vehicles was not explained. Many of the new-car dealers who were selling used cars may not have actually been in the used-car business because they were selling their customers' secondhand cars on consignment, a common practice until about 1909. Car dealers who offered to sell privately owned cars without taking legal possession of them avoided both the expense of paying for the used car and the complications of having to find a second buyer at the right price. The Packard Motor Car Company of New York, for example, followed a 1903 list of secondhand vehicles for sale with the notation: "The above slightly used cars *belong to customers* who have purchased the celebrated Packard transcontinental touring cars."[24] Similar ads spoke about selling cars "for our customers," cars that customers had "left" at the dealer and cars "returned" for a new model.[25]

It is unclear exactly what it meant for a car to have been "returned" for a new model, though some early dealers did indeed buy back "returns" (at a steep discount) from dissatisfied drivers who did not understand how to run them.[26] Direct purchases of customers' current cars as part of the deal for a new car were taking place by 1907. That is approximately when the term "trade-in" came into use and used-car dealers emerged as a distinct retail category.[27] Thus, a recognizably modern used-car market had developed before 1910, when the husband in a short story tries to mollify his wife by telling her that the $2000 he spent on their first car will make all the subsequent ones considerably cheaper because of the allowances he will get for his trade-ins.[28]

Over the next few years, the secondhand car business blossomed as used-car dealers refined the kind of promises that had previously been made to horse buyers. They "guaranteed" that cars had been "thoroughly overhauled" and were in "perfect running order" and promised "any reasonable offer considered."[29] However, when the used-car dealer was buying rather than selling, the value of vehicles suddenly plummeted. In 1914 a man who had accepted a used car as payment for a $250 debt was shocked by a dealer's offer of $31.50. The dealer said there was no demand for that model car, and he was offering the value of the windshield, speedometer, and headlights, accessories that he could salvage and sell separately.[30]

The rise of a market for used cars led salesmen and manufacturers of high-priced automobiles like Packard to use their brand's "second-hand value" as a selling point.[31] Curiously, Packard had a firm rule against taking cars as trade-ins on the purchase of its new cars, but other companies recognized that accepting trade-ins was an incentive to buy their brands and encouraged their dealers to trade. "Your old car is worth more now than it will be next spring," promised an ad in November 1917. "Trade it in now as part payment on an Overland or Willys-Knight car."[32] In a pitch for manufacturers and dealers to buy more magazine advertising in 1914, the Curtis Publishing Company reminded them that the buyer with a trade-in was actually a seller, and unlike the dealer who had to move his inventory, the buyer could always wait if he did not get the price he wanted.[33]

Just about the only quality that distinguished the period from 1909 to 1917 from the 1920s was the absence of the label "used-car problem."[34] While some dealers before the war sought to take advantage of the used-car market as a way to make additional sales, others recognized that secondhand cars used as trade-ins had the potential to erode profits on the new-car sale. A speaker at the 1912 National Automobile Dealers Association convention reminded his fellow dealers that the "ever-increasing percentage of sales involving trades . . . means usually the making of two sales in order to make one profit."[35] Another dealer chided the industry for the secondhand car "situation" that he called "a curse which motor car dealers have largely brought upon their own heads." The solution, he suggested, was a central clearinghouse that bought and valued all trade-ins.[36] The clearinghouse solution would be proposed repeatedly over the next thirty years as the "situation" became universally perceived as a "problem."

Trade-In Allowances and Over-Allowances

The secondhand automobile "situation" became a used-car "problem" in the 1920s because the car market became much more competitive. Qualitatively, there was nothing very different in the used-car market pre- and postwar, but quantitatively, the hidden cost of trade-ins was much harder to ignore. Over-allowances had become almost standard practice by 1922, when it is estimated that dealers lost an average of $56 on each trade-in. The problem accelerated through the decade as the proportion of used to new cars sales increased, with used cars taking the lead for the first time in 1927.[37] Over-allowances had been an issue even before World War I, when one manufacturer warned in 1912 that overpriced trade-ins were no way to sell new cars, and a study in 1914 found that price-cutting was taking place through discounts, free accessories, free service, and over-allowances.[38] A Ford dealer who adamantly asserted he never varied a penny from the official list price nevertheless admitted, "We might over-allow a little on the used-car appraisal to close a deal."[39]

On the eve of American entry into World War I, a popular how-to book for car dealers featured an illustration of a "prospect information sheet" that showed the salesman penciling in "$400" on the "amount offered" line, while noting separately that the car was worth only $350; the over-allowance was simply taken for granted.[40] The situation accelerated in the 1920s. Packard, which had prohibited trade-ins before the war, did an about-face by cutting wholesale, not retail, prices to allow its dealers to give higher trade-in allowances than their competition while maintaining the semblance of an unvarying list price.[41] Other manufacturers less concerned with dealer profits simply demanded so much volume that the Federal Trade Commission accused them of forcing their dealers to give over-allowances.[42] Ford, on the other hand, tried to hold back the tide by suggesting that its dealers just ignore the problem by not accepting trade-ins at all.[43] One way to do that was to sell to buyers who did not own cars. The factory urged Ford dealers to canvass aggressively for first-time buyers, pointing out that doing so eliminated the "bug bear" of used cars.[44] However, first-time buyers were a rapidly shrinking pool, a fact that was recognized at the time—albeit reluctantly at Ford's home office.[45]

Unlike Ford, General Motors, which promoted rapid turnover with its annual model change, pressured its dealers to take trade-ins.[46] In case the implied message was too subtle, local factory representatives openly recommended that dealers make over-allowances in order to keep their volume up. By 1938, factory reps were telling a GM dealer in New Hampshire that he should give as much as forty dollars per car as an over-allowance to boost his sales numbers.[47] Thus, over-allowances, which lay at the core of the used-car problem, may have originated with dealers but were encouraged by some manufacturers who reaped the benefits of increased volume without having to bear the cost of reduced profits.

By the 1920s, the horse-trade model had become integral to the way cars were sold. No individual dealer could refuse to buy his prospect's used car and expect to have many customers. Advice for dealers and salesmen constantly referred to customers using the trade-in allowance as a bargaining point, threatening to buy elsewhere if they did not get what they wanted. A three-city survey in 1931 found that almost three-quarters of salesmen spent their time "horse trading" over the allowance rather than "selling" the virtues of the new car.[48] The marketing professionals could insist all they liked that cars should be sold on their merits; the men on the lot knew that sales were made by negotiating prices, usually for the trade-in.

Salesmen were often advised to respond to demands for an over-allowance by appealing to the customer's sense of fair play. Charging one customer more than another for the same product violated the ethical norms of twentieth-century retailing, and dealers tried to invoke the department store ethos to shame haggling customers. Salesmen were told to explain that an over-allowance would unfairly cut the dealers' profit and that legitimate dealers never gave discounts. "It is absolutely unfair to buyers on straight sales (where there are no cars traded in) to ask them to pay full price and full profit," argued a *Manual for Ford Salesmen*. In fact, the manual continued, because of the extra work involved in a trade-in, "if anything, the man who gives the clean deal is the one who should get the reduced price."[49] When a referred customer "forced" a Connecticut Dodge dealer to give him fifty dollars more on a trade-in than his friend had gotten, the dealer felt obliged to send the first customer a fifty-dollar refund. Both the dealer and the original customer felt sullied by the "dishonest" transaction.[50]

When appeals to customers' sense of fairness failed, as they usually did, dealers were told to protect themselves by being careful businessmen. It was not enough to sell cars; they were reminded to make sure that their accounting and appraising procedures meticulously factored in all the costs of the purchase and resale of the trade-in, lest they be "headed for bankruptcy."[51] The best way to establish realistic allowances, said the experts, was to have them firmly set by a staffer who was a used-car specialist and could accurately estimate what the dealer would get for the trade-in.[52] Striving for high volume at the cost of profits was self-defeating, retail advisors warned, ignoring the fact that the push for high volume was often a dealership's attempt to meet factory-imposed quotas in an increasingly saturated market.[53]

With the advent of the Depression, the "problem" in the used-car problem was no longer reduced profits from over-allowances, but the absence of new-car customers altogether. Aside from a brief respite while the National Industrial Recovery Act was in effect, dealers in the 1930s believed that the only way to sell more new cars was to reduce what they called the "glut" of used cars.[54] There was a nightmare theory in the car business that every car taken in trade could be resold infinitely. Although it did not explore the regression beyond the second generation, a study in 1935 concluded that for every new car they sold, dealers had to sell 1.5 used cars: one they had taken in trade on the original new car, and one they had taken in trade on the sale of the original trade-in.[55] The ratio of used to new cars being sold was actually much higher, because the 1.5 figure does not include person-to-person sales or sales by exclusively second-hand dealers.[56] Each time a car was traded in, the industry was losing an opportunity to sell a new car. Consequently, "used-car loss control" became the major concern of new-car dealers during the Depression.[57] Periodically throughout the 1930s, regional and national groups came up with plans for "the extermination of superannuated automobiles."[58]

At the beginning of the Depression, Chevrolet and Ford had set up programs to buy and scrap cars that had been used as trade, and in 1930 the National Automobile Chamber of Commerce (the manufacturers' trade organization) consolidated the scrapping schemes into a national plan. This particular scheme, which remained in operation for about three years, had manufacturers contribute to a fund used to pay dealers for scrapping trade-ins that were in running condition. A contemporary report on this plan explained that the "running condition" requirement was necessary in order to prevent dealers from acquiring cars from junkyards and turning them in for cash, adding laconically, "It must be admitted that some dealers are not nice."[59] This observation was borne out by a report that dealers still found a way to game the system by picking up wrecks from junkyards, nursing them back into barely running condition, and then turning them in for the bounty.[60]

The drive to rid the road of used cars paused between 1933 and 1935 while the NRA regulated trade-in prices, but picked up again during Roosevelt's second term. NADA promoted a trade-in buying plan in 1938 that would have been similar to the Auto Chamber of Commerce scheme of 1930. Dealers loved the idea, but manufacturers were no longer willing to pay to scrap functional old cars, and the plan never got off the ground.[61] The *Milwaukee Journal*, in conjunction with local dealers, ran a voluntary junking plan in 1938. That scheme, like the earlier one, stressed the safety issue of getting "jalopies" off the road and featured bonfires in which dozens of obsolete cars were burned in front of forty thousand spectators. Milwaukee's *auto da fe* (as it were) prompted a short-term uptick in used-car sales—presumably of better quality than those burned at the stake—but without manufacturer support, the dealers had to find some device other than culling to grapple with the used-car problem.[62]

Controlling Over-Allowances

Short of a law that prohibited the resale of automobiles, dealers understood that used cars were not going to disappear from the market. Junking jalopies might have been marginally useful in expanding the market for new cars had it worked, but the underlying problem for dealers was not too many used cars, but over-allowances, which was their backhanded way of cutting prices on new cars. List-price cutting risked angering the manufacturer, because it made it harder for the car companies to feature prices in their national advertising and made their automobiles look less desirable to the public when they saw local advertisements trumpeting discounts. If they became sufficiently annoyed, the manufacturers could discipline errant dealers by canceling their franchises or being slow to deliver desirable models. Furthermore, because car dealers did not compete by advertising lower retail prices, many buyers in the 1930s may not have known that list prices were negotiable, although almost all knew they could shop around for the best trade-in allowance.[63] Trade-ins per se were not problems—allowances were. (See fig. 3.)

Programs to coordinate used-car buying and control over-allowances began a full decade before the "problem" label was routinely used. In 1911 auto executive A. O. Smith said that overpriced trade-ins were a bad way to boost new-car sales. He blamed the dealers, not the customers, for initiating the trade-in practice and said the only way that it could be brought under control was to establish a single clearinghouse with the sole authority to determine the value of a used car.[64] Smith may have been familiar with another attempt to rein in high trade-in allowances that had begun earlier the same year. The licensed auto dealers of New York City, worried that over-allowances had the potential to "greatly hamper the automobile industry," had met and pledged to abide by the so-called "Philadelphia plan," described as "a uniform basis for the trading in of second-hand cars."[65] A year later the dealers agreed to stop buying trade-ins and accept them only on consignment, giving the buyer of the new car simply what the dealer could fetch for the old one.[66] The New York arrangement was unable to survive the competitive pressures of the retail car business, but the dream of controlling used-car allowances lived on.

Attempts to coordinate allowances blossomed again once the post–World War I demand for cars had been satisfied. There were reportedly "hundreds of dealer groups" that participated in cooperative marketing exchanges in the first years of the 1920s, and many survived until the start of World War II.[67] In some cases these appear to have been actual centralized buying and selling sites, while in others they were a voluntary weekly exchange of information on used-car sales prices. One such exchange had started in Saginaw, Michigan, in 1914 and was copied by others after World War I.[68] The sales figures exchanged by the dealers could be used both to avoid unintentional overpayment on trade-ins and to show buyers that their cars were not worth as much as they thought.[69] The voluntary approach peaked in the second half of the 1930s when dealer groups all over the country drafted complicated plans as part of the movement to pass price-maintenance legislation. In 1935 the NADA enlisted many of the major manufacturers in a scheme to pressure dealers to report all of their used-car sales so the association could issue an "official" price guide.[70] At the same time, a private firm, Chamberlain Associates of Detroit, sought to act as a regional price coordinator, taking a commission from the sales of participating dealer groups to oversee used-car allowances.[71]

The various plans to create central buy-back clearinghouses or standardized consignment programs invariably failed after a few months, but the idea of exchanging information was able to take root. A Chicago company had been selling "red books" of used-car prices to local dealers since 1911. The concept was picked up and repeated in major market areas across the country.[72] Most famously, Les Kelley, a Los Angeles used-car dealer who had distributed a list of cars he wanted to buy, began publishing that list as the *Kelley Blue Book* in 1926. His color choice became the generic term for more than a half-dozen used-car guides that developed into fixtures of the secondhand car business.[73] The guides were compiled by surveying regional used-car sales and then publishing average prices based on model, age, and condition. They were intended to give salesmen realistic numbers on which they could base their allowance offers, but salesmen were quick to show them to customers to justify lower-than-expected offers. The offers were often so low that both sellers and buyers referred to the blue books as "shock appraisal guides," and in 1939 the Federal Trade Commission charged that some blue book values were deliberately understated so that salesmen could use them to make lower offers.[74] Deflated values, however, undermined the usefulness of the books to dealers, and in any event, most drivers had such inflated ideas about the worth of their trade-in that even an honest evaluation was bound to be a shock.[75]

Industry hopes for controlling over-allowances got a boost when President Franklin D. Roosevelt signed the National Industrial Recovery Act into law on June 16, 1933. The law created the National Recovery Administration (NRA), which supervised the "codes of fair competition" that allowed industries to establish certain parameters of conduct without running afoul of the antitrust laws. The members of the retail automobile industry leaped at this opportunity to use the power of the government to do what they had not been able to do by themselves—put a ceiling on the amount paid for trade-ins. New-car dealers were the first retail industry in the nation to approve a fair competition code and would later look back on the period "as one of the best in their history."[76] The National Automobile Dealers Association drafted the NRA code that made it a violation to sell at less than the list price established by the manufacturer. This provision was especially important in "straight" (or "clean") deals where there was no trade-in, because it stopped the savvy buyers who had been able to play one dealer off against another from getting discounts of as much as eighty or ninety dollars.[77]

List-price discounts were not the major problem for dealers, however; over-allowances were. Only if dealers could standardize the payments for trade-ins could they make the list prices the real cost of the car. For many years prior to 1933, manufacturers of less-popular brands had given their dealers large wholesale discounts, some of which could be given away as an over-allowance.[78] At the beginning of the Depression, Ford tried to resist this shell game, but ultimately it had to play along by upping its own dealer discount.[79] While the Ford factory reluctantly acknowledged that trade-in bargaining had become standard operating procedure, the company did not provide its sales force with any suggestions on how to negotiate effectively.[80] Over-allowances were like sex—you might not be able to stop your kids from doing it, but you had no obligation to teach them how to do it well.

Once the NRA code went into effect, the allowance issue disappeared, because the prices for used cars were established by NADA in its *Official Used Car Guide*, which was updated every sixty days and informally known as the "brown book" (temporarily displacing Kelley blue as the industry's emblematic color).[81] The prescribed trade-in prices varied by region, but all retailers who operated under the code were supposed to follow it. "Your code and the official interpretations of your code are federal law," NADA told its members. "Traitors, snipers, chiselers and weaselers must be rooted out" and sent to "jail where they belong."[82] Dealers believed that in this brave new world they could compete on brand merit and manufacturers' list prices, but would stop competing through "commercial bribery in the form of a padded trade allowance."[83]

The code may have prohibited "commercial bribery" (otherwise known as price competition) on the up side, but there were no limits on the downside. The figure in the official used-car guide, less about 10 percent for reconditioning and handling, was the maximum that dealers could allow on a trade-in, but they could give less if the customer would accept it. From the dealers' point of view, it was a no-lose situation. The dealers told their salesmen not to offer the book price, but to show it to customers and then explain why their particular car was not up to the standards required to get the maximum trade-in amount.[84]

Dealers loved the NRA code because it installed a downward ratchet on used-car allowances. However, most seemed oblivious to the incongruous sound of their complaints when they talked about how customers would have to be weaned away from their attempts to get higher prices for their trade-ins. "The buying public has got to be re-educated. Car buyers will have to be taught that they must abide by prices prescribed," said a large-volume dealer. "They will have to be made ashamed of 'chiseling' or forcing a dealer to violate a code."[85] When customers sought better prices, they were "chiselers"; but when a salesman charged full list price and low-balled the code allowance, he was acting appropriately. The term "chiseler" would remain a common pejorative epithet for about a decade for any dealer who gave over-allowances.[86] Even within the restrictions of the NRA, the FTC reported that some dealers sought to undermine the fixed-price system by "giving away equipment as an inducement to make sales." Alternatively, in an act of creative rule avoidance worthy of the horse-trading tradition, the salesmen "made foolish side bets with customers" that they knew they would lose, and the wager payoff became the discount on the price of the new car.[87]

The Supreme Court declared the NIRA unconstitutional in May 1935, and the experiment in federal price-fixing ended. For those two years, car dealers had stopped complaining about the used-car problem. It would be unfair to call the depths of the Great Depression a golden age of car retailing—the number of new cars sold was still disturbingly low—but it most certainly was a golden age for dealer bargaining. The law prohibited new car discounts and trade-in over-allowances but permitted under-allowances. There was a floor but no ceiling on profits. With the demise of the NRA, dealer organizations attempted to recreate its benefits at the state level by supporting retail licensing laws. The dealers hoped that by linking licenses to standardized trade-in allowances they could put an end to what they had begun to label "wild trading."[88]

By 1939, twenty-three states and three municipalities had passed laws requiring automobile retailers to obtain licenses to buy used cars. Dealers who "willfully or habitually made excessive trade-in allowances for the purpose of lessening competition," in the words of the Nebraska statute, could have their licenses revoked.[89] The Wisconsin law, which called for the licensing of salesmen and finance companies along with dealers, said that "consistent and material over-allowances on used car trade-ins" would be considered an "unfair trade practice." As the secretary of the Wisconsin dealers association put it, perhaps too candidly, "This means Wisconsin dealers will save two and one-half million dollars which they otherwise would have passed on to new car purchasers."[90]

The somewhat frantic efforts to restore NRA-like market restrictions inevitably attracted the attention of the Federal Trade Commission, which had previously, but unsuccessfully, objected to the price controls under the NRA. A 1938 congressional resolution asking the FTC to investigate the industry led to a series of conferences and hearings that determined that there was no way for retailers to control trade-in allowances without running afoul of antitrust regulations.[91] To the industry, the schemes were a way to control "wild trading"; to the government, wild trading was simply a dysphemism for competition, and the FTC report detailed what it called the "History of Automobile Dealer Plans to Restrict Competition."[92]

The commission found that the dealers were aware that their attempts to limit allowances would play badly with the car-buying public, which was why many of them cloaked their efforts in secrecy. "When a prospect voices the opinion that, due to the similarity of the bids, the dealers are together on a plan," the director of one joint appraisal bureau said, "the best thing to do is deny all knowledge of the plan."[93] The plans to limit over-allowances were so clandestine that they sometimes took on the trappings of a secret fraternal order.[94] For example, dealers who wanted to join the Wisconsin Automotive Trade Association had to swear an oath before a notary public and "almighty God, and this assembly of automobile dealers" that they would "not mention, or refer to, the association, code book, or plan at any time or place when in communication with anyone." Members who violated the association's rules would be "termed an outlaw" and be cast out of the secret brotherhood of price-fixers.[95]

Attempts to reestablish a legal basis for fixing used-car allowances became moot after the beginning of World War II in Europe. The great enthusiasm for government regulation of industry prices waned in direct proportion to the return of a sellers' market.[96] New-car production officially ceased in January 1942, and the available supply was depleted by the end of 1943.[97] Consequently, the demand for used cars increased dramatically, which caused one of the more improbable shifts in automobile retailing. While not significant in the overall history of car dealing, 1942 and 1943 did witness a reversal of the chronic dealer complaint that customers demanded over-allowances. At the beginning of the war, it was the *customers* who complained that *dealers* were demanding that they trade in their used car if they wanted to buy a new one.[98] Because new-car (but not used-car) prices had been frozen by the Office of Price Administration on January 1, 1942, by September 1943 used cars were actually selling for more than their brand-new equivalents.[99]

Used-car prices were especially strong in the West, where defense workers needed autos to drive to work, had the money to pay for them, and were less constrained by gas rationing than people who lived in the urban East. The used-car market in the West was described as a second gold rush. Dealers' representatives would sidle up to drivers on the street, offering them significant premiums if they would sell their cars, "no questions asked," and then upping the offers if they were rebuffed. Earl "Madman" Muntz, the legendary Glendale, California, car dealer who came to personify exaggerated advertising in the 1950s, got his start in this overheated wartime market. Les Kelley, the Los Angeles dealer who had started the Blue Book in 1926, could not keep up with the demand. He imported a thousand secondhand cars a week from the East, tacked on several hundred dollars in shipping costs, and sold them for more than they had cost new. Kelley's fame and business future were ensured when the Office of Price Administration used his Blue Book, not NADA's brown book, as the official standard for used-car values during the last year of the war.[100]

In July 1944, the OPA finally moved to put a cap on what really was wild trading by establishing maximum prices for used cars. The rule applied both to dealerships and to individuals. To enforce the price ceilings, drivers had to turn in "certificates of transfer" before they could get gas rations for their recently purchased vehicles. The techniques worked to keep dealer prices in check, but the long-established tradition of person-to-person used-car sales quickly morphed into a black market. There was no practical way for the OPA to control private car deals. Even the incentive that buyers could collect triple damages from sellers if they reported overcharges—and get to keep the car—could not stop the private black market.[101]

Both new and used-car price controls ended along with the war in 1945, and with the return of market pricing, there was a more open acknowledgment of the role of bargaining in determining the allowance. Ford, which in 1936 had barely recognized the reality of over- allowances, was cautiously embracing them in 1954. A Ford sales manual published that year cautioned the salesman not to give the buyer an allowance offer until he had given the full sales pitch for the new car. Tell the customer that "your boss won't let you look at the old car. . . . Or, if you're the boss, tell him your wife won't let you do it. Tell him anything, but show him your merchandise before he shows you his." But once the salesman had presented his case, if the buyer balked, the salesman was told, "Find out what he will take—what he thinks is a fair allowance. If it's reasonable, then sign him up."[102] They had little choice, because private surveys for Ford found that customers said price and trade-in were the most important reasons they bought a Ford, not, as the company would have preferred, performance, design, economy of operation, or brand loyalty.[103]

When the MSRP sticker first appeared on 1959 model cars, some dealers tried to convince buyers that it was a legally mandated list price and that the only figure open to negotiation was the trade-in allowance.[104] Claims of that sort did not persist for long, and within a few years, salesmen and customers were learning how to deal with haggling over the trade-in and the new car price in a combined negotiation.[105]

Cheating: "Buyers Are Liars"—And So Are Sellers

A typical car sale is a "lying contest," explained a veteran salesman in 1987: "The customer lies to you, you lie to the customer, the customer lies to you, you lie to the customer. . . . The better liar prevails."[106] Automobile salespeople live by the motto "Buyers are liars" because, as sociologist Joy Browne points out, it is a way for them to rationalize their own dishonesty.[107] Nevertheless, the axiom has real roots in the multitude of ploys buyers use to get a better deal on both the new car and the trade-in. They lie about their credit; they lie about their budgets; they lie about having to check with their spouses before signing a contract; they lie about some other dealer's new-car price or used-car allowance; they lie about the condition of their current car, and so on. By drawing attention to this behavior, sales personnel seek to create a moral equivalence between themselves and their customers. The irate buyer in a 1909 joke returned to the used-car lot where he had just purchased a car, "thundering" complaints about everything from a cracked block to wobbly wheels. The dealer responded by suggesting that he not shout so loudly about the car's shortcomings or else he would never be able to sell it himself.[108] The joke affirms the continuation of a cultural assumption that started with horse trading: any man, public or private, who was selling personal transportation would lie to hide its faults.

Dealers voiced the same complaint in every decade that followed.[109] "Do not be influenced, in the slightest degree, by what the second-hand owner says," cautioned a salesman's manual in 1915. "He is the seller in this case, even if he is trying to make a trade deal."[110] W. J. Boone, a Chicago car dealer in the mid-1920s, expressed the sellers' perspective poetically. His lament starts with the prospective customer telling him what a wonderful car his trade-in is and how "they ain't built nowadays like this one." After lying about the car's condition, he follows up by lying about offers from other dealers:

In the very next block a firm just offered me
Almost twice as much and an extra tire free,
They'd throw in a bumper, a spotlight and lock
And I believe by insisting they'd give me a clock.

The poem ends with the dealer discovering that the necessary cost of reboring the trade-in's cylinders would wipe out any profit on the deal.[111]

This was old-fashioned horse trading in every sense of the term; no quarter asked and none given. Salesmen were told to use a form of moral and tactical jujitsu to beat the customer by "playing on his emotions, his greed, his avarice, his desire to cheat you!"[112] A customer whose greed was satisfied by an over-allowances could be fooled into accepting a very high new-car price.[113] There was no deceit to which buyers would not stoop, the sellers asserted. They would lie about trade-in offers from other dealers (even during the regulated days of the NRA) or pretend to have a heart condition, bringing along a fake "doctor" to strengthen their position.[114] "The customer will absolutely tell you fifty lies to every one of yours," explained a used-car salesman. Compared to him, "an Arab street merchant in the Casbah is a novice."[115]

Advice to customers on how to sell a used car lent support to the dealers' view that buyers were liars. For example, since dealers made money from financing the car, they would often lower the price on the car itself, making up the difference in the finance charge. Why not use that knowledge to get a better price? suggested one expert. Drive away with the car and then return a few hours later to pay off the contract in full. "While this may seem a bit underhanded," he said, "it's perfectly legal"—legal, perhaps, but clearly not ethical.[116] Owners were also advised to carry out cosmetic improvements on their cars that went well beyond simple cleaning and polishing.[117] During the immediate postwar car shortage, a *Popular Science* article recommended, among other tricks, covering the rust on the back of bumpers with silver paint, and coating engine hoses with rubber dressing and engine parts with black paint.[118] Others suggested bringing a used car in for appraisal in the evening on a rainy day so that the paint job would look less faded and scratched.[119]

Customers who doctored their cars so that they could get a higher trade-in were participating in the time-honored technique of horse trading. Yet there was something less playful about car-doctoring, and amusing anecdotes were rarer. One that made the rounds told of a dealer who agreed to accept a cream-puff (lightly used) car as a trade-in. When the time came to deliver the new car, the buyer returned with the same make and model car, but it was a rattletrap that had been driven to death; he and his wife owned "twin" cars, and the one used in the original deal had been hers.[120] Other showroom tales involve similar but slightly less outrageous substitutions before delivering the trade-in: tires and batteries switched, or additional mileage racked up on a quick drive across country.[121]

The buyer-liar with a trade-in was in fact a seller-liar. Buyers might feign indifference or plead poverty to force down a price, but their options were limited. It was the seller who had the opportunity to do the serious lying, and the buyer who risked getting stuck with a "lemon" (a neologism created to describe a poor-quality used car). There were a variety of American terms for broken-down horses, including: plug, nag, hack, and jade. A horse with hidden problems that could be bought back at a discount was sometimes called a snide, but that term never gained the common usage of lemon. The earliest print example appears to be a 1907 display advertisement in the *New York Times* in which a used-car dealer boasts that his vehicles are not "lemons" because they have gone through extensive reconditioning.[122] For the word "lemon" to be used without any explanation but with quotation marks means that the term was already in popular use (at least in New York) to refer to cars that looked good superficially but had some underlying defect.

The issue here is not that used cars might have problems. Buyers expected that; they were, after all, secondhand, and there was no implied warranty on used vehicles. The issue is that sellers would lie about or hide their autos' problems. As early as 1904 used-car dealers were trying to deny their inherited horse traders' reputation by assuring buyers that they were not "gyps" and did not deal in "junks" or "misrepresentations."[123] The disclaimers were necessary because many used-car dealers had in fact adopted horse trader's techniques. Automobile ads, for example, picked up the "distress sale" motif without missing a beat. For example, several early New York City dealers sold shined-up poor-quality used cars from warehouses, claiming they had to be sold at a loss because the owners had died.[124] Just after World War I, *Literary Digest* noted that the "Automobile Exchange" section of newspaper classified ads "carried more misery and misfortune to the square inch than any other circulating medium." Every used car on the market was there because the owner had experienced a personal tragedy. "Bereaved widows, orphans in reduced circumstances, suffering families of hospital victims, business bankrupts, consumptives hastening West, or similar unfortunates" were the only people selling cars, and always at a great loss.[125] In the 1920s some dealers used automotive equivalents of snides, which they called "decoys." When buyers discovered their good-looking decoys' hidden problems, the dealers would agree to take them back as down payments on other, more expensive vehicles.[126]

Thus, when early car experts spelled out the various mechanical systems that buyers should check out before they purchased a used vehicle, they were not just extending a word of caution about secondhand machinery; they were raising red flags about the ethical behavior of used-car sellers.[127] The appellation "gyp" migrated seamlessly from horses to cars. By 1919 readers were being reminded of the term's ethnic etymology when they were warned not to buy "gyp tires," which could be worse and more dangerous than the broken-down nags sold by Gypsies.[128] Careful buyers of cars, like careful buyers of horses, were urged to have the perspective purchase evaluated by an independent professional, although some sellers were known to give kickbacks to "engineers" (mechanics) to certify unsound cars as mechanically fit.[129] (See fig. 4.) Sixty years later, according to a New York City Consumer Affairs investigation, seller scruples were still in short supply. Rather than fixing deficiencies brought to their attention as the result of mechanical inspection, dealers just tried to pawn the car off on the next prospect without disclosing the problem.[130]

From the first to the last decades of the twentieth century, used-car buyers were given specific advice on how to check for hidden problems. Beware of tires that look too new, or body paint that looks too shiny, or engines that look too clean—or, in the same order, too bald, rusted, or greasy.[131] Use a magnet to check for non-metallic body patches.[132] Check under new seat covers and floor mats for signs of wear. Look for gas and clutch peddles that are too worn or too new. Smell the oil dipstick for a burned scent, and so on.[133] "Detailers" who specialized in cosmetic makeovers became so skilled by the mid-1960s that one Los Angeles dealer complained, "It's getting so tricky, even dealers have been fooled. I've bought several clunkers myself at auction."[134] And in 1976, *Car and Driver* writer Warren Weith related his own cautionary tale of buying a "cream puff" of a Fiat with only fifteen thousand miles on it from a neighbor "leaving the country." Weith wanted the car so much he overlooked the telltale signals that it was sucker-bait. He never saw the "neighbor" again, and the car started falling apart the following week. Weith patched it together and announced, "My next move is to put a low price on it, an innocent look on my gypsy face, and a dishonest man in my sights. He won't be hard to find."[135]

Weith's "Gypsies" were professionals acting like amateurs, and when he sold the car to the next victim, Weith was an amateur acting like a professional. Anybody and everybody who sold a used car was suspect. Individuals could buy books that walked them through the steps used to cover up a car's problems. Most of the suggested modifications were superficial, but the spirit was larcenous. "Applying lube stick won't eliminate the squeaking noise permanently, but it will keep the belts quiet for a week or two while you're trying to sell your car," advised one such publication in 1977.[136] If a buyer sarcastically noted that he wished he could have seen the engine before it was steam cleaned, the same author suggested that the seller reply, "I'm sorry, but I've always kept my engine clean so that I would be able to recognize anything wrong developing," and then "give him an angelic look."[137] He warned, however, that rolling back the odometer was impractical, illegal, and "morally wrong," because "there's a big difference between 'horse trading' and lying."[138]

Professional car dealers, especially those who worked on used-car lots, emerged as the quintessential embodiment of the flashy, fast-talking, conscienceless purveyor of shoddy merchandise that was hidden under a coat of cheap paint and a blanket of lies. "I've been wondering if they'd dare to try to pull anything on me—me being on the cops," mused a policeman in the market for a used car in 1942. "If J. Edgar Hoover bought a car from them, they'd try to skin him," replied his mechanic.[139] Every generation of buyers was treated to a new round of stories about the swindles run by used-car dealers. If you left your car with them on consignment, they would lie about how much they had sold it for.[140] Or they would pretend a car they owned was on consignment and hold mock negotiations with the "owner" in a false telephone call to convince the buyer that he could not possibly get a lower price. Or they would take a deposit on a car, but the car, the seller, and the deposit would be gone when the buyer came back to pay the balance.[141]

There were, of course, dealers who tried to be honest with their customers. "If a car has had use, it will make noise," observed a sales manual in 1923. Treat your customers as friends and "sell it noise and all," advised the writer: "There are still a great many people who believe that used-car selling is a swindler's game. Don't encourage that reputation."[142] A Wheeling, West Virginia, used-car dealer said in 1937 that he had never tampered with an odometer in twenty-three years of business and sold every car with a twenty-four-hour money-back guaranty and a thirty-day guaranty on parts and labor.[143] His was a lonely voice in the wilderness of secondhand car dealing, which is why it was always a "man bites dog" news story when a used-car dealer sold good cars, honestly.[144]

No part or function of the car was safe from the used-car dealer's nefarious arts. While some of the tricks of the early years were more blatant then those that came later, the basic techniques used to hide faults remained surprisingly consistent from the beginning to the end of the twentieth century. To be sure, it is unlikely that a dealer in the 1990s would back a car with no reverse against a wall so the test driver could only move forward. Certainly, if he forgot and drove it into the storage space front first, he would not have his mechanics crouch down behind it to pull when the buyer shifted into reverse, as did one dealer in about 1910.[145] Furthermore, the earlier practice of boosting a car's performance by spiking its gasoline with ether disappeared, but the same effect could be achieved by using extra-hot spark plugs and coils.[146] Heavy oil or grease, paraffin, fuller's earth, sand, sawdust, powdered resin, and pulverized cork were inserted over the years into one or another of a car's strategic parts to temporarily mask the symptoms of major mechanical problems. A bit of judiciously applied spot welding to hold a car together long enough to get it off the lot, a final spray of "new car smell," and the car could misrepresent itself as well as any bishoped, gingered, and nose-plugged nag in a road trader's string.[147]

Odometers—or speedometers, as they were popularly called—became the icon of used-car deceit. Technically, an odometer measures the number of miles a car has traveled, while a speedometer measures how fast it is going. Because both calibrations depend on measuring wheel rotation, they were combined into a single instrument early in automotive history and were widely available as accessories after 1908. Unlike horses, cars came with the functional equivalent of birth certificates. Registrations and serial numbers made it relatively easy to know what year any given vehicle was made, so unlike the horse, the age of a car was never in question. Like a horse buyer, a car buyer could take note of the general condition of a vehicle and try to make an informed judgment as to how hard it had been used. However, once odometers became standard, there was an even better way than age (which might be unimportant) and appearance (which might be tampered with) to judge the wear and tear on a car, and that was by how many miles it had traveled. Unfortunately for buyers, odometers, like cars, could run in both directions. In 1961 an investigative reporter estimated that 80 to 90 percent of the twelve million used cars sold in America had their odometers altered.[148]

Turning back odometers was such standard practice that buyers were advised never to accept their numbers at face value. Laws governing the treatment of odometers varied across jurisdictions. Before 1973, when federal law finally prohibited dealers from tampering with odometers, it was illegal in only a handful of states (two in 1961, seventeen in 1972), so cars were routinely shipped from regulated to unregulated states to have their odometers rejuvenated.[149] The ubiquity of the practice prompted a suggestion by the FTC in 1939 to ban rolling back the speedometer—except all the way to zero.[150] In other words, the FTC wanted to make it illegal to lie a little, but perfectly legal to lie absolutely. The proposal was never implemented. Nevertheless, turning back the speedometer to zero was so widely practiced that its sheer audacity allowed sellers to transcend legal, if not moral, charges of lying for another thirty years.[151]

The 1960s and 1970s appear to have been the zenith of odometer tampering. Some rollback specialists worked out of fixed locations and were available to individual owners. Others traveled from dealer to dealer, making a good living by the automotive equivalent of grooving an old horse's teeth. (In the automotive version of actual grooving, there were specialists who cut deeper treads into balding tires to make them look younger.) It was not unusual for a car's odometer to be moved backward three times in the course of a sale: first by the owner who was trading it in, second by the new-car dealer who took it in trade, and finally by the used-car dealer who bought the trade-in at a wholesale auction.[152] In 1967 a rollback artist, sometimes called a "spinner" or "clocker," could doctor as many as one hundred cars a day with a kit of tools that cost less than fifty dollars. Spinners found a ready market for their skills at used-car lots and at new-car showrooms, where dealers would crank back the mileage on demonstrators and sell them as new.[153] Since the number on the odometer had to agree with the mileage on its title, a rollback support group called "title washers" emerged to produce false car titles that showed mileage consistent with the new numbers on the dashboard.[154]

Manufacturers attempted to thwart odometer tampering by introducing technical innovations to make it more difficult to run the gauges backward, and the federal government increased penalties for odometer tampering in 1976.[155] More sophisticated anti-tampering devices merely generated more sophisticated tamperers. For example, between 1976 and 1978 half a dozen free lance rollback artists in New Jersey pleaded guilty to altering mileage readings on thousands cars a year for dealers and private citizens, and charges were brought against a score of dealers on similar allegations.[156] The disappearance of mechanical mile counters and the advent of electronic readouts do not seem to have made much difference. By the mid-1990s odometer fraud was reportedly costing consumers anywhere from two to four thousand dollars a car, which some authorities claimed reached a cumulative total of four to ten billion dollars a year.[157] Carfax, a private company that keeps a computer database of registered automobiles, does appear to have made it more difficult to wash registrations. However, when cars are not registered and are sold privately, or when buyers do not bother to check, used-car con artists continue to demonstrate that in the retail automobile business, numbers still lie.[158]

Used cars were the element in car dealing that ensured the persistence of the horse-trading traditions in automotive retailing. It is conceivable that if the industry had figured out some way to segregate used-car sales, new cars could have been sold at a single price set by the dealer and posted on the vehicle. Something approximating that situation obtained until the 1930s. There was, to be sure, wide-spread but low-profile dickering over posted prices, but those were prices set by the factory. If the dealers had been free to advertise lower one-price-to-all figures, it seems possible that auto sales could have been conducted in a style similar to that of other high-priced manufactured goods, which is to say that some aggressive shoppers might get a reduction from the posted price, but protracted bargaining would not be an integral part of every transaction. Used cars, however, undermined that option. The price of each used car had to be negotiated on an ad hoc basis, and once that sale was linked to the purchase of the new car, the horse trading over the price of the trade-in became horse trading over the price of the new car. In this way over-allowances before World War II laid the groundwork for the horse-fair environment of the postwar auto sales.

CHAPTER FIVE

The Triumph of the Price Pack

Selling the Deal

World War II is often cited as the beginning of the deterioration in automobile retailing methods, but little of the retail intemperance of the postwar world was new. The situation appeared to change after 1945 because of the pent-up demand created by wartime savings and wartime shortages. "Never was there a time," said a finance company executive in 1946, "when so many paid so much for so little," and he cautioned dealers not to become greedy lest they generate bad feelings that would carry over from the sellers' to the inevitable buyers' market.[1] He was right; the greed unleashed by the opportunity to cash in on the car shortage created a retail culture that tainted the industry from that day to this.[2] The period between the end of the war and 1959 became the benchmark era for unethical retailing, and the price pack, a method of inflating the car's cost to the customer, became the emblem of the era.

While the companies that made things came out of the war in good financial shape, companies that sold them needed to make up for lost time. Delays in the production of new cars and the continuation of price controls through 1946 frustrated auto retailers' ability to take advantage of the high demand and gave rise to a widespread black market. Businesses that had cars could easily sell them for more than the legal limit by disguising the overpayment. A favorite device of car dealers was to give *under*-allowances on trade-ins. They would refuse to sell to any customer who did not have a trade-in and would pay significantly less than the car would bring in the hot used-car market. The poetic justice of this inversion of forty years of over-allowances appears to have been lost on most buyers. Nevertheless, they willingly participated in the charade of throwing in their old car as boot to get a scarce new one.[3] A congressional committee charged that in the first seven months of 1948 alone, dealers had mulcted buyers out of 250 million dollars through under-allowances.[4] Taking their cue from the car dealers, some creative landlords in New York City in 1946 required a used car as well as a deposit as a condition for leasing scarce apartments.[5]

Certainly large numbers of automobile dealers, perhaps most, played by the rules. They could sell every car they could get their hands on, and many were reluctant to risk alienating their future customers for a short-term gain. Individual dealers as well as dealer groups ran advertisements in newspapers all over the country explaining how they used first-come-first-served waiting lists to allocate cars, promising fair prices for trade-ins and urging buyers to shun unscrupulous black-market sellers.[6] Until the end of 1946, the honest dealers had the legal backing of the federal Office of Price Administration and of local authorities.[7] However, by the beginning of 1947, when the government lifted all legal restrictions, only factory regulations and social restraint stood between consumers and sky-high prices. Manufacturers' threats to cut back shipments or rescind franchises were serious disincentives to price gouging, but the desire for profits was a powerful force, and many dealers sought ways around the factory restrictions.

Customers had to wait a year to eighteen months for a new car in 1947 and 1948, and buyers regularly offered dealers all sorts of financial incentives to move their names to the top of the ubiquitous queues. When they played fair, the dealers not only forewent significant additional profit, but they might see that profit being made by somebody else, often the very person who had been complaining that dealers were not sticking to the rules. Buyers who valued money over transportation could immediately sell their new (now used, if only for a few miles) cars at a substantial markup, either to private parties or to used-car dealers who would mark them up yet again.[8] The result was used cars selling for substantially more than new ones. "I'll be damned if I'll pay $600 or $700 more for a "used" car than for a brand new one," screamed one would-be customer who could not get a car from the regular dealer but could find one being sold by an unauthorized outlet.[9] Some dealers tried to stop this practice by requiring their customers to sign an option agreement to give the dealer first rights to buy back the car, but to little avail.[10]

Unwilling to pass up the opportunity for windfall profits but wary about alienating customers and manufacturers, some dealers followed the horse-trading logic of a certain Quaker farmer who had a recalcitrant mule. The farmer explained to the beast that it had better get to work, because while as a man of peace he would not beat it, he *would* trade it to a Methodist. That was the relationship between new and used-car dealers beginning in 1947: what the new-car dealers would not do themselves, the used-car dealers would. By selling their new cars at a premium directly to used-car dealers, new-car dealers could cut out the customer "middleman." Nobody really knew how many cars went into this "gray market," a term that automobile dealers said they had invented to describe postwar "bootlegging."[11]

Bootlegging had first arisen in the 1930s when factories were forcing dealers to take more cars than they could sell. Dealers discovered that one way to move cars and not risk losing their franchise was to sell them to used-car dealers at a steep discount. The used-car dealers would, in turn, sell them to the public below list price.[12] The new bootlegging, or gray market, reversed the Depression-era process. Postwar gray market transactions were over, not under, list price and may have involved as much as 80 percent of new car production, although some calculated the number as low as 5 percent. The disparity of estimates reflects both the volatility of the market and the emotional impact of the situation.[13] Such deals violated some local ordinances, and a few factories cracked down on authorized dealers who resold their allotments to nonfranchised retailers rather than to customers.[14] The market, however, overcame all attempts at control, perhaps because many manufacturers did not care all that much who sold their cars at retail as long as they were moving out of the factory.[15]

In addition to offering under-allowances for used cars, sellers demanded "tips" of as much as $500 to facilitate the delivery of new cars and began to charge "fees" for putting a customer's name on a waiting list or supplying a car out of turn.[16] The fee gambit worked so well that dealers invented all sorts of payments as way to pass on sometimes real and sometimes imagined business costs to their customers. Eventually, these included document fees, delivery fees, dealer preparation fees, and even advertising fees, as though customers should directly shoulder the cost of the advertising used to lure them onto the showroom floor in the first place.

Price Padding with the Pack

The final way of padding the customers' bills was called the "pack." Like many informal trade terms, the definition of pack varied somewhat from user to user. The name itself may have come from high-profit accessories "packaged" with the car or from the additional profits "packed" into the invoice. The point, however, was to inflate the bottom line with extraneous items and charges. Pack profit was usually thought of as over and above the standard profit on a sale and could therefore be reduced during the haggling process without seriously compromising revenue.[17] The pack came to be identified with dealer duplicity because customers rarely understood which accessories were standard, which were installed at the factory, which were installed by the dealer, and what the manufacturer's suggested list price was for any of them. For example, a dealer advertisement for a 1956 Pontiac offered to include a radio, seat heater, automatic transmission, two-tone paint job, whitewall tires, power steering, and power brakes all for one cent each. Thus the ad stated that the consumer would pay seven cents for accessories worth a total of $575. However, since the ad did not include the price of the car, the buyer had no idea what the accessories actually cost.[18]

Early car magazines were full of advertisements for gadgets to enhance performance. As inventors and independent entrepreneurs dreamed up improvements, many manufacturers incorporated them into production models. Henry Ford, however, did the opposite. Rather than selling his Model T with the latest automotive gizmos, he sold it stripped down and cheap. A list of options for the 1917 Model T, which were standard on most other cars, included a speedometer, a steering wheel horn, an engine thermometer, demountable rims, shock absorbers, an electric starter, electric headlights, a windshield, rearview mirrors, and door locks—and that list does not include front and rear bumpers and spare tires, which were extras on most cars.[19] As late as 1926, Ford defended its bare-bones base model by pointing out that nothing on a new car was really free, but by buying only the options needed, "you know how much you are paying when you buy from us."[20] That policy ended the next year when Ford introduced its Model A that included most of the features that had been optional on the Model T, and Ford dealers quickly embraced the practice of forcing buyers to purchase even more accessories if they wished to buy one of the very popular new cars.[21]

When the new-model enthusiasm waned and the economic vise of the Depression tightened, Ford dealers and others tried to continue to use the pack to squeeze the last dollar of profit out of their increasingly rare sales.[22] The practice became common enough to first be called "packing" during the 1930s. Although the early definition was a bit loose, it usually referred to artificially low nationally advertised prices. When the buyer tried to purchase a car at the advertised price, the dealer would inform him that there were a variety of extra charges for transportation, handling, and documents. Furthermore, the dealer would explain, there was an additional fee for the bumpers and spare tire, which was the only way that the car came. In response to an FTC investigation, dealers said that price packing was the only way they could make money in an environment that practically forced them to grant over-allowances. The commission was able to extract an agreement from most of the manufacturers in 1939 that they would no longer publish misleadingly low prices, and with the war and the return of prosperity, the packing issue temporarily faded from view.[23]

When it reemerged after World War II, the pack grew to become something of a national scandal and a proximate cause of the 1958 legislation that was supposed to reform the way cars were sold. At first the pack joined the *under-allowance* as a way for dealers to increase the cost of the cars without appearing to violate the manufacturers' list prices. In the car-scarce days of the late 1940s, if customers wanted a car, they bought it the way it came, with all the high-priced accessories. Between the manufacturers' and the dealers' add-ons, most cars came decked out with more baubles than a Christmas tree.[24] Customers complained about the added costs, and dealers feigned innocence. In January of 1947, the official line from the dealers' association was that no customers would get less than their trade-in was worth, pay more than the "established" list price, or be "required to purchase any extra equipment that he did not desire."[25] In the summer of 1947, eager for profits, the dealers hedged their no-profiteering promise with the observation that "many of these so-called 'unwanted accessories' were items such as radios, heaters, etc.," which "throughout the years have been considered desirable additions." And by 1949, dealers were being told to explain to their customers that factory list prices never included automatic transmissions, heaters, radios, backup lights, and seat covers; but these accessories were all highly attractive, and besides, that was the only way the cars came.[26]

As long as there was an acute car shortage between the end of the war and about 1949, customers complained about the pack because it forced them to spend more than they wanted to on a new car. Once autos became more plentiful, the source of customer dissatisfaction was less explicit but seemed to boil down to a generalized sense that dealers were not "playing fair." Before the war, widely posted list prices gave buyers a starting point to judge how well their price negotiating was going. The practice of manufacturers' publishing their suggested list price for cars disappeared along with the cars themselves during World War II. After the war the cars came back, but the prices remained missing in action. "The public was accustomed to fair prices established by the factories," noted an industry observer in 1958, and "didn't realize that universal fixed prices had fallen out of official favor."[27] If customers asked for the list price, what they got was a number concocted on the spot by the salesman, based on his estimation of what the traffic would bear. As long as they did not have to worry about the factory disclosing prices, dealers were on their own. A confidential survey done for Ford in 1956 noted that advertisements from "authorized dealers seldom mention specific prices."[28]

A tacit understanding had evolved in which the car companies refrained from advertising specific numbers and local dealers added the cost of various options onto the prices they quoted to customers. In the case of General Motors, it was more than an understanding; it was company policy. Harlow Curtice, the president of GM, explicitly (but not publicly) condoned price packing in 1953, and GM divisions actively recommend that their retailers use the pack as a way to inflate prices on the showroom floor.[29] When Chrysler customers complained of price packing at the beginning of the 1954 model year, the company responded by running national ads with factory list prices. However, a company spokesman told the Justice Department that retail dealers "brought so much pressure to bear on us that we discontinued the factory retail prices at Detroit."[30]

In the 1950s, local automobile dealers believed that aggressive, often misleading, and frequently over-the-top local advertising was the way to satisfy the demands of the factories for increased sales, and the pack was a vital component of that strategy. Come-on advertisements promising to sell cars for pennies over cost were backed up with false factory invoices, and dealer-published price lists were fat with packing that could be bargained away as needed. Without factory list prices for base models, optional accessories, and shipping costs, the consumer was cast into what *Advertising Age* called "the economic jungle of a Middle East bazaar in which everything, including price, is a mystery." The magazine complained that car "customers are no longer customers in the traditional American sense."[31] The haggling was bad, but the absence of list prices was positively un-American.

The window price sticker took the edge off the complaints about packing after 1959.[32] While the haggling did not stop, the dealers at least had to list the suggested list price of the car, including the prices of all accessories. The practice of packing, and sometimes the term itself, persisted as dealers sought ways to increase the cost of the car beyond a low advertised price designed to lure customers into the dealership. These additional charges included preparation, document, and advertising fees as well as mandatory options. The major difference was that after 1958 these added costs had to be itemized on the window sticker.[33] Failure to do so was against the law, though some dealers kept doing it anyway.[34]

After-Sales Packing

At the beginning of the twentieth century, King Camp Gillette realized that he could make more money from selling his disposable safety razor blades than he could from selling the blade holder. Although automobiles entered the consumer market at exactly the same time as the Gillette safety razor, nobody imagined that car companies could make money from a machine that cost thousands of dollars the way Gillette did from a machine that cost less than one dollar. Yet there were times in the history of car retailing when dealers lost money on the sale of the car itself but made up for it with after-sale add-ons, finance charges, and vehicle maintenance.[35] In 1989 and 1992, for example, the average American dealer earned less than a hundred dollars per new car sold, and in 1990 and 1991 they actually lost money on every sale of a new car.[36]

In the post–price sticker world, customers had to be told what they were paying for add-ons. Accessories installed at the factory came with manufacturer recommended prices, but those put in locally could be posted at whatever price the dealer thought he could get. Even better, if the items were added after the car was sold, the dealers could charge whatever they thought the customer would pay.[37] Most aftermarket add-ons were essentially cosmetic, consisting of things like pinstripes, fancy wheel covers, and splashguards. Some, however, were arguably more useful, such as improved heaters, sound systems, and alarms. A 1985 list included more than two hundred firms that would provide items for dealers to install in more than a dozen categories.[38] Useful or not, at least these accessories could be seen, so the buyers knew they were getting something for their money.

Other add-ons, called "appearance maintenance" items were inherently invisible. "Think about it," urged a dealer's magazine piece praising aftermarket chemicals and protectants: "What other service do you offer that can average $75 an hour with unskilled labor?"[39] And that was if the work was actually done, because sometimes it wasn't. How could the customer know if the car had been undercoated or that fabric guard and paint sealer had been applied? An industry whistle-blower who had worked as a salesman said he had frequently seen these services paid for, but had never seen them performed.[40]

Automobile financing, a major aftermarket profit center for most dealers, is one of the few car business practices that has no horse-trading precursors. Installment buying did evolve from the older pattern of local store owners allowing their customers keep a running tab. Such "book credit," however, had no legally enforceable repayment schedule and depended on a personal relationship between the shopkeeper and the customer who was running up the bills.[41] For that reason many of the early department stores, where the customer was anonymous and everybody paid the same price, explicitly rejected this tradition and made a point of not extending credit to anybody. They proudly labeled themselves "cash stores." A few of the more expensive department stores, however, did set up their own formal systems for extending credit to their best customers. Storeowners, who had moral or economic scruples about letting people use their purchases before they were actually paid for, set up layaway plans that permitted customers to pay installments in advance while the store set aside the desired item so that it would be available when the full price was paid.

Critics of the bicycle craze attributed at least part of the bursting of the bubble in 1895 to dealers who had extended too much credit to too many people who did not pay off their debts and had to forfeit their bicycles.[42] Some early car dealers took that warning to heart, but trying to sell cars without extended financing was like trying to sell houses without mortgages: it was possible, but it severely limited the potential customer base.[43] Before about 1914, men who wanted a car they could not afford might embezzle the money from their employers, like one Washington husband who was upset because his friends' cars had more lamps than his. Or, more conventionally, they could take out loans on their homes and possessions to raise the funds. Some few lucky ones could find a dealer willing to extend credit by mortgaging the car itself. That is, the dealer would accept 25 percent down and the balance in monthly payments, with both the car and the previous payments to be forfeited if any installment were missed.[44]

After about 1914, however, buyers of automobiles could obtain financing from small loan companies and larger established banks as well as from dealers.[45] General Motors stole a march on its rival Ford in this area, as it did in so many others, by setting up a wholly owned subsidiary to finance both dealer purchases of cars from the factory and customer purchase of cars from the dealer.[46] During the 1920s, installment purchasing of big-ticket items, including automobiles, became the consumer standard. By the end of the decade, at least 70 percent of cars were sold "on time," and that was actually a lower percentage than some other consumer items such as furniture and phonographs.[47]

Economic historian Lendol Calder has suggested that the rise of readily available credit was not a sign of a hedonistically self-destructive nation, but rather it contributed significantly toward a society in which Americans could use debt to improve their lives while maintaining traditional values of "discipline, hard work, budgeting, and saving."[48] Calder's persuasive argument for consumer credit as an instrument of personal economic discipline would have been lost on Henry Ford. Like most traditionalists in the 1920s, Ford felt that borrowing money was morally dangerous. He fiercely resisted suggestions that his company follow the GM lead to extend credit to new-car buyers and would go no further than approving a "Weekly Purchase Plan," which was a layaway plan in which the buyer paid in installments in advance. This quaint scheme made as much progress against the GM time-payment plans in the 1920s as the aging Model T did against GM's snappy new Chevrolets. Ford gave up both his beloved Model T and his old-fashioned ideas about thrift and spending in 1927 when he introduced the Model A and finally agreed to a factory-sponsored finance operation.[49]

Ford's belief that installment buying was morally reprehensible may have been nurtured by the way many non-auto businesses in the 1920s concealed the cost of credit when they advertised "low monthly payments." Thus, it was considered worthy of note in 1925 that Chevrolet actually told buyers how they could figure out what portion of advertised prices were finance charges and therefore how much they could save if they paid cash.[50] This uncustomary burst of candor did not become the norm. Reports from the 1930s indicate that car dealers regularly hid fees and true interest rates from buyers.[51]

Padding and disguising finance charges continued through the war and into the 1950s. Reports from the mid-fifties claim that aggressive dealers would charge hundreds of percent interest and bury the figures so deep in the contracts that buyers never knew what they were paying. Indeed, it was common to fast-talk the customer into signing a blank contract and then add usurious rates after the fact.[52] The system worked because higher backend profits meant that the dealers could offer higher trade-in allowances, thus leading naïve buyers to think they were getting a good deal when they were actually paying top dollar.[53] Despite accusations of consumer exploitation and lopsided dealer profits from financing, time-payment charges were not included among the costs that had to be listed on window stickers.[54] Hiding the cost of credit would remain a standard device in all areas of consumer borrowing until Congress passed the federal Truth in Lending Act in 1968.

What set the questionable finance practices of the retail car business apart from equally questionable practices in other industries was that auto finance charges could be folded into the whole negotiating package. Along with the price of the new car, the size of the used-car allowance, and the cost of accessories, the cost to the customer of borrowing money from the dealer fluctuated with the bargaining skill of the buyer. A consultant's report prepared for the Ford Motor Company in 1956 claimed that buyers who financed their purchases through the dealers "were emotionally handicapped in bargaining with authorized dealers." The report suggested that customers were embarrassed by asking for credit, which they regarded as a favor, and were therefore less willing to press the dealer on prices for either the new car or the trade-in.[55]

After 1968, state and federal legislation made it increasingly difficult to hide the true cost of financial services, but that did not stop dealers from developing an elaborate endgame that could mean the difference between a small and a large profit on a given sale. In the 1970s, for example, while dealers earned less than 2 percent return on new-car sales, they realized over 8 percent on finance and insurance.[56] Customers with poor credit who could not get third-party loans remained a major source of backend profit.[57] In the most recent (but surely not the last) financing fraud, dealerships have called buyers with poor credit ratings to inform them that their cars would be repossessed because their loan applications had been turned down. However, the dealers add helpfully, they would be able to arrange a different loan package at a much higher rate.[58]

Although F&I (finance and insurance) was often handled independently, some dealerships allowed their sales staff to negotiate the entire package simultaneously so that not only could the cost of the new car and the trade-in allowance be played off against each other, but so could the cost of dealer-added accessories, finance charges, and insurance packages. In such situations, the negotiating seller could take buyer's preferences into account by adjusting any one of the numbers up or down as needed, while recouping the profit by moving another component in the opposite direction; some dealers referred to this as the "waterbed theory": when you pushed down in one area, it just rose in another. Most dealers, however, chose to separate F&I from the initial sales process and use a distinct sales representative, usually called the finance or credit manager, to pressure customers into buying credit life insurance, accident and health insurance, service contracts, and other income-producing F&I products. Anything the F&I manager could add to the contract was gravy.[59]

Finance and insurance price packing became a chronic irritant and a significant part of the retail experience. Because it usually occurred after the customer had negotiated a deal, it played a less prominent role than false advertising, accessory packing, and high-pressure salesmanship in the periodic outbursts of public indignation about the way that automobiles were sold. That indignation reached a climax in the 1950s and led to the window price sticker that seemed at the time like a significant legal reform but turned out to be just a minor deviation in the continuing course of transportation sales.

The 1950s: ". . . for Thieves to Sell to Mental Defectives"

In 2002 General Motors ran a series of print and television ads that featured the ghost of Harley J. Earl touting the auto giant's new Buick line. Dressed in World War II–era clothing, the spirit-Earl must have perplexed all but the oldest car buffs. In his day (obviously one still fondly remembered in Detroit), Earl was the legendary head of styling for GM and the creative genius behind tail fins, two-tone paint jobs, wraparound windshields, and chrome, chrome, and more chrome. The 2002 advertisements were a strange obeisance to the auto gods, imploring them to bring back the glory days of the 1950s, when the American car business burst into full bloom in all its sparkly, multicolored expanses of sheet metal glory—and General Motors reigned supreme.

While some industry insiders may have remembered the 1950s fondly, most others have viewed the decade with ambivalence or outright disgust. It was a time when factory-dealer-customer relations entered into a triangular war, with each side fighting the other two. Social critic John Keats called cars of the fifties "insolent chariots," referring to them as "overblown, overpriced monstrosities built by oafs for thieves to sell to mental defectives."[60] Keats's acerbic critique of cars and car culture became a touchstone for a generation of Detroit bashers who had never ceased to mourn the demise of the Model T and who saw the arrival of small European imports like the Volkswagen as a hopeful sign of the imminent end of the great American land yacht.[61]

Among the most frequent accusations still being leveled against manufacturers by the retailers was one they had been charging since the 1930s. The dealers protested that company rivalry for market share led to unrelenting factory pressure on them to compete with each other solely on volume, which they could achieve only with over-allowances and high-pressure sales methods. The high-pressure sales techniques perpetuated the evils of the pack and led to garish and misleading local advertising that was a pastiche of smoke and mirrors.[62] Industry historian James Flink lists almost a dozen distinct abuses that characterized retail auto sales in the early 1950s, although many of them, including the pack and the use of sales closers, predate the postwar era by at least twenty years.[63]

Like a drunk muttering, "I really shouldn't drink this," then drinking it anyway, the auto industry was aware of what was going on but seemed powerless to end it. The participants themselves called attention to the abuses, issued pleas to stop them, bemoaned the loss of public confidence, castigated those who participated in the process, and then proceeded to ratchet up the behavior to new levels. The National Automobile Dealers Association, which had been working since 1917 to improve the public image of car dealers, spoke out strongly in favor of curbing activity that threw the industry into disrepute. At their 1951 convention, NADA's Dealer-Customer Relations Committee staged a skit in which an old-school father had to step in to rescue his son from customer service gaffs that included high-pressuring a clergyman into buying unwanted accessories and getting fresh with a woman customer in a bathing suit. (Conventioneers were apparently expected to suspend disbelief for the benefit of dramatic license—and cheesecake.)[64] A second presentation depicted a predatory dealer taking every advantage he could of customers and justifying his actions as natural expressions of market system. The piece closed with the warning that such firms would soon be out of business.[65]

The Korean War had much less impact on the auto business than had World War II, although it does seem to have led to a temporary lull in the chorus of criticism, perhaps because supplies dipped and profits rose during the years of the conflict.[66] The election of Dwight Eisenhower and the Korean armistice allowed the car market to heat up once again and led to a new round of complaints. An Indiana Ford dealer charged that in the years after the Korean War "we reached a new low in false and misleading advertising, give-away programs, blitz merchandising, price packing, finance loading, and the bootlegging and cross selling of new automobiles."[67] Speaking to the 1954 NADA convention, Eisenhower's Secretary of the Interior, Douglas McKay, warned the dealers that they were alienating the public with these kinds of "huckster" methods. Then, in words that echoed Quaker founder George Fox, he said, "I think that we should be able to send our wives and daughters to buy a car and not have them robbed."[68]

High on the list of concerns that the dealers themselves had about the wild trading of the 1950s was a reoccurrence of the longstanding charge that some dealers were, with factory complicity, selling on "nothing but price and discount." Radio ads announced, "Profit is no aim . . . we want volume and will give our profits to you," and not only the public but also competing dealers believed these retailers were giving away the store.[69] The complaint in this case was not that the advertising was false—but that it was true. It appears that the misleading come-on ads were not sufficiently misleading, fooling rivals into thinking that the cut-rate dealers were truly making only the pittance they advertised.[70] As had been the case previously, especially during the Great Depression, dealers hated market conditions that forced them to sell below the manufacturer's list price or clinch a deal by giving an over-allowance on the trade-in. This time, however, in the unbridled spirit of fifties merchandising, creative dealers introduced discounts disguised as free vacation trips and other non-cash premiums.[71] Manufacturers felt ambivalent about this aggressive price-cutting. On the one hand, they did not want to anger their dealers or cheapen the public's image of their cars, but on the other, they wanted to keep up volume, especially during a period when GM and Ford were competing head to head for bragging rights about which had the most popular cars in the country.

The battle for sales leadership that emerged in the wake of the Korean War generated a rebirth of the late-1940s gray market, now once again called bootlegging. In the 1930s bootlegging had referred to new-car dealers selling cars below list price to gray marketers, but in the late forties, the definition had reversed to mean wholesaling cars to unauthorized dealers at inflated prices that the used-car dealers could mark up even more. By 1954, however, the situation had turned upside down once again and reverted to its original meaning. There were not enough buyers for the cars Detroit was producing, yet the manufacturers demanded that their dealers absorb everything they made. Rather than risking factory ire and endangering their franchises, many dealers would buy what they considered (or what they were told by factory representatives) were their quotas, knowing that they could not sell them to the public. Instead, they would resell them at a steep discount to gray market resellers who would then undercut the standard retail price.[72]

Car buyers perceived the gray market as somehow unethical, although there was nothing illegal about it. In fifty years of franchise selling, manufacturers had instilled customers with a sense that buying from an unauthorized dealer was asking for trouble. Dealers claimed that they provided "the final steps in the manufacturing and assembly process" and that a car bought from a bootlegger would be unfinished and therefore unsafe. In a culture of cold-war paranoia, the family car had to be kept in a state of good repair because one never knew when it might be needed "for evacuating our citizens in the event of an enemy attack" with one of the new "potent instruments of war, such as the A bomb and the hydrogen bomb," explained a NADA official in 1956.[73] Less apocalyptically, customers worried that there would be trouble with the licenses or the taxes if a bootlegged car were being shipped across state lines. Or they worried that it would not really be a new car but a low-mileage used car with the speedometer rolled back. Finally, there was the sense that buying a prestige item from a shady character was just not good form, "something like for a millionaire or a bank president to be caught at a lunch counter."[74]

On the other hand, bootleg sellers were much more willing to openly compete on price. Like their horse-trading antecedents, the gray marketers reduced the transaction to its economic essence. They were not selling ambiance, service, or long-term relationships. They were selling cars and selling them on price alone. While authorized dealers almost never advertised prices in the 1950s, bootleggers usually did. Moreover, the unauthorized dealers seemed to be more willing to give larger allowances on trade-ins, perhaps because they were in the used-car business and felt more confident of the price they could get when reselling them. A confidential report prepared for the Ford Motor Company in 1956 concluded that customers who wanted the best deal and were willing to do aggressive comparison shopping could save hundreds of dollars by buying their new cars from a gravel lot rather than from a showroom floor.[75]

Authorized retailers suspected that the factories were deliberately supplying the gray market by designating certain franchises "stimulator dealers." Regular dealers charged that the factories established and underwrote the stimulator outlets that competed with older, more established enterprises. They alleged that the manufacturers provided the upstart stimulators with hundreds more cars than they could possibly sell in their territories with the full knowledge that the stimulators would discount them to bootleggers. The factory would then hold up the stimulators as models and accuse other dealers in the region of not selling hard enough.[76]

Advertising and Blitz Marketing

The industry often referred to misleading advertising after World War II as "wild" or "blitz" advertising. Given its association with the recent Nazi blitz-krieg assault tactic, the name had particularly negative connotations. On one level, the sales blitz was a coordinated series of events designed to attract a large number of customers to the lot and create a buying frenzy. A Ford factory merchandising bulletin in 1953 used martial imagery while urging its dealers to build showroom traffic with marching band parades, free Polaroid photos, free lunches, searchlights, and promises that a hundred cars would be sold. Other manufacturers also exhorted their dealers to sell at any cost.[77] Razzle-dazzle tactics with their accompanying big print and noisy broadcast advertising may have been tasteless, but they were not dishonest. What was dishonest were the accompanying false promises of maximum trade-in allowances, low prices for nonexistent new cars, offers of free premiums with every sale, and phony cash-back offers that were nothing more than loans whose value was tacked on to the sales price.[78]

The most outrageous of these gimmicks were borrowed from used-car dealers like Earl Muntz, the self-diagnosed "madman" whose craziness consisted of "giving away" cars regardless of profit. As they had since before World War I, used-car dealers continued to be major violators of advertising ethics after World War II. Used-car dealers had become such icons of postwar marketplace dishonesty that even used-car dealers made fun of used-car dealers. Sailor Main, a San Diego used-car seller, conceded that his cars were clunkers but claimed that unlike other dealers' cars at least they ran. Similarly playing against type, Wilkie Buick in Philadelphia announced it would *not* sell its used cars for less, would *not* extend easier terms, and would *not* offer unusual guaranties because these were always dishonest come-ons. Ironically, these little flashes of honesty came at a time when new-car dealers were beginning to adopt the sales techniques of used-car dealers.[79]

During the Depression era, used-car dealers had used bait-and-switch advertising in which the great bargain advertised had always "just been sold" when a customer answered the ad. Free gas, free licenses, high allowances, and similar advertised benefits somehow never seemed to materialize when the sale was actually consummated.[80] In the 1950s, new-car dealers adopted the same techniques. They presented themselves as innocent victims of factory pressure, claiming that just as over-allowances and bootlegging were the result of factory pressure to produce unrealistic volume, so too were the over-the-top advertising techniques that accompanied them. It was the car companies' "greed for leadership" that was "forcing the dealers to cast away all ethics of salesmanship and enter into eye-gouging tactics to deliver new cars," testified one Chevrolet dealer.[81]

The Chevy dealer's complaint was in response to a questionnaire from Democratic Senator A. S. Mike Monroney of Oklahoma. Dealer complaints had prompted Monroney to send out questionnaires to forty thousand car retailers in the fall of 1955 asking their opinion about manufacturers' sales practices. Based on the answers he received, Monroney convened a Commerce Subcommittee hearing in January 1956 to investigate the extent of the problem.[82] The hearings accelerated a round of introspection that had begun earlier in 1955 when NADA and the Better Business Bureau (BBB) had agreed to work together to draw up a code of advertising ethics. The leaders of this reform movement held out hope for success because they said that "discount schemes, phony offers, meaningless contests, and countless gimmicks" had also plagued the retail furniture business, which had been able to work with the BBB to clean up that industry's ads. Their optimism may have been somewhat premature since the furniture campaign had itself just begun and its success seems to have consisted mostly of printing and distributing advertising codes.[83] Nevertheless, the BBB could provide some sort of oversight for the process that promised to eliminate two acknowledged problems. The first was bait advertising, in which a nonexistent low-priced car was advertised to draw in customers. The second was "bushing" (a term with etymological links to "bush league," "bushwhack," and "ambush") that was used to describe a variety of techniques that increased the price of the car after the buyer thought a firm deal had been concluded.[84]

The NADA-BBB code listed sixteen specific kinds of "grotesque and exaggerated claims of alleged savings" in advertising that were unacceptable. Leading the list were misleading profit statements in which dealers claimed they were selling cars for only a pittance over their costs. The code also condemned claims that a minimum number of cars "must be sold" during a specific period, as well as false assertions of distress, such as "overstocked" or "need cash." In addition it denounced misleading finance claims like that of the Chicago dealer who "announced on the radio that he would sell cars on the basis of ten cents a day for the first year" without ever disclosing the final cost.[85] The code condemned excessively vague promises about the value of trade-ins, and dealers were specifically warned against referring to themselves as "supermarkets," having special factory ties, or implying that their large volume allowed them to buy their cars from the manufacturer for less than their competitors. Finally, in a category called "additional phraseology," the code listed twenty-six advertising expressions to avoid. They included virtually the entire vocabulary of automobile retailing. Dealers were told not to claim to have the "best deal in town," "lowest prices," or "highest trades." Besides not promising specific dollar amounts in discounts or allowances, the dealers were warned against referring to themselves as "wheeling and dealing," or claiming that "we will not be undersold."[86]

The breadth of the prohibitions was awesome. Had they been obeyed, car advertisers would have been struck dumb. Within a year, however, the Better Business Bureau was reporting that charges of unethical practices in the automobile business had increased 30 percent. Fifty field investigations by the BBB found that dealers were still advertising unavailable cars and bushing the customers who took the bait. One dealer promised to "give away" one 1958 car with every 1957 model he sold—at a price, of course, that more than covered the cost of both. Another ran ads that asked, "Why pay $1,988 when you get your brand new car at 1884?" It turned out that 1884 was the dealer's street address; the car cost $2,150.[87]

The Monroney hearings extensively documented the deceptive nature of blitz marketing, and representatives of the manufacturers, dealers, public, and Congress all agreed that such retail practices hurt consumers and "legitimate" dealers. When Monroney confronted Ford vice-president (later president) Robert S. McNamara with examples of blitz advertising from the company's largest dealer, McNamara called the ads "disgraceful."[88] Nevertheless, the committee's bill did not address advertising, and in the absence of specific legal prohibitions, car dealers continued to run ads that were garish, noisy, and intentionally deceptive.[89] NADA revised its "Recommended Standards of Practice for Advertising and Selling Automobiles" in 1962 and urged newspaper publishers to refuse to run "false, misleading, and unethical automobile dealer advertising, which continued to be a leading cause of public dissatisfaction with the industry."[90]

The grossly misleading advertisers were in fact a minority, according to the Chicago BBB, which had a special automobile division funded by the Chicago Automobile Trade Association. The BBB division limited its criticism to the most blatant forms of deceptive ads, but it still found plenty to complain about. Although the BBB said that the offending dealers constituted less than 8 percent of the area's auto retailers, that small group "included a disproportionate ratio of heavy advertisers"—so heavy that the Bureau's buyers' guides included special sections on decoding car ads.[91] They warned against "lowball" advertisements that promised "full factory equipment," which meant the car came *without* any desirable accessories, or an extremely low price for a current model car that neglected to mention that it was secondhand. Similarly, consumers were told how to spot misleading promises, such as guaranteed high trade-in allowances, free color televisions, thousands of gallons of free gasoline, or even a free kitchen stove with each car sold.[92]

These kinds of ads played hide-and-seek with growing state regulations requiring truth in auto advertising. Since almost all the deceptive advertisements were run by local new and used-car dealers, not national manufacturers, local governments drafted a variety of restrictions in an attempt to stop the retailers from lying outright.[93] By 1988 twenty states had passed some sort of rules. Among other things, the regulations required that all mandatory charges (except taxes and registration) be listed in advertised prices, that the pictures and the text be about the same model car, that tiny footnotes could not contradict promises set in large type, that no specific offers could be made about trade-in amounts, and that if dealers said they had the "best prices in town," they had to have evidence to verify the claim. The states responded to the bait-and-switch ploy by requiring ads to say how many cars were available at the advertised price and sometimes to identify them by specific invoice or vehicle numbers. It really made no difference, because, as one salesman explained, the identified cars were invariably sold before the newspapers hit the streets, either to a friend of the person who took the ad to the paper or by a friend of the person at the paper who took in the ad.[94]

Critics of false advertising from within the automobile industry often fell back on the charge that price advertising was inherently bad business because it combined price competition, which dealers hated, with blitz techniques, which were despised by the public.[95] As they had been since the teens of the twentieth century, dealers were urged to sell their product and themselves, not the cost of the car, because that road led to reduced profits. Yet dealers were operating in an economy where retailers of almost every other product sold on price. Consumers expected to be able to comparison shop and buy identical manufactured products on the basis of price. The difference was that the advertised price for products other than cars was the price that the consumer paid. The advertised price for cars (if any) was only a vague lowball approximation of what the buyer would pay.

Posting a Price

In 1939 the Federal Trade Commission had recommended that all car sales be accompanied by a detailed invoice that listed the price of every component of the sale: accessories, taxes, advertising and handling charges, title fees, and so forth.[96] It is not clear if FTC expected the invoice to be available before the salesman and customer shook hands on the deal, but at least two car companies, General Motors and Packard, took the suggestion to heart and ordered their dealers to attach such an invoice to each vehicle at the start of the 1940 season.[97] Nineteen-forty was the penultimate year for car production prior to World War II, and by the time the war ended, the industry was so caught up in the frenzy of the postwar sellers' market that anything like an itemized invoice that might have eaten into the profits from the pack was forgotten.

As the sellers' market faded in the early 1950s, the impact of bootlegging, price packing, over-allowances, and blitz advertising was further confused by the way manufacturers levied delivery fees on their dealers. That dispute between the factories and the retailers did not have a direct effect on price negotiations, but the arcane accounting questions of who should pay how much for shipping a car from Detroit or from a closer assembly plant did affect what costs the dealers passed on to their customers.[98] The end result of all this pricing complexity was an environment of mutual distrust among the three groups involved. The dealers wanted protection from the factory and from each other. The customers wanted protection from the dealers and the manufacturers.

At the Commerce Subcommittee hearings, Monroney spread the blame around. He accused what he had called "a few unscrupulous dealers" of lying to their customers about the list price of cars, but he also got the manufacturers to admit that they had contributed to the circus-like atmosphere of blitz advertising and price packing.[99] Tired of their poor public image and unable to control the excesses on their own, the dealers endorsed the idea of government-mandated price labels on new cars.[100] The Automobile Information Disclosure Act (Monroney Act), which President Dwight Eisenhower signed into law in early June, went into effect in the fall of 1958 with the introduction of the 1959 model year cars. The law required that new cars display a label with the vehicle's serial number, final assembly point, and to whom and how it was shipped, along with the transportation charge, the manufacturer's suggested retail price (MSRP) of the basic car, and the price of each factory-installed accessory but not the cost of taxes, license fees, and any items installed by the dealer.[101] By passing the bill, Congress enshrined in law what had evolved in practice: cars would continue to be sold differently from all other manufactured goods. Other manufacturers could, if they wanted, suggest a retail price, but only carmakers were required by federal legislation to post such a price on their product.

The MSRP was a *suggested* retail price. Retailers could charge whatever they wanted, but they could not alter the window sticker. At the hearings, Monroney had been quite explicit that the law would continue to allow what he called "the great American sport of bargaining."[102] The *New York Times* article that announced the implementation of the law invoked the equine precedent when it explained that all sides "freely acknowledged that the same old horse trading between dealer and prospective customer will prevail."[103] At the time, observers believed that the MSRP would become a de facto price ceiling and that customers would attempt to bargain down the price from there.[104] The older system, in which the dealer inflated the initial asking price with a hidden pack would no longer be possible.[105] However, the dealer was assured that if he could "find a customer gullible enough who can be convinced that the suggested list price is not binding, he can even sell the car at over list."[106] That the author of this statement assumed that any buyer who paid over list was "gullible" is some indication of how deeply ingrained price haggling had become. By not publishing list prices and encouraging dealers to inflate them through packing, while at the same time cutting prices through bargaining and over-allowances, the automobile industry had educated the public to expect discounts.[107]

Every person who spoke in favor of the law, both before and after it was passed, emphasized that it would do away with the pack. The pack had been the law's raison d'être, and the law would be the pack's coup de grace—at least, that was the plan. The problem was that there were multiple definitions of the pack, or to put it another way, there was more than one kind of pack. When he introduced the bill, Monroney defined the pack as the extra cost built into a false list price that would then be given back in an over-allowance.[108] That little shell game, in which the salesman closed the deal on the basis of price he offered for the buyer's old car, not the price he offered for the new one, did go away with the new law, because now the buyer had a factory-supplied number to measure his allowance against. However, there was nothing particularly new about the buyer's knowing the factory list price. Manufacturers had routinely advertised car prices before World War II, and that had not prevented a second form of price packing.

Prior to World War II, the term "pack" never referred to a fictitiously high list price precisely because of factory price advertising. Rather, the pack usually meant forcing the customer to buy accessories he did not want (both factory and dealer-installed) and padding the invoice with dubious charges for such things as delivery, preparation, advertising, and documentation. The Monroney Act nibbled at the edges of some of these tricks, requiring, for example, that the delivery cost to the dealer be included on the sticker. Nevertheless, the dealers could still pack the car with retailer-installed services, or with high-profit factory-installed accessories, for that matter, except that the prices of latter, but not the former, would be listed on the sticker. Dealers could still invent creative "fees" to add to the bottom line and do almost everything else they had always done to manipulate the consumer's price. The only difference was that now some of those additional charges showed up on the sticker along with the MSRP.[109]

Initial reaction to the new law was uniformly positive. Customers liked having a factory-supplied list price because it gave them a basis for judging the real value of a trade-in allowance. Dealers said they liked being more honest about the lower price of both new cars and trade-ins.[110] However, one confused Connecticut dealer complained that customers "study prices by candlelight to save electricity and hold us up. They come in with a chip on their shoulder. They cannot dicker about the list price, which the government controls, so their chief concern is the trade-in."[111] The dealer was, of course, wrong about the government controlling the list price, but that, no doubt, was what he wanted his customers to think.

Consumer advisors constantly reminded buyers that the sticker price was the beginning not the end of price negotiation, and that only the "most naïve" would pay it. The net effect of the Monroney sticker was to make the negotiations over the price of the car somewhat more transparent. Both sides now had an "official" starting point from which they could bargain and could have a rough idea of just what part of this complicated product, and equally complicated transaction, was costing what.[112] But beyond that, the process continued to be, as it had been previously, one of multiple simultaneous negotiations involving the base price, the cost of options, finance and insurance fees, and the trade-in allowance. The final price to customers was usually so far off the sticker price that the FTC spent several years, starting in 1969, investigating whether to require that window stickers reflect actual selling prices.[113] The plan was never implemented, but in 1973 the California attorney general's office did require

General Motors to post a "Notice to Buyer" on each of its cars to the effect that the MSRP was not necessarily the price the cars were actually selling for.[114]

The governmental worry that price stickers were misleading consumers reflected the continuing deeper concern that car buying was not fair. By providing all consumers with the same MSRP, the Monroney sticker made the bargaining process more equal, but the underlying issue was not a more level playing field for the negotiators but the fact that there was negotiating at all. Compared to standard retail transactions, car sales treated people as individuals, not as equal members of a consumer class. Nineteenth-century advocates of a one-price policy had referred to this as "undemocratic." People wound up paying widely different prices for the same goods because of who they were (good or bad bargainers). The writer of a consumer advice book in 1970 raised the issue by asking if it were "unethical" for one consumer to demand a lower price than others. It was indeed "unfair" for one person to pay hundreds of dollars more for a car than another, he said, but he consoled any buyers who might be conscience-stricken by assuring them that dealers suffered no pangs of remorse when they stuck it to a "nice trustful guy" to make up for the money they lost on a "chiseling fink."[115]

The Great Warranty War

Some particularly innocent buyers may have thought the Monroney sticker was a standard price tag (and no salesman would disabuse them of that idea), but most customers understood that cars had to be bargained for. Moreover, just as cars had no one-price policy, they could not be returned. Luxury automaker Peerless had offered a one-year warranty and a two-day money-back guaranty in 1931—the same year it went out of business.[116] A half-century later, in 1980, Chrysler, also faced with imminent demise, briefly experimented with a "30-day satisfaction money-back guaranty," following the lead of a suburban Minneapolis dealer who had been extending that protection on his own for six years.[117] The federal government bailed out Chrysler, and other manufacturers declined to follow Chrysler's lead.

When an unhappy automobile buyer wanted her money back from a Washington, D.C., dealer in 1995, a local newspaper columnist suggested that in the future all car salesmen read a "hey, you bought it" statement to every customer: "You have just bought a car. You have not rented it, borrowed it, or leased it. It is yours until you sell it. The dealership has no intention of taking it back under any circumstances." The writer's sarcastic language was an expression of exasperation with a female shopper who did not understand that different rules applied in the male world of car sales. The suggested statement did end with one promise: "We will, however, stand behind our factory service warranty in case of mechanical trouble."[118] Just how much protection that afforded varied over the course of automobile history, yet it seldom played an important role in price negotiations.

In horse trading, warranties were integral to the bargaining process because they constituted a promise about a particular animal's qualities. In a horse trade, the default assumption was caveat emptor, and the buyer tried to get the seller to make specific promises. As manufactured products, cars automatically came with a warranty of merchantability, and the sellers (both manufacturers and dealers) usually tried to provide just enough buyer protection to satisfy the law or the marketplace—whichever was less. With cars, there was never a buyer's right to return or exchange the purchase, and until the 1980s there was not even any assurance that whatever limited warranty the manufacturer had given would be sufficient to satisfy an unhappy buyer. The line between the legal rights of the buyer under commercial law and the retail return privilege was a blurry one in most consumers' minds except when they were buying cars. Then it was bright and sharp: there was no right to return the product.

In the beginning, as recently invented and highly unreliable mechanical devices, new cars were a bit of a gamble to own, and drivers could not demand much more than that a machine called an "automobile" should in fact propel itself.[119] Nevertheless, as early as 1908 Studebaker drew particular attention to its "well-known Studebaker guaranty (the most liberal ever written)."[120] After 1910, as supply met demand, other manufacturers pressured their dealers to stand behind the products they sold, often offering free maintenance and service during the first year of ownership.[121] This relatively generous warranty coverage eroded in the 1920s to an industry standard of ninety days.[122] The ninety-day warranty was modified slightly for the 1932 model year when the auto manufacturers collectively agreed to adopt a ninety-day or four- thousand-miles standard except for the tires. This new standard was hailed as "the most liberal guarantee of manufacturing perfection and the broadest promise of free service attention ever offered in the history of the automobile industry," although in fact, individual companies had done better before World War I.[123]

The ninety-day/four-thousand-mile warranty remained unchanged for thirty years. Manufacturers jousted with their dealers over which of them would cover the costs of various repairs, but the cost of parts and labor for the buyer was zero. The warranties themselves did not play a major role at the retail level until the 1960s, when manufacturers started to increase buyer protection as a marketing tool.[124] The new industry standard for 1961 models was 12/12, that is, twelve months or twelve thousand miles. Chrysler upped the ante the next year when it offered a five-year/fifty-thousand-mile (5/50) warranty on its power train components (but only a 12/12 guaranty on all the other car parts). Other firms countered with 24/24 protection on the entire vehicle; Chrysler saw their 24/24 and raised them 5/50 on the power train. The others matched Chrysler once again, and by 1968 all the companies were offering 5/50 on the power train and 24/24 on the rest of the car.[125] For seven years the auto companies sought to outbid each other for customer trust. Unfortunately for them, the products put out by their engineering and manufacturing personnel could not match the self-confidence of their marketing departments. The manufacturers tried to protect themselves by larding their warranties with limitations and exceptions, but that only angered the buyers, who were bringing their poorly constructed American cars back to the shop in record numbers. The cost to the factories became prohibitive, and in 1968 the carmakers abandoned the extended warranties and reverted to 12/12 coverage.[126]

The fluctuations in new-car warranties reflected broad market conditions that included the lack of mechanical reliability of American automobiles and legal interpretations about the meaning of implied warranties. With the end of the industry's brief experiment with extended warranties in the 1960s, horror stories of badly designed cars that could not be fixed and would not be exchanged filled the papers once again. Starting with Connecticut in 1982, states began to pass "lemon laws" that gave consumers specific rights if they were stuck with a chronically troublesome new car. By 1994 every state in the union had a law that required manufacturers to replace a malfunctioning new car if it had not been fixed after a certain number of attempts.[127] The lemon laws were a legislative response to an industry that not only refused to offer a money-back guaranty, but had also developed a reputation for refusing to live up to the commonsense meaning of merchantability. While not exactly shrugging their shoulders and invoking caveat emptor, neither had the car companies treated their customers as purchasers of manufactured products that would be replaced if they did not work.

Used cars, on the other hand, occupied a different legal position; caveat emptor was still the rule. Some early used-car dealers promised, "Customers are

protected by ample guaranty." The norm, however, was lots of talk but no assurance that anything the salesman said would actually be honored once the car
had been driven off the lot.[128] "Driven off the lot" could be taken quite literally.
Author Milton Mayer remembered buying a used Ford in his youth before
World War II. The car died as he was driving it off the lot—halfway off the lot.
He knows it was halfway because the salesman came out with a tape measure
and determined that it was more than 50 percent over the property line and
therefore sold.[129] Warranties on secondhand cars remained relatively rare, although every decade or so industry leaders would try to convince dealers to
guarantee their used cars and even allow returns for credit.[130] Ford, for example,
recommended in 1939 that its dealers inspect trade-ins and "certify" those that
met certain standards. The dealers would then repair for free any problem with
a certified car that was brought to their attention during the first ten days of
ownership or, at the dealer's discretion, refund the buyer's purchase price.[131]
The idea of premium-priced warranted used cars continued, but consumer advocates thought all secondhand cars should carry some kind of buyer protection
information.[132]

Economist George Akerlof won the Nobel Prize in 2001 for ideas that originated in an essay that explained why poor-quality used cars (lemons) drove
down the price of good-quality used cars. Akerlof argued that sellers knew more
than buyers about the condition of cars and that this asymmetrical knowledge
meant buyers always had to assume a car for sale was flawed, an insight, he said,
that "had been central to the horse trading profession for centuries."[133] Horse
buyers had attempted to compensate for their lack of knowledge by asking for,
but seldom receiving, a warranty. Secondhand car buyers were hardly better off,
but their plight could have been remedied by a government requirement for
greater disclosure of a car's problems. Legislators, however, were even slower to
protect used-car customers than they had been to protect new-car buyers. The
first tentative steps to impose honesty on those who sold used cars and provide
protection for those who bought them took place in the 1930s and barely increased over the next forty years.[134] Not until after 1975 was there any shift in
the assumption that neither sellers nor buyers of used cars could take anything
the other party said at face value. In the mid-1970s, however, six states passed
laws that prohibited used-car dealers from excluding or modifying the implied
warranty of merchantability and fitness as it applied to used cars. The laws, however, did not define what the implied warranty should cover or how long it
should last, leaving that issue to be hammered out in case law at the local level.[135]

Taking its lead from the states, for a dozen years, from 1976 to 1988, the Federal Trade Commission sought to hammer out a federal policy to protect used-car buyers. In its initial finding, the FTC confirmed the reasoning behind the state laws by charging that dealers engaged in "pervasive misrepresentation" by making minor cosmetic alterations that led buyers "to make erroneous assumptions concerning the prior use and care" of the vehicles. In addition, the commission said that sellers advertised that certain cars had had "only one owner," neglecting to mention that the one owner had been a rental car company, a taxi-cab business, or a police department.[136] The report further charged that salespeople made verbal promises about standing behind their products, while the written contracts disclaimed any responsibility for vehicle malfunction. Therefore, on January 2, 1976, the FTC proposed that all used-car dealers, but not individual sellers, be required to attach a window sticker that would spell out known flaws, past use, and warranty specifics.[137] No immediate action was taken, and two years later the FTC recommended that all used cars be required to undergo a sixty-point safety inspection, with results posted on a window sticker.

The National Independent Automobile Dealers Association (NIADA), the organization that represented nonfranchised used-car dealers, was much more receptive to the idea of disclosure than their colleagues who also sold new cars. The independent used-car dealers accepted all the FTC's categories of disclosure in principle and even added a couple of specifics of their own. They did, however, request a "no disclosure" option for buyers who were willing to pay a lower price for "as-is" vehicles.[138] However, NADA, the organization that represented franchised car dealers, argued that repair lists on better cars would make them look worse than as-is cars with no posted repairs, thus increasing "rather then decreasing the likelihood that the purchaser will select a defective vehicle."[139] In 1981 the FTC suggested a rule that would allow dealers to sell used cars as is and would require them to spell out the details on any warranty that was being offered but said nothing about inspections.[140]

The dealers, however, would not accept a face-saving compromise; they wanted unconditional surrender and knew that their opponent was seriously wounded. The Reagan Era attack on government regulation had already cut the FTC off at the knees. In 1980, Congress passed a law giving itself the power to veto commission regulations. Fortified with massive campaign contributions from the used-car industry, Congress took this as its first opportunity to exercise the veto option, prompting humorist Russell Baker to observe that Congress was doing its part to help Americans stay in touch with their roots "by keeping alive the memory of the Old West horse trader in a thousand concrete cities."[141]

When the courts subsequently declared the congressional veto of commission rules unconstitutional, the FTC itself backed down and temporarily dropped the regulation in favor of a public education campaign.[142] Ultimately, in 1988, the FTC did issue a rule that required a used-car window sticker. It was a pale reflection of the original 1978 staff proposal and went into effect without a peep of objection from the industry. The "Buyers Guide" sticker on every used car has to say whether the vehicle is for sale "as is" or comes with a warranty. If there is a warranty, the coverage and limits must be spelled out. That's it: no inspections, no information on mechanical condition or previous use.[143] Some states continued to extend additional protections to used-car buyers, but at the federal level all the used-car sticker did was tell buyers whether they were buying a pig in a poke, the modern equivalent of horses from shifty road traders.

Consumer information labels on cars for sale and seller warranties were responses to the postwar triumph of the pack. Bargaining practices carried over from horse trading into car dealing by the trade-in system flourished in the late 1940s and 50s when manufacturers stopped publishing new-car list prices. The myriad ways in which auto retailing violated the conventional retail model irritated consumers (and to a lesser extent, dealers and manufacturers). Governments at various levels stepped in to tinker with the way cars were sold, but nothing they did altered the fundamental system of negotiated prices. Window stickers, limited warranties, and lemon laws may have ameliorated some of the worst excesses, but the public still hated the process and continued to think of the people who sold cars as the bad guys.

Figure 1. The mule-swapper on the right examines one animal's teeth to check its age, while the man on the left may be looking for rubbed areas that indicate that this mule would pull in a harness. William M. Brewer, "A Horse Swapping Convention," *Cosmopolitan,* October 1899, 582.

THE FARMER'S FAILING—IT USED TO BE SWAPPIN' HORSES.

FARMER STUBBLE.—Henry, I'll tell ye what I'll do! I'll give ye this tourin'-car of mine, an' a plow I ain't used none, fer that new runabout o' yours an' fifty dollars. Come now!

Figure 2. A couple of farmers demonstrate the same penchant for swapping cars that they previously had for horse trading. "The Farmers' Failing," *Puck*, 16 October 1912, 7.

Figure 3. A cartoon in an auto dealers' magazine warns against giving generous allowances on trade-ins so dilapidated even junk dealers would not take them. "Profitable Operation Depends on Ability to Reject Deals," *N.A.D.A. Bulletin,* August 1937, 3.

Buying a Secondhand Car Is Almost as Risky as Buying a Secondhand Horse

Figure 4. World War I–era used-car buyers were cautioned to treat salesmen with the same suspicion they had for horse traders. Ray Goldman, "How to Buy a Second Hand Car," *Illustrated World*, January 1918, 742.

THE NEW RITUAL.

GENTLEMAN IN BLACK.—Who giveth this automobile away?

SALESMAN (*stepping forward*).—Considering the standing of our firm, our well-known guarantee, the low price asked, and the decreased vibration, rich black body, sweet running qualities, increased power, and unsurpassed flexibility of the machine—I feel that, to all intents and purposes, I am giving her away.

GENTLEMAN IN BLACK.—John Smith, do you take this automobile for better or worse; for uphill or down; for rough roads or smooth? Do you promise to nurse her over hard going and to be tender with her tires? Do you promise to keep her in magnetos and carburetors and bearings and lubrication and enamel? To baby her when she falters; to repair her when she breaks down; and to blow about her superb running qualities all the time to everybody till the second-hand dealer do you part? . . . . . In that case, by the authority vested in me by the Automobile Fanatics of the World, I pronounce you One!

Figure 5. Humor magazine *Puck* makes fun of men's attachment to their cars and salesmen's patter about giving good deals. Gordon Grant, "The New Ritual," *Puck*, 16 October 1912, 7.

Figure 6. The title of the *Business Week* article illustrated by this photo announced that this ancestor of the Internet was "A Machine That Sells Cars." *Business Week,* 17 April 1954, 62.

CHAPTER SIX

Bad Guys

Historically, the buying public used the terms "salesman" and "dealer" as though they were synonymous. The conflation makes sense because in smaller dealerships the owners commonly worked the sales floor. In larger firms, however, and especially in franchises that operated out of multiple locations, there usually were sales managers and other levels of personnel between the salespeople and the owner (dealer). Just as the negotiation over price was a zero-sum game between the buyer and the seller, so was the division of profits between the salesman and the house. While it might make no difference from the customer's perspective if the person trying to squeeze the last penny out of the deal was the owner or an employee, that distinction had great significance from the seller's side: what the salesman got, the dealer lost. The three-way conflict among the customer, the salesman, and the dealer contributed significantly to the masculinized culture of the showroom floor.

The Car Seller's Career: Nasty, Brutish, and Short

Almost from the beginning of the retail car business, franchise owners debated the best way to compensate salesmen. Salesmen always received commissions, occasionally they got an advance against commissions, and sometimes they even got a salary augmented by commissions. The formulas for determining the commissions varied widely. They were variously based on the number of units (individual cars) sold, on the price of each unit sold, on the net profit for each deal, taking into account both the selling price and the trade-in allowance—all of which could be modified by additional commissions from financing, insurance, and dealer-installed accessories. In addition, there were often sliding scales that increased commissions as the number of cars sold increased, bonuses based on various sales contests to reach certain individual or collective goals, or to sell slow-moving models, or almost anything else an executive could dream up to motivate the sales staff.[1]

Dealers often made it a practice not to let the staff see the car invoices, so salesmen had no idea what sort of margin they were working with. Just as the salesman was expected to squeeze the last dollar out of the buyer, the dealer would squeeze the last dollar out of the salesman by withholding the information he needed to cut a fair deal with the customer and calculate his own commission.[2] The competing interests of salesman and management, combined with the generally no-holds-barred culture of the showroom floor, meant that the relations between the sales staff and the dealer could become positively toxic. The heartbreaking collapse of Shelley Levine, the real estate salesman in David Mamet's play *Glengarry, Glen Ross*, could have been the story of almost any car salesman, except that Shelley was at the end of a long and successful professional life, a rarity among cars salesmen. Automobile salesmen worked in a Hobbesian environment where professional lives were typically "solitary, poor, nasty, brutish, and short." One ex-salesman noted that while their customers regarded them as cheats, pickpockets, cutpurses, and con men, their bosses thought of them as "something akin to itinerant fruit pickers" who could be fired as soon as the crop was in and sometimes refused to pay them the money they had earned.[3]

Becoming a car salesman was rarely a prime career move, although the industry fought a losing century-long battle to elevate its status. In his description of the origins of the modern sales profession, historian Walter Friedman accepts the automobile industry's view that by the 1920s their products were being sold in a modern and scientific way.[4] The carmakers did indeed picture their ideal salesman as the antithesis of a horse trader. He was a man who knew both his product and his customers and who, with hard work and a positive attitude, could, claimed Chevrolet in 1930, be in the top 6 percent of all wage

earners in the nation.[5] The real situation was very different from the corpora-
tions' preferred image, however. Successful car salesmen were not particularly
knowledgeable or helpful, and most were not successful.

One salesman who *was* successful illustrates the difference between the ideal
and the real. In the 1960s and 70s, America's ultimate car salesman, Joe Girard,
would regularly sell more than a thousand cars a year. Girard *personally* sold
more cars than 96 percent of the *dealerships* in the country.[6] Yet Joe Girard's approach to sales was neither particularly modern nor scientific. He violated two
fundamental principles stressed by manufacturers and dealers: first, he knew
very little about the technical features of the Chevrolets he was selling, which
made sense because he also violated the second principle by always selling the
price, not the product. Girard understood that car selling was as much about the
deal as the car. What he did not know about engine torque, he made up for with
his understanding of accessory packages, trade-in values, and anything else that
would let him cut the price until he nailed the sale.[7] The factory and the house
might have thought that customers bought cars, but Girard knew that they
bought deals, and he was *a* dealer even when he was not *the* dealer. As the quintessential transportation salesman, Girard was a trader who could have sold
horses in the 1890s or cars in any decade after 1910.

Pre-1910, cars were sold as novelties. Writing in 1911 about the "olden
times," an automotive executive said that early car salesmen did not know very
much about their products beyond being able to drive them. Time and again
those seeking to professionalize the cars sales vocation dismissed this first generation of salesmen as not being able to do anything more than take prospects
for joyrides and let the excitement of speed and power sell itself.[8] By 1911,
though, times had changed. Manufacturers, dealership owners, and industry
pundits began to insist that the new-car salesman had to be professional, with a
"vast amount of knowledge" and a genuine concern for the long-term well-
being of the customer.[9] Vocational schools and how-to books promised to provide the necessary instruction for a career in what one called "this big money
making field."[10] The manufacturers themselves created short courses, work-
shops, books and pamphlets, training films, and other educational devices that
gave the official view of how retail car salesmen were supposed to operate. Most
of these instructional aids were intended for franchise owners and sales managers, but at least one manufacturer ran a school for salesmen where it paid the
men to take courses not only in salesmanship but also in technical subjects that
trained them "to assemble and disassemble the various parts of the car."[11]

By World War I, however, the importance of technical knowledge was being soft-pedaled because "mechanical talk always leads to confusion and argument."[12] The new emphasis was on selling skills, not axle bearings. The salesman's job was now to go out and find the prospect and say to him: "Good morning! Mr. So-and-so. I understand you are thinking about buying an automobile. (Don't stop here to allow him to answer this question until you finish by saying, 'Of course you're thinking of buying one. Everyone is.')" The salesman was then to recite his car's virtues while starting to fill out the order blank and shrugging off the prospect's protests that he was not ready to buy.[13]

From the end of World War I to the end of the century, the official script for the sales process remained essentially unchanged and was notable for the absence of any reference to negotiating prices. Roughly in this order, the ideal salesperson was supposed to:

1. *Canvass for prospects:* reach out to find customers, not wait for them to walk in the door.
2. *Qualify the prospect:* make sure the prospect was ready and able to pay.
3. *Present the vehicle:* find a car the prospect wanted and demonstrate it in a way that emphasized the buyer's needs and desires.
4. *Close the sale:* turn the prospect into a customer by getting him or her to sign a purchase contract.
5. *Offer the allowance:* get the buyer's current car appraised and present the trade-in allowance.
6. *Sell aftermarket accessories:* convince the buyer to purchase financing, insurance, and extended warranties through the dealership.
7. *Deliver the car:* turn the car over to the buyer in a way designed to make the customer feel that he or she had gotten a great car at a great price.[14]

By never mentioning price haggling, the factory-authorized sales scenario perpetuated the myth that every new car should sell at list and every trade-in should bring a fair profit as a separate transaction. This was true not only before World War II, when the entire industry pretended that all cars were sold for what the manufacturer suggested, but also in the wild and woolly 1950s, when the manufacturer's list was practically a trade secret. An academic expert on salesmanship told the dealers at the 1959 NADA convention that the salesman who begins "dickering and haggling, too often settles for a loss or goes away defeated."[15] Both factory and dealership management clung to the fantasy that any day now the auto retail business would be staffed by polite, technically knowledgeable, low-key professionals who would eschew what a NADA executive called the "manipulative or adversarial tactics that chase away today's customers."[16] These benign sales staffers would help their customers define their transportation needs and then fill them so smoothly that list prices would be selling prices and fair trade-in allowances would always prevail.[17] Not only would the customers pay top dollar, they would return every couple of years to buy a new car from the same salesperson and recommend this paragon of retail service to all their relatives and acquaintances.[18]

The Sales Game: Tactics

For there to be an ideal car seller, there had to be an ideal car buyer who paid full price and accepted whatever was offered in trade. Salesmen often referred to such buyers as "lay downs" or "barefoot pilgrims."[19] Sometimes the barefoot pilgrim's route led to the showroom door, but sales staffers were also expected to go out into the field and entice them in. A department store did not expect its clerks to find customers. The customers came into the store, and the clerk offered to help them find what they were looking for. Dealers had "stores" (although the industry did not use that word to describe showrooms until after World War II) but did not have customers; they had "prospects." Prospects were not necessarily people who wanted to buy a car from the salesman. Prospects were people who needed to be convinced that they wanted to buy a car from the salesman.

Dealers have never thought that their salesmen should act like department store clerks waiting for the customers to come to them; they should go to the customer—originally, with the product itself. Into the 1930s, sellers would first meet prospects at their houses to show them sales brochures and then return with a demonstrator car to take the prospects for a test drive. Until the mid-1920s, the salesman himself did most of the driving. Prospects stayed in the passenger seat—either because they did not know how to drive, or because the salesman knew how to drive the car in a way that emphasized its strengths and hid weaknesses such as an inability to climb hills.[20] When the short-story character Reginald Randolph decided to buy his first automobile in 1910, he and his wife enjoyed several extensive drives through the park with the salesmen of competing brands. One was bold enough to suggest that Reginald take a turn behind the wheel. The novice driver, who could not tell the knobs and levers apart, applied the emergency brake when he meant to shift and produced "a horrible grinding, as if the car was being torn asunder." When he did shift, he almost drove into a tree while shouting "Whoa! Whoa!" at his mechanical steed.[21]

It pained dealers to see their staff sitting in an empty showroom waiting when they could be working the phones or ringing doorbells.[22] Sales supervisors believed that there were plenty of people who would buy that car if a salesman took the initiative to approach them the way insurance, encyclopedia, and vacation-home salesmen did. In the 1920s and 30s, when salesmen had no leads, they were advised: "Solicit everybody in your community on the theory that some time or another everyone is a prospect for a car"; or, only slightly more specifically, "Pick out a street or group of streets and cover each home or business house systematically. In rural communities go up one country road and down another."[23]

The idea of wandering up and down rustic roads and knocking on farmhouse doors like an old-time Yankee tinware peddler held little appeal for the average car salesman because they thought canvassing was a lot of effort for very little return.[24] Nevertheless, the pressure to hustle for prospects was relentless.[25] If it wasn't country back roads, salesmen were told to cruise downtown office buildings, either in person or by telephone. Dealers had all kinds of ways to encourage or coerce their sales people to drum up leads. Some paid their staff on a per-call basis; others would not let them have access to walk-ins (called "ups") until they had scheduled a certain number of sales presentations by phone.[26] A Kansas City Ford dealer, who required ninety minutes of telephone calls daily from every member of his sales staff, said it was either that or "have six guys standing on the showroom floor waiting for something to happen."[27] In 1915, a time when few people had telephones and fewer had cars, one would-be buyer made the mistake of mailing off magazine coupons for catalogs of cars he was idly considering. Instead of catalogs, he got a steady stream of automobile salesmen ringing his doorbell.[28] Other popular techniques included talking to owners waiting to have their cars serviced, following up publicly reported car thefts and garage fires, contacting car owners when they had paid their final installment, and soliciting names from current and past customers.[29]

In New York City at mid-century, particularly aggressive salesmen congregated at passenger piers and airports to high-pressure servicemen returning from overseas into signing contracts for new cars.[30] The New Yorkers called this process "bird dogging." The term "bird dog," however, usually referred to people like tow-truck drivers, garage mechanics, insurance men, parking-lot attendants, and auto parts supply store clerks who could give salesmen the names of people who probably needed a new car.[31] Salesmen also lured potential buyers into the showroom with "would you take" offers. As early as 1919, salesmen were walking the streets and placing tags on parked cars asking if the owner would accept a specific sum as an allowance on a new car.[32] Handwritten and geared to the particular vehicle, the tag would promise a price far in excess of what the car was worth as bait to bring the curious car owner onto the salesman's home turf.[33]

Dealers and manufacturers grumbled that salesmen refused to make cold calls, distribute "would you take" tags, or even send out personal postcards because they were just plain lazy. "Every time we run an ad for salesmen," said one sales manager, "we get a large supply of drifters, loudmouths, and failures." He said they refused to "make phone calls. They won't send out literature. They won't line up bird dogs. All they want to do is live off the floor traffic."[34] What was laziness from the dealer's perspective was commonsense conservation of energy from the salesman's. As a rule, experienced salesmen refused to do anything that they thought had a low probability of resulting in a sale, including talking to some walk-ins, which is why they often ignored women, poor people (often ethnic minorities), and obvious "looky-loos" (people "just looking").[35] Exasperation with car salesman laziness would be a perennial motif in dealer commentary and was one reason some managers preferred to hire salesmen from outside the auto industry. Inexperience with automobiles was good, one said, because "in this business, experience amounts to a set of bad habits."[36]

The would-you-take gambit to get prospects into the showroom was a classic version of the so-called highball, which had its natural reciprocal, the lowball. The terms, apparently borrowed from the names of baseball pitches, varied somewhat in meaning from time to time and place to place.[37] Ultimately, however, they implied the same thing: the salesman was offering the customer a price much lower than the dealer would possibly give. The terms first became common in the 1950s, although the techniques themselves are as old as car bargaining itself.[38] Most commonly, a lowball was an unrealistically low quote on a new car, offered either on the phone to bring a prospect into the showroom or to the prospect as he was walking out to bring him back. A highball was a similarly unrealistic price offered for a trade-in, either in a would-you-take offer or as a parting enticement to get a customer to return. "You are a salesman, not a store clerk," thundered a car sales instructor. "If you know that you can only discount the car another $100, then discount it up to $300 in order to get the commitment."[39] The salesman knew that $300 was a phony offer but would take it back after the "commitment" when he sat down with the prospect and told him to "be reasonable."[40]

A particularly nasty version of the lowball involved a "purchase order" that included a trade-in allowance and a deposit (but not a sales contract). The customer would wait for the car, which would never show up. Whenever he contacted the dealer to ask what was happening with his order, he would get a double-talk response and the suggestion that he come in to the showroom where they just happened to have a model similar to the one he wanted but with additional accessories (a pack). The dealer counted on the buyer's expectation of driving a new car and exasperation with waiting to break down his resistance to the higher-priced vehicle.[41]

Dealers and salesmen who tried to deport themselves honestly often disavowed lowball and highball offers. This was especially true for dealers who sought repeat business and tried to avoid making customers angry.[42] However, the temptation not to lose a prospect was strong, and even in more honest stores the subjunctive mood of horse-trading promises persisted in the language of negotiation. "Would you take" was joined by "what if I could," "I'll try to get," and "it could be worth"—and of course the classic "What will it take to get you to buy this car today?"—expressions that did not actually promise anything but left the impression that they did.[43] Technically (if, indeed, one can be "technical" about the argot of unethical commerce), an over-allowance was not a highball, because the customer actually received the proffered amount. Of course, what the right hand gave for the trade-in, the left hand took away in an inflated price for the new car. Moreover, the hand that gave and the hand that took away in car dealerships often belonged to two different people. In the parlance of postwar car dealing, the prospect was "turned over" to a second salesman to close the sale.

The "turn-over" (sometimes referred to as the "take-over," and often as the "TO") to a "closer" is considered by many, both inside and outside the industry, to be the heart of high-pressure auto sales and the symbol of postwar excess. Yet like most of the other components of car dealing, turning a customer over to a closer was an established practice in the industry long before the 1950s. In June 1914, Ford's corporate sales manager wrote to every dealer, rhetorically asking, among other things, "Do you have one man in the salesroom office who is known as the 'Inside Closer,' and who devote[s] all of his time in actually closing prospects when salesmen bring them into the showroom?"[44] Ideally, the closer would do his work in a specially designated "closing room," where "there is nothing to distract the prospect; it is quiet. He cannot but listen to you."[45] Similar processes have been used at least since the 1920s by other big-ticket retailers, some of whom might also trim the tag price if pushed.[46] Price negotiation does not require a turn-over, and turn-overs can exist without price negotiation. However, only the automobile sales system was built on the underlying logic of the turn-over. The auto system assumed that almost all customers would haggle over price and that the best way to get maximum profit from bargaining prospects would be to wear them down with a roster of serial negotiators.[47]

The owner of a Ford dealership in the Bronx, for instance, prided himself in running "a company where customers feel they are not being abused or mistreated." "We do not use any pressure," explained Vic Goldsmith, the firm's vice president, in 1956. Apparently Goldsmith did not consider their automatic double turn-over "pressure." It was the salesman's job, Goldsmith explained, to "beat the bushes, scrape the barrel, qualify and put [the deal] on paper," for which he would receive one silver dollar, whether or not a sale was made. It was then the assistant manager's duty to bring the salesman's promise "into the realm of acceptance." In other words, the prospect was lowballed by the salesman and then bushed by the assistant manager. Having jacked up the price once, the assistant manager was required to make a second turn-over to the sales manager, "the true expert in his field, to make it a profitable transaction. It is up to these men to work for that extra $10 in a deal because they are more skilled closers," concluded Goldsmith. This tale of triple-teaming all customers to wring the last ten bucks out of them was featured in Ford's own dealer magazine as a positive object lesson for other store owners.[48]

The Monroney price sticker had no impact on the TO system because both sides in a car sale still expected to haggle over price. Rather than decrease the haggling, the sticker made the buyers even more price conscious, so as one salesman observed in 1959, "Car buying, always a horse-trading game, has developed into a fight for the last drop of blood between the seller and buyer."[49] Indeed, there were dealers who believed that if they did not turn over a customer to a second salesman, the customer "would suspect he didn't get the best possible deal."[50] The final attempt to raise the price, even if only a few dollars, was known as the "bump." As one Ford dealer observed, "There is always a little more gross obtainable from a buyer." And if the bump failed, it still had the effect of convincing the customer that he had gotten the best deal possible.[51] The idea that buyers *wanted* to work their way through layers of salesmen because it convinced them that they were fighting hard for the last dollar reflects the ritualization, or scripting, of the bargaining process. In this sales model, both the buyer and seller expected to proceed along a predetermined path. They both understood the steps involved, and for the ritual to reach a successful conclusion, both sides had to abide by the unspoken but mutually understood rules.

The car buying drama involved a certain amount of improvisation, and the exact climax (the net price) was not in the script. Furthermore, there was always a small percentage of the public who did not know the parts they were supposed to play. The salesman's role in the performance varied according to the size of the dramatis personae. Where there was a long list of players, some of the salesmen in the process did not do any negotiating. For example, in the late 1960s a Los Angeles Ford dealer explained that the first-level "sales order" was no such thing, but was "similar to those used in the real estate field." By this he meant that the manager was analogous to a homeowner, and the salesman was merely the agent conveying the prospective buyer's *offer* (not order). Management would automatically reject the offer, and the prospect would be handed off to the turn-over man, who would proceed with a "friendly renegotiation."[52] The role of the closer before World War II was to overcome customers' doubts about the product. In the postwar marketplace, however, the closer became a distinct negotiator, whose job it was to increase the price to a customer who had already agreed to buy.[53]

Dealerships using a fully developed TO system might have six (or more) turn-overs for each sale. The first sales staffer a walk-in prospect would meet was the liner or greeter, whose job it was to make the customer feel welcome and to determine what brought him (or, increasingly, her) onto the lot. The greeter would then introduce the customer to a "qualifier" (turn-over number one), who would try to determine if the buyer were serious or just a looker and get some idea of what kind of the car the customer wanted. Assuming the customer was "qualified," he or she would be introduced to a salesman (turn-over number two), who would try to find a car in stock that the customer liked as well as to secure some kind of a written commitment that the customer was willing to buy the car at some price, no matter how unrealistically low.

At this juncture, two other employees would enter the picture: the salesperson's manager and the used-car appraiser. The initial sales staffer would introduce the customer to the manager (turn-over number three), who up to this point had may have been "consulted" by the salesperson in frequent trips to the back office. Industry lore says that the closing room in which the customer and salesperson had been dickering was frequently bugged so that the manager could monitor the negotiations and eavesdrop on conversations between couples when they thought they had been left alone.[54] The manager would continue to negotiate new car and used-car prices and, if the customer were a hard bargainer, might turn the prospect over to yet another manager for another round of haggling (turn-over number four).

The second TO manager would sign the official purchase agreement, shake the buyer's hand, and turn the customer over to the finance and insurance (F&I) manager, who was in fact a specialized sales staffer (turn-over number five). The F&I manager drew up the actual purchase contract but also negotiated loans and attempted to sell finance insurance, extended warranties, and a variety of dealer-installed options such as undercoating, paint protection, and fabric guard. In a truly unscrupulous house, the customer might be turned over to a sixth person, who actually delivered the vehicle and would attempt to extract one final bump in the form of a delivery or service fee. This total of six turn-overs assumes that the customer had not been originally prospected by a sales staffer or turned over to the used-car appraiser for a separate set of negotiations.[55]

In its more extreme form, the TO system transformed the first-level floor staffer's role back to something resembling that of a standard store clerk. The salesperson was there to be friendly, knowledgeable about the product, and helpful in filling the customer's needs. He or she was a nice person who might gently suggest that the prospect's offer on the new car and allowance expectations were somewhat unrealistic, but he or she would be positioned as the customer's friend.[56] Just as the sales staff in a standard retail outlet had no control over the price, neither did the first-line salespeople in a TO house. Their job was to sell the product, not the deal, and to be part of what one critic called "institutionalized patience."[57]

Car sales techniques could range from the multiple turn-overs in high-volume urban stores, to situations in small dealerships in which the same person greeted prospects and worked with them at every step until the final sales contract was signed. Compensation systems varied according to how many individuals participated in a sale. Thus, depending on the sales structure of the particular firm, the salesperson might be locked in combat with the buyer or be operating as the customer's semi-ally against the house, as represented by the sales manager.[58] Similarly, the salesperson might be cooperating with various other levels of staffers to keep ratcheting up the price of the deal or working alone against the prospect. The salesperson would also be in competition with other salespeople to get good "ups." Some houses gave floor staffers turns with walk-ins, while others had an "open floor," where salespeople competed with each other to attract the attention of likely looking prospects and tried to hand off people they regarded as non-buyers, referred to as "flakes."[59]

The Sales Game: Strategy

Conscienceless car sales have a long, if not exactly venerable, history. For example, while passing on selling tips to others in 1924, an award-winning salesman explained that when he left the showroom to visit a prospect at his office, he never turned down a deal because he could not give the expected trade-in allowance. Instead, he said, he wrote up the order with the customer's figures and took a deposit: "The prospect now thinks he has bought a car and goes home and tells his family and maybe some friends." When the sales manager rejected the deal, the salesman would return to renegotiate, placing the blame on the house.[60] At about the same time, in the mid-1920s, a Ford salesmen displayed even lower standards when he sold an ill and impoverished young father a new car, taking the family's last $200. When the man died and his widow could not meet the car payments, the dealer repossessed the family's sole asset and sold it for costs. "I know this sounds pretty tough," he admitted, "but when it's a case of your own scalp or some other fellow's, you can't afford to be too particular." He assuaged his conscience by donating twenty dollars toward the sales victim's funeral.[61]

As these stories illustrate, the twenties, not the fifties, was the decade when aggressive sales techniques became the industry standard, and their use grew over the next thirty years. Until the 1950s, industry voices regularly called for honesty and restraint, and for selling cars on their merits, not on their prices. But after the war, they were drowned out by the noise of the Hull-Dobbs-customer-disassembly-line.[62] Horace Hull and James Dobbs started their Ford business in Memphis, Tennessee, just before the war. They expanded rapidly during the war by selling used cars and parts that they had presciently stockpiled. They also initiated an incentive pay scheme that became known throughout the industry as "the system."[63] It worked so well that Hull-Dobbs grew into a regional chain of more than twenty outlets and is often credited with being the industry's first mega-store. The Hull-Dobbs system combined existing techniques that emphasized pressure and misdirection. Customer satisfaction was sacrificed to sales volume. The essential element was an unrelenting pressure to buy now! Multiple turn-overs were one way to apply that pressure, but there were others. When novelist Benjamin Cheever, who was between jobs and between books, took a turn at selling cars in 1997, one of his colleagues spoke approvingly of a salesman "who once threw a customer up against the wall and said, 'You're not leaving here until you buy a fucking car.'"[64] That was the spirit, albeit in an exaggerated form, behind the system.

Reduced to its simplest formulation, the system was bait-and-trap, a coercive variation of the more traditional bait-and-switch. Advertising fantastic prices that did not exist was the bait. The trap kept the prospect from turning into a "be-back" (from "I'll be back") who would never return. The multiple turn-over was the most common trap, but the most renowned trap involved actually holding prospects in the store against their will. Involuntary detention is one of the few areas where car sales generated the same kind of folklore as horse trading. Salesmen claimed to have heard of colleagues who would lie down in front of a car to prevent a prospect from leaving or hang on to the door handle as though they could physically hold the customer on the lot.[65] It would be easy to dismiss such stories as an amalgam of salesman machismo and buyer paranoia, but even the legendary "lost key" delay tactic has a basis in fact. In 1994 a Nissan dealer in Texas was fined over five million dollars for, among other things, keeping a deaf-mute customer trapped in the showroom for more than four hours by telling him they had misplaced his keys.[66]

Prospects who handed over their keys so that their trade-ins could be appraised might find that their keys had been "lost," but prospects who handed over their certificates of title could lose their cars. Stories abounded about people who had been induced on one pretext or another to give their titles to salesmen. Sometimes the owners signed them, other times their signatures were forged, but in either case the dealership would sell the car while they were looking at a new vehicle. When the prospects asked for their cars back, they would be told that a "mistake" had been made and the car had been sold, but the seemingly chagrined salesman would promise a particularly good deal on a new car.[67] Again, it would be easy to dismiss this oft-repeated tale as apocryphal, but H. J. Caruso, a southern California dealer, was convicted of doing exactly this (and a lot more) in 1957.[68]

Lowball and highball offers functioned as both bait and trap. The promise of a great discount on the new car or a great allowance on the trade-in would entice prospects into the store and keep them negotiating once they were there. Prolonged bargaining gave the prospects time to think of the car as theirs and created a sense of invested effort that the buyers were increasingly loath to waste by walking out. Invested money was even better than invested time to keep the prospects talking. Sales experts advised that when ostensibly accepting a customer's unacceptable offer, a salesman should ask for a cash deposit that he could show to his manager as a token of the buyer's good faith.[69] The deposit was a key link in keeping the buyer in chains. Now the customer would have to get the money back before walking.[70]

The Hull-Dobbs system stressed deals, not cars, and the deals were often made on the size of the monthly payments, not on the final cost. By selling the payment, the dealers kept the customers from knowing the new-car price. One salesmen's guide noted that at some point the prospect would probably "want to know *exactly* what he is obligating himself for—and 'dollars-per-month' is the most palatable way to give this to him."[71] Selling the payment was intended to confuse the customer, because in addition to talking about the price of the new car and the trade-in allowance on the old car, the customer was bargaining over finance rates and dealer-installed options. Keeping the confusion level high and the customer off-balance was an essential part of the process. Dealers instructed new salesmen how to jump back and forth among the various components to prevent the buyer from nailing down the cost of any one of them. To keep the customers in the dark, one Los Angeles dealer trained his men to break their own pencils and grab the customer's pencil if the prospect began to keep track of numbers by jotting them down.[72]

The salesman was supposed to control the numbers as part of the process of controlling the prospect through every step in the process. To keep track of the figures, salesmen used a worksheet that often took the form of a paper divided into four squares by crossed lines. One square was for the price of the new car; the second was for the trade-in allowance; the third was for the down payment, and the monthly payment was in the fourth. Using a heavy marking pencil, the salesman entered numbers in each cell of the four-square worksheet. "Good penmanship is essential," instructed a manager. "This makes it harder for them to negotiate." Ultimately however, even big, bold, and carefully written numbers had to be adjusted. "When you negotiate, this sheet should be covered with numbers," the manager continued. "It should be like a battleground. And I don't want to see the price dropping five hundred dollars at a pop. Come down slowly."[73] The idea was to keep adjusting the numbers in the boxes so that the monthly payment figure was one that the buyer could afford. By bouncing around among the cells, crossing out old numbers and adding new ones as the relationships changed, this crude spreadsheet was used to confuse the buyer about everything except the monthly payment.[74]

Car Dealers' Reputation and Character

Not every franchised dealership was a high-pressure-system house, and many new-car dealers wanted the buying public to respect them as legitimate purveyors of a high-quality product. Used-car dealers, on the other hand, inherited the soiled reputation of horse traders from the very beginning. Horse traders, however, were sometimes depicted as clever scamps, while used-car dealers could not extract even that minor concession from public opinion. When Roald Dahl had to choose a job for the nasty father in his 1988 children's book *Matilda*, he made his character the speedometer-tampering proprietor of the Wormwood Motors secondhand car lot.[75] At the Democratic presidential convention of 1960, Kennedy supporters carried posters with a glowering portrait of Republican candidate Richard Nixon over the caption, "Would you buy a used car from this man?"[76] Although they did not know it, the Democrats were using the same ploy their party had used almost a hundred years earlier against Abraham Lincoln when they predicted he would be defeated in the election of 1864 and return to Springfield to swap horses. It is telling that the Nixon jibes referred to a "used" car. New-car dealers and salesmen retained a smidgen of good character in the public's opinion, but used-car salesmen occupied the darkest corner of the shady retail world.

Used-car dealers were publishing protestations of their credibility as early as 1909, and their reputation as untrustworthy had been firmly established by World War I.[77] Buying a used car "is almost as risky as buying a horse, and perhaps more people are cheated every year in purchasing an automobile than were victimized with worn-out horse flesh," warned a 1918 article on "How to Buy a Secondhand Car."[78] Used-car dealers, like horse traders, existed on the unsavory fringe of the transportation business, occupying vacant lots on the outskirts of town or wedged in the perpetual gloom between big city buildings. They drew attention to themselves and their stock with flashy signs, flashy lights, and flashy clothes. If you foolishly choose to buy a used car from a dealer rather than from a private party, advised a postwar writer, "mentally sneer at everything he says. Know in your mind that he is trying to cheat you out of every possible dollar, and fight him all the way."[79]

This advice to buy from a private party needs to be seen in the context of the wartime and immediate postwar used-car business, which achieved a national reputation for outrageousness. Earl "Madman" Muntz earned his notoriety as the Barnum of the car business through his advertising man, Mike Shore, who ran a series of radio and billboard ads for Muntz during the war in which he quoted the dealer as saying: "I want to give them away, but Mrs. Muntz won't let me, she's crazy; I buy 'em retail, sell 'em wholesale—it's more fun that way; and, just sound your horn, we pay by ear."[80] At the same time, a Dutch-American used-car dealer and an Italian-American used-car dealer were battling in New York for the right to do business as "the Smiling Irishman." (A local Irish-American also doing business under that name remained litigiously aloof.) The Dutch-American, Tony Holzer, also operated a used-car lot in California under the moniker "Hog Wild Tony Holzer, a Bundle of Bedlam in Beverly Hills." What set Muntz apart from characters like Holzer was the friendship between Shore, his publicity agent, and joke writer Allen Woods, who made Muntz a running gag for the comedy team of Abbott and Costello. That is how the "world's largest used-car lot" became a stop on tourist bus tours of Los Angeles.[81]

After the war, Muntz became a dealer for the short-lived Kaiser-Frazer brand automobile and then moved on to sell the television sets that broadcast the even more outrageous sales stunts of his successors. Live and late at night, a new generation of used-car dealers performed ridiculous pranks and offered unbelievable deals to attract prospects to the lot. Of course, when they got there, the customers always found that the advertised car had been sold. That is, except for one memorable moment when a customer lay in wait for used-car dealer Les Bacon, raced in front of the live camera waving his money, and demanded the featured bargain.[82] The absurdist nature of the advertising gimmicks was both a latter-day reincarnation of the game-playing misdirection of horse traders and the hyperbole of carnival barkers and snake-oil salesmen. Customers recognized that most of the claims were ridiculous, but the fast-talking pitchmen caught the attention of potential buyers and lured them into the store where the salesmen could work their wiles.

Even before the war, some reformer was always trying to clean up the used-car business and the image of its salesman. "There is a large potential market for a different type of used car," a marketing book promised in 1929. It would have to be one that is not "improperly conditioned, misrepresented, and sold by unreliable dealers."[83] In 1950 an ad for an Akron, Ohio, used-car dealer boasted, "I can go home at night with a clear conscience."[84] Fabulous Sam, another dealer of the same era, put up huge billboards that promised, "If I can't help you,

I won't hurt you."[85] Just in case the customers for some reason did not believe sellers like this East Coast dealer decked out in cowboy duds and smoking a big cigar, the National Used Car Dealers Association and the National Independent Automobile Dealers Association (both representing used-car dealers) expended a lot of effort to convince the public that their members did not deserve their terrible reputation.[86] New-car dealers, almost all of whom sold used-car trade-ins, smarted at being lumped into the same category as independent used-car dealers. When a San Francisco Plymouth dealer spoke about his used-car operation to the 1953 NADA convention, he opened his talk by saying, "Ladies and Gentlemen," then assured them he used the term "gentlemen" because he knew it was true. "However," he asked, "how would our public address this assembled group?" They would say, "Good afternoon, you . . ." and he listed: chislers, camouflage artists, millionaires, price extortionists, and misleading advertisers.[87]

Every decade or so another representative of the used-car industry would step forward to assure the public that while things may have been bad in the past, a new leaf had been turned.[88] The public would have none of it. Cartoons, jokes, movies, and countless cautionary articles continually reinforced the image of the duplicitous used-car dealer. "Don't go to almost any used-cars-only dealer," warned a long how-to article in 1968, "the 'almost' being the best concession you dare make for the absolutely ethical men, of which there are some in the business."[89] One of those "almosts" must have been the angel standing on a cloud in a 1987 *New Yorker* cartoon who says to his friend, "I was a used-car salesman, but I was terrible at it."[90] "The used-car industry stood for everything shifty-eyed and raffish in American business. It skulked on the margins of respectability and swarmed with pomaded torpedoes named Rudy or Sid," recalled an industry journalist.[91]

While new-car salesmen may not have been perceived as the salt of the earth prior to the war, neither were they automatically assumed to be Satan's spawn. That changed in the 1950s. If, as the *New Yorker* cartoon implied, only ineffective used-car salesmen went to heaven, the opposite was true for new-car dealers. They worried that their success at selling new cars meant they were going to hell. A skit put on by car dealers for car dealers at the 1951 NADA convention opened with an offstage voice telling the onstage dealer it was "the voice of your conscience." "Oh, no, not my conscience!" the dealer cries. "I don't want any conscience following me around. Good Lord, man, I've been an automobile dealer!" "Don't worry," the voice replies, "I'm not talking to you from hell. I'm right here on earth with you."[92] Like similar convention skits and speeches in the 1950s, it went on to remind the audience of the many ways that dealers were honorable citizens and businessmen. The skits spoofed coarse and unprincipled sales techniques as a way of reminding the conventioneers to control themselves and their salesmen lest they perpetuate the negative stereotype.[93]

Much to the new-car dealers' frustration, their reputation hardly improved over the next half-century. They were willing to concede that the situation might have gotten out of hand in the 1940s and 1950s but insisted that things had changed. "The last 30 years have been spent bending over backwards to clear the car dealer's tarnished reputation," a dealer's wife pleaded in 1995, why wouldn't the public let bygones be bygones?[94] In 1979 one optimist had predicted that in twenty years car salesmen would be licensed, bonded professionals governed "by an enforceable code of conduct."[95] However, 1999 came and went, and car consumers saw no change. A steady stream of polls and studies, including those sponsored by the industry itself, confirmed the public's opinion. While the auto journalist who suggested that car salesmen "were slightly above child molesters in the public's opinion" may have been overstating the case, polls showed that the public had little good to say about car sellers.[96]

A seller-to-seller how-to book in 1982 admitted, "We have all been conditioned not to trust most people—*especially* salespeople, and *especially, especially* automobile salespeople." Then he added, "Our reputation is well deserved."[97] Dealers could not catch a break. When the Honda corporation introduced a humanoid robot to the public in 2002, the Associated Press referred to it as the "most honest car dealer ever."[98] Like their used-car brethren, new-car salesmen were perceived as having both the morals and the fashion sense of riverboat gamblers. To counter the constant barrage of negative press, the new-car dealers borrowed a technique long used by secondhand car sellers; they advertised the fact that they were honest. Like a drug-free bodybuilder or a well-dressed academic, an honest used car-dealer was considered worthy of note. Only an auto dealer could be proud enough of simple honesty to brag, "No ridiculous claims to get you in," "No lowball prices to get you to come back," "No misquoted payments."[99]

The industry also tried to counter its negative image with promises of reform. On both the national and regional level, and with depressing regularity, the retail car business sought to cultivate a more favorable reputation by adopting codes of conduct and ethics. In 1955, during the run-up to the Monroney hearings, NADA promised fair prices and accurate advertising, along with support for highway safety.[100] In 1961, without much enthusiasm, the regional dealers' group in New York adopted a set of "Standards for Advertising and Selling of New and Used Automobiles" that promised an end to the lowball-highball abuse.[101] A year later the state association in Washington passed a ten-point code, eight of which were pledges not to lie, cheat, or steal.[102] NADA was back at it in 1971 with a "Program of Self-Regulation."[103] Finally (thus far), NADA introduced a sales staff certification plan in 1990, which it rejuvenated five years later with a strengthened ethics and law component.[104]

The codes and certification programs, however, merely confirmed what they were trying to counteract since they promised nothing more than the kind of straightforward and honest behavior that customers simply assumed were the norm in other retail transactions. Explaining the meaning of his "certificate," a Florida Ford salesman said, "This lets the customer know you're there to take care of them and to abide by the law."[105] Members of the retail automobile industry may have bristled at the popular assumption that an honest car salesman was an oxymoron, but what else could they expect when the salesmen took pride in the fact that they had been "certified" to obey the law?

The structure of the car business made car sellers different from other sales personnel. The classic outside sales person (a manufacturer's representative) had a comfortable, easygoing relationship with his or her customers. The sales rep returned regularly to introduce new products and renew existing orders. Pressure to make a sale may have come from the sales manager, but the reps had to maintain friendly continuing relationships with their customers. The classic inside sales person (a store clerk) was also disinclined to engage in hard-sell techniques because the whole department store environment assumed that customers could choose what they wanted at a single posted price—and in smaller stores there might also be a personal component in the customer relationship.

The most common exceptions to the low-pressure sales tradition were in businesses where the sales personnel worked on a high commission, where the expectation of a repeat business was very low, and where the salesperson came to the customer, not vice versa. Door-to-door vacuum cleaner, encyclopedia, and vacation property sellers were typical of this category, and they followed the trail blazed in the nineteenth century by lightening rod salesmen who were infamous for their use of high-pressure scare tactics to sell expensive devices of dubious merit for farfetched needs.[106] The early history of car salesmen having to visit their non-driving customers combined with the continuing insistence by dealers that their salesmen actively canvass for prospects to create a retail environment conducive to a high pressure ("You have to buy now"), rather than a low pressure ("How can I help you?") shopping environment. As a result, the public came to view car salesmen as an unpleasant combination of the worst techniques of door-to-door sellers with all of the guile but none of the wit of their horse-trading precursors.

It was, of course, every sales person's job to convince prospects that they need the seller's merchandise, and car salesmen could hardly be faulted for aggressively representing their products to potential buyers. Furthermore, sartorial bad taste was not a violation of business ethics. The problem with so many car salesmen was deeper than noisy enthusiasm and plaid suits; it was the underlying assumption that the maximum amount of money had to be made on every deal. Salesmen who referred to themselves as robbers without guns may have been joking, but car buyers had every reason to believe that salesmen saw them as "marks," targets of an elaborate con game that the customers had a responsibility to understand, because it was going to be played whether or not they knew the rules.[107]

Stealing from customers was a time-honored tradition in the car business. A longtime Ford dealer, reminiscing about the good old days when new Fords sold for $678 with no discounts or over-allowances, remembered a used car that had been sold by a hot young salesman at a mislabeled price that was actually more than a new car would have cost. He had no pangs of conscience then or later about keeping the money.[108] Other salesmen proudly told stories of deliberately selling befuddled buyers poor-quality cars several times over so that, as one salesman reported, a retired man who spent a total of $5000 for a car worth $2000 would be "paying out of his social security check forever."[109] In 1970, when a novice asked a veteran salesman if he gave discounts to his friends, the veteran laughed and said, "Man, I make most of my money off my friends. They aren't looking for you to screw them, so you can really sock it to them." He elaborated by explaining that he had made one of his most profitable sales to his sister, who bought a fully-loaded big car for top dollar.[110]

Screwing your sister, even figuratively, and then boasting about it, indicates a certain detachment from mainstream values, but moral obtuseness was virtually guaranteed by the structure of the business. Discriminatory pricing meant that salespeople could maximize their income by increasing the numbers per unit as well as the number of units. Narrow margins on hard-fought deals were recouped by "the fool who pays the full list price because he doesn't know any better, the guy who lets you steal his trade-in."[111] It was the dogma of the sales floor that showing compassion would only result in somebody else plucking the prize. One salesman recounted the cautionary tale of feeling virtuous after convincing a young couple with a baby that they really could not afford a new car. The next day he looked out his window to see the same couple leaving a neighboring lot in a brand new car.[112] When a different salesman expressed his concern about an F&I manager finagling an additional $10,000 from an elderly customer, he was reminded by a colleague, "You can't be a salesman and expect to go to heaven."[113]

Images of heaven and hell appear frequently in the incidental discourse about car sales because the process plays hob with conventional norms about marketplace morality. Whatever the legal fine points of implied warranty, car selling violates the broader assumption that a business should not take advantage of a customer's ignorance, to say nothing of the retail precept that "the customer is always right."[114] For car salesmen, however, moral principles could be just another set of tools to be used against the customer—as they were for an Atlanta car salesman who said that "most people think car salesmen have plaid jackets, white shoes, and Elvis hairdos and that they lie." He claimed that he never lied and informed self-professed Christian customers that he attributed his success to "a higher power." "In the car business," he explained, with an auto seller's off-kilter sense of values, "you have to build the rapport before you go for the jugular."[115]

Dealers resented their disreputable image and made periodic attempts to improve it by promoting ethical sales behavior, but they were trying to climb out of a deep hole. For example, *CBS Evening News* featured NADA's sales certification course as "'a school for scoundrels,' a 'seminar where showroom sharks come to confess their sins and repent,' and an attempt to 'save what's left of salesmen' souls.'"[116] The real school for scoundrels, however, was the showroom floor. The store owners wanted to be both respected businesspeople and successful car sellers. The sales staff cared only about selling cars. Staffers looked to each other, not to the broader business community for instruction and standards.[117] An industry consultant described automobile sellers as "ego-driven people with low self-esteem [who] get into the business because they can't do anything else."[118] There is plenty of solid evidence to back up the view of the typical car seller as a reasonably personable young man with little interest in either his customers or the product he is selling, who compensates for his low self-esteem by being highly manipulative of others.[119] A 1988 survey sponsored by NADA found that 97 percent of cars salesmen were male, more than half were under forty, and more than two-thirds had been in their current jobs for fewer than three years. In fact, salespeople frequently left after just a couple of months on the job, and in some geographic areas dealerships had almost a 100 percent turnover of sales staff every year.[120]

Rather than being trained in professional courses like the NADA certification program, most salespeople were informally instructed on the job by veterans who passed on the techniques and values of the sales floor.[121] The culture of the sales floor was expressed in a distinct vocabulary that was unusually elaborate for a job without specialized tools or technically unusual activities. Vocational argot is a universal phenomenon. Horse traders, for example, used it so that they could talk about various animal vices without alerting the buying public.[122] Professional jargon in the retail auto business, however, was so abundant that authors writing about the trade often felt compelled to include glossaries.[123] Some of the terms, such as turn-over, up, and lowball/highball, have become more or less industry standards. Others, however, appear to have been limited either by region or time period. Poor-quality used cars or trade-ins, for example, have been variously known as junkers, jalopies, dogs, sleds, rats, rough, iron, tin cans, shit boxes, yechs, and crappers, to name just a few of their colorful designations.

The lexicon of car sellers contributed to the game-like environment in which each sale was a contest to be won by making the maximum profit. This was different from non-auto retail environments, where the sales process was about serving the customer. Appliance sellers, for instance, earned their commissions when they found a refrigerator that filled their customer's needs at an affordable price; paying was a mere formality. In contrast, finding a customer a car that he or she wanted to buy was only a preliminary to the main event. The car seller's commission and the store's profit would depend on his ability to beat up the customer in the closing room. That is what Chandler Phillips learned when he did a stint as an undercover salesman for the car Website Edmonds.com. Phillips had assumed he would tell the interviewer that he wanted the job because he knew and loved cars and could communicate that to his customers. No, said his editor, just tell him you are in it for the money.

Phillips took the advice and told the sales manager doing the hiring, "I want to make a lot of money." He reported that the sales manager "smiled and relaxed, as if I had said the password to enter an exclusive club. If this had been a cartoon, dollar signs would have appeared in his eyes accompanied by a loud 'cha-ching.'"[124] Phillips's report, probably the best of its kind, lays out how, a half-century after the Monroney Act, car selling had hardly changed. The high-volume, high-pressure dealership for which he worked wanted salespeople who could use a procedure (the system) that "wasn't to help customers make informed decisions, [but] was designed to catch people off guard, to score a quick sale, to exploit people who were weak or uninformed."[125]

CHAPTER SEVEN

Bargaining and Gender

For customers, buying a car evokes strong feelings, not only because they are spending a lot of money but also because they have to engage in the process variously known as trading, dealing, negotiating, bargaining, haggling, and dickering. The practice is both unfamiliar and fraught with symbolic meaning, which is why it is frequently described with metaphorical labels like hunt, battle, contest, and game. Both men and women say they dislike negotiating, but men understand it as part of the meaning of owning the car. An Atlanta Cadillac dealer explained that his poor male customers who realized they were being tricked into paying more than they could afford did not "even have sense enough to walk out." By that time, he said, "the guy is so ashamed he buys it anyway and then lies in the street. He tells everybody he paid this real low price because he doesn't want to admit he got taken."[1]

Getting cheated on a car purchase and losing "street cred" is a direct carry-over of horse trading patterns into the new transportation market. The buyer lost status by paying too much; the seller gained status by charging too much. Early Ford dealer John Eagal took horses in trade for his Model Ts in 1909. He had a hostler on staff who not only knew how to polish up an old horse to make it look new but was also a first-class bargainer.[2] Eagal was conflicted about bringing horse-trading techniques over to the car side of the business. On the one hand, he said he never cut list prices, but on the other, he admitted he would give over-allowances to close a sale. The willingness to sweeten the deal by upping the allowance on a trade-in permitted customers to walk away thinking they had beaten the dealer and done better than their acquaintances. If you want to impress your friends, "talk prices," suggested a piece in 1915. Tell them "by knowing the ropes and working one dealer against another you got a big shave."[3]

"The Great American Sport of Bargaining"

Consumers and dealers believed, and numerous field studies have confirmed, that buyers who bargain pay less than those who do not.[4] For male customers, the opportunity to boast about a good price may have been as important as the money. "All men like to be called 'shrewd,'" a Ford sales manual advised in 1926.[5] Shrewd meant getting a better price than expected, a better price than friends, a better price than the dealer wanted to charge. Beating the dealer gave the buyer bragging rights.[6] It did not matter if the buyer won the concession on the price of the new car or the allowance on the old one, just as long as there was the appearance of victory. "If John Smith can get 5 per cent reduction, he is pleased, not merely because he saved $100 but because he beat the game," reported an industry study in 1932: "The chief satisfaction that he gets from the reduction is when he whispers to Henry Jones, his neighbor, that he was clever enough to get 5 per cent off."[7]

Dealers understood that customers perceived car buying as a contest and cultivated devices to make them think they had beaten the house. "You have to make the customer feel that he has won a victory," said a Chevrolet salesman in 1979.[8] "It is a cardinal sin to give the prospect an unearned concession," advised a sales manual a dozen years earlier. "He will value it little unless he feels he has earned it. Give him the satisfaction he seeks. Let him earn the savings he wants to brag about."[9] Salesmen would bolster the egos of even weak negotiators by telling them they were tough customers who were beating them up, or getting them in trouble with their managers. The managers would use similar language, joking about how the customer was stealing the car or was out to ruin the salesman's reputation.[10]

The need to make the buyer feel like a winner was one of the incentives for price packing. By inflating the cost of the new car, the dealers could give over-allowances on the trade-in, making the buyer believe he was a shrewd bargainer. In 1939, a West Coast dealer asked fifty buyers to whom he had just sold a car how much they had paid for it; only three knew. However, forty-eight knew exactly how much they had gotten for their trade-in.[11] Once the customer brought up the question of his current car, what ensued was "a real battle of wits," explained a Cadillac sales manual in the 1920s. If you showed weakness, the prospect would pounce, and if the prospect showed weakness, you had to be ready to pounce.[12] The language of the hunt, along with the language of sexual conquest, distinguished the salesmen's discourse, while people outside the industry usually preferred game terms. At the hearings that led to the MSRP sticker legislation, Senator Mike Monroney referred to "the great American sport of bargaining over the prices of both the new car and the trade-in."[13] Monroney should have said, although in 1958 it was probably taken for granted, that he meant the great American *manly* sport of bargaining. A study of male car buyers in the late 1950s found that men who shopped at more than one dealership (and who were presumably more aggressive bargainers) had more stereotypically masculine personality traits than those who went to a single dealer. Specifically, they were more achievement oriented, more dominant, and more aggressive.[14] The salesman's job, therefore, was to let these (and all other) buyers think they were winning a contest, whereas in fact, the salesman remained in control.[15]

The contest was a game of strategy, a psychological contest, and the seller learned to dominate without appearing to be domineering. The salesperson never followed the customer around the lot but always led the way, and he did so without looking back, forcing the prospect to trot dutifully behind the alpha dog.[16] The seller set the pace, urging the prospect to move on to the next stage in the system but forcing the customer to wait in the closing room for protracted periods while the salesperson was ostensibly consulting with the manager about a price offer. The salesperson used long silences to make customers uncomfortable and force them into verbal concessions that could be turned into price bumps. Emphasizing the need to control the prospect, one trainer bet his class of salesmen that he could make the next customer on the lot climb into a car's trunk and shut the lid. He did so—by explaining it was the only way the prospect could appreciate how much luggage capacity it had.[17]

Advice to buyers was often couched in combative game terminology. Typically, Michael Royce's excellent how-to book was called *Beat the Car Salesman*, and the first chapter was "Understanding the Game."[18] Unlike the salesman who hoped he could metaphorically *kill* the customer, the customer just hoped he could *beat* the salesman. It is a "mind game," explained Gary Carr in his book *How to Outsmart the New-car Salesman.* Carr described strategies that could be used to unsettle sales staffers as they used each of the standard bargaining tactics. Although Carr avoided the fight-to-the-death language that salespeople used among themselves, the ex-salesman made sure his readers understood that car buying was not a transaction in which a fair price could be paid for a fair product. It was a contest, a challenge: "To be second means that you still lose. In the game of cars, unless you come in first, the dealer and his staff win."[19]

Both sides in the bargaining game claimed they did not want to participate. Dealers said they played only because buyers expected discounts. "We don't want any horsetrading," said a dealer in 1965, "but most of our customers force us to horsetrade."[20] The evidence is as mixed and conflicting as the attitudes. A 1986 survey done for the National Highway Traffic Safety Administration reported consumers were "angered by, if not intimidated by, the bargaining process which they feel they must engage in with dealers."[21] But a study in 1995 found that more than 80 percent of those asked knew that car prices were negotiable, and about half said they liked to bargain over prices.[22]

The other half were presumably those described by salesman Chandler Phillips as responding to his cheerful "Good afternoon" with fear: "They were afraid they would be cheated, ripped-off, pressured, hoodwinked, swindled, jacked around, suckered or fleeced."[23] "Buying a car," said a self-confessed car-lover "is an exercise in degradation and humiliation."[24] What did he find degrading and humiliating? To judge from complaints to the Better Business Bureau, it was the haggling.[25] "Horse trading tactics" created a "customer beware" attitude among car buyers, said American Motors' president George Romney in 1956.[26] An unpublished summary of consumer complaints from Ford customers during the same period found that almost all buyer criticisms were related to the bargaining process. Customers objected to sharp trading, deception or misrepresentation, undue pressure, objectionable attitudes, would-you-take offers, and bushing. However, they also objected to "excessive prices" and "failure to grant concession."[27]

Smarting from forty years of terrible press, the auto industry embraced the customer satisfaction movement of the 1980s.[28] Questionnaires administered by outside monitoring agencies like J. D. Powers became de rigueur for dealers, and firms that did well would boast about their high CSIs (customer satisfaction indexes). But "happy" did not necessarily sell cars, and an article in an industry magazine in 1998 was subtitled "Making Nice versus Selling on Price." It found people hated shopping at big high-pressure stores, but that is where most of them bought their cars because that is where the cars were cheapest.[29]

In the non-auto retail environment, large high-volume outlets attract customers with price. First referred to as "discount stores" after World War II, they kept costs low with some combination of low prices from suppliers, small numbers of low-paid staff, bare-bones stores in low-rent districts, and aggressive price advertising. Car retailers could not duplicate this cost-cutting model. Auto manufacturers fixed their wholesale prices. Salesmen were already practically free by working solely on commission. Space requirements already required "auto rows" to be on cheaper land outside of downtown. Service was a profit center to build up, not an operating cost to reduce. Like discount stores, high-volume car dealers made a little profit on a lot of sales. Unlike discount stores, they sometimes made a lot of profit on a portion of them because some buyers did not know they should bargain or how to bargain well.

Individual buyers were amateurs playing a game with professionals. The deck was stacked, the dice were loaded, the playing field was uneven, but the game could not be avoided. In 1917 the *New York Tribune* published an exposé of dealer tricks and made it available as a special booklet that readers could order by mail. The *Tribune's* advice pamphlet, which covered "Contracts, Warranties, Service, Salesmen, Used Cars and Freight," was an unusual example of car consumer education before the World War II.[30] Manufacturers and dealers advertised list prices in the prewar era and tried to stick to them. The dealers disguised most discounts as over-allowances on the owner's used car, and dickering on used-car prices was so much a continuation of the informal horse-trading market that it was taken for granted. However, when the postwar Hull-Dobbs system with its hidden retail prices rubbed buyers' noses in the differences between buying a car and buying other manufactured goods, warnings and car-buying instructions appeared with increasing frequency.

Barefoot pilgrims were always welcome, but they did become rarer. In 1953 the NADA magazine happily reprinted a newspaper column that described how the writer had indignantly walked out of nine dealerships where salesmen began bargaining over price. Instead, this proud victim bought at a tenth store, accepting the first price quoted for the new car and the first offer for his trade-in. He said he was pleased the salesman could discuss the car's technical characteristics and even more pleased that the salesman helped rather than pressured him.[31] If the approximately 6,081,000 other people who bought cars in 1953 had acted in the same way, new-car dealerships would have operated like other retail businesses; presumably, buyers would have been happier (but poorer), and dealers would have been happier and richer.

Consumers, however, had been dickering with car dealers for fifty years, and the nine bargaining salesmen were much more typical than the laid-back one. Anxious to make up for lost sales during the war, car dealers in the 1950s intensified their negotiating system. Consumers reacted with anger, and consumer advocates responded with advice. The defensive tone of one Better Business Bureau's counsel was typical of postwar advice: "The majority of automobile dealers are legitimate," the Bureau warned in 1958. "However, there is an unscrupulous element using dishonest sales practices coldly calculated to fool and cheat the buyer." The steps the BBB suggested were classic advice to the consumer venturing into a hostile marketplace of get-rich-quick schemes and other snares for the unwary. They were not the recommendations given in a retail environment where the customer was always right. Don't allow yourself to be rushed or pressured, the bureau advised; don't sign contracts with blank lines; watch for price packing; stay with your trade-in and guard the keys to prevent car-napping; get proof the car you are buying is really new; and check out the dealer's reputation.[32] The 1958 Monroney law was supposed to protect the customer from these abuses, but consumer advocates continued to issue similar advice through the end of the century.[33]

Before the 1960s there were few if any suggestions of how to bargain for the best price. Rather, consumers were warned about sellers who violated the conventions of the one-price marketplace. However, no such marketplace existed in the automobile industry. The advisors recommended that customers shop carefully and compare prices but implied that marketplace haggling was unseemly and alien. Between the wars, industry critics of price negotiating invariably used the same imagery to condemn the practice. It was, they said, like an Oriental bazaar. The implication was that arguing over prices was not only un-American, it was un-Western, and quite possibly un-Christian. The locations invoked in this image were almost always Middle Eastern, with the insinuation that the metaphorical marketplace was populated with Muslims (or, perhaps, Jews).

The few American markets in which there was regular price dickering in the 1920s and 1930s were in predominantly Jewish urban neighborhoods like Manhattan's Lower East Side, or Chicago's Maxwell Street. Moreover, the verb "to jew," which had been used as a pejorative to characterize hard bargaining since early in the nineteenth century, was still in wide use. The car-buying public was caught in a cultural trap. Purchasing a new car required them to negotiate the price, something for which they had no training. It was, moreover, something that suffered from the taint of foreignness and impropriety. Bargaining was not playing the shopping game by the regular rules, but for cars it was the only game in town, and people had to learn it. By making the Hull-Dobbs system the industry standard after World War II, the dealers created a new cohort of customers tutored in the methods of aggressive bargaining. Faced with a larger number of knowledgeable buyers, salesmen had to work even harder to make up from innocent buyers what they were forced to concede to more sophisticated consumers.

This distinction between the knowledgeable and unconstrained buyers on the one hand, and naïve or culturally bound buyers on the other, expressed itself very clearly in the way women and minorities were treated in the postwar market. Women felt intimidated and uncomfortable shopping for cars, because even as their numbers increased, cars continued to be male-gendered objects and buying them was framed as a contest. As we shall see, the evidence on whether or not women were taken advantage of when they ventured into the car market is unclear, but there is no doubt that a century of one-price retailing had eliminated bargaining from the standard set of female skills. And while men were not exactly trained from childhood to haggle over prices, they were generally more comfortable with adversarial negotiations.

Ethnic and racial minorities also expressed the belief that they were discriminated against in the automobile marketplace. Here too the evidence is unclear. No reasonable observer doubts that there is a history of economic discrimination against African Americans, but the ways in which racial prejudice expressed itself can be hard to pin down. Economic class and geographic factors complicate analyses that seek to describe racial discrimination. Although he did not address race, ethnicity, or gender, Allen Jung did demonstrate in a series of studies that salesmen charged naïve buyers more than those who bargained and that urban dealers charged less than those in outlying areas.[34] Everything else being equal, lower prices in cities should have helped black buyers, so that finding does not fit the expected pattern. However, Jung's second conclusion, that non-bargainers pay more, does provide some evidence for understanding racial price differentials.

For African Americans, buying a car became a particularly ironic historical exception. Early in the twentieth century, African Americans had demonstrated a clear preference for shopping at department stores with their posted one-price-to-all, even though they risked being treated discourteously by the white sales staff. They may have been discouraged, for example, from using the fitting rooms, but when they did buy something, they paid the ticket price and did not have to worry that a prejudiced store owner was hiking up the price of the goods.[35] Because they could never be sure how they were being perceived by white sellers, blacks may have been more reluctant than others to violate the retail rules that called for paying the posted price. The rules were what protected them from price "discrimination"—in both the social and economic senses of the term.

A survey in 1991 found contemporary evidence for this historical pattern. Two-thirds of black respondents—double the white rate—did not know that automobile sticker prices could be negotiated, and among whites the rate for women was higher than the rate for men.[36] Because the pattern of overcharging holds true for both non-white and female sales staff, researchers Ian Ayres and Peter Siegelman have suggested that sales staff who quoted higher prices to blacks and women may not have been manifesting racial or gender prejudice but may simply have been taking advantage of people they assumed would not demand lower prices.[37] Whatever its causes, the pattern of discrimination continued after the sale when blacks were charged more for financing.[38] Anecdotal evidence suggests that ethnic minorities from bargaining cultures in East and South Asia do not suffer from the same price discrimination—and are heartily disliked by cars salesman for it.

Accustomed to paying the price on the ticket for all their other purchases, the buying public first had to be assured that negotiating over car prices was socially acceptable and a "fair game" to play.[39] Next they had to be told how to play it. Although the Hull-Dobbs system had been around since the late 1940s, it took almost thirty years for consumer advocates to give car buyers specific instructions on how to bargain. Before the 1960s even *Consumer Reports* refrained from providing negotiating advice. In a 1955 article titled "How to Shop for a New Car," the magazine recommended that car buyers test different brands and different models of the same brand on all kinds of roads and in various parking situations. It suggested that all the drivers in the family go over dozens of details—from the size of the trunk and the glove compartment to the location of the cigarette lighter—and it said not one single word about negotiating for price or even comparing prices, though the latter may have been taken for granted.[40]

Reader's Digest was an exception to the no-bargaining advice position, perhaps because it did not accept any advertising (a policy that also allowed it to be the first national publication to expose the dangers of cigarette smoking). In

1957 the magazine ran a pre-Monroney article called "The Art of Buying a New Car," illustrated by a cut of a farmer buying a horse from a flashily dressed horse trader. Most of the article explained how dealers inflated the value of new cars with a pack, but there was also an underlying message that prices for new cars were as flexible as prices for used cars.[41] Aggressive shoppers took this kind of advice to heart, and reports in the late 1950s indicate that some had started asking for written price quotes at each of a series of dealers to provoke a bidding war for their business.[42] This approach required a high degree of buyer discipline and was an open invitation to lowball offers, at which point the buyer would be back to one-on-one bargaining.

Until the 1960s consumer advice was either defensive (watch out for shady operators), or traditional (compare prices). After that, however, there was a slowly growing recognition of the long-established reality of new-car price negotiation. Writers began to use the words "haggle" and "horse trade" when describing how to get the best price on a new car. Just a year after the window sticker became law in 1959, *Popular Science* (which did carry automobile ads), told its readers, "The price sticker that legally must be posted on new cars is not a firm figure. It is subject to discount. The dealer expects you to haggle."[43] For its part, *Consumer Reports* reminded its readers in 1963 that the sticker price was not the selling price but merely a "uniform starting point for bargaining."[44] However, it did not give any suggestions as to how that bargaining should be carried out. A few years later, the magazine did offer a confused description of the bargaining process in which it suggested that the dealer "trades up from the tissue [wholesale price], not down from the sticker," exactly the opposite of what actually occurred.[45] The magazine's advice was finally straightened out by 1973, when its annual auto issue opened with an essay on "Dealing with the Dealer" that explained, "Most dealers start with an inflated price because they expect you to bargain." The article gave some general advice about getting a fair allowance for the trade-in but no specifics on the closing-room combat that hammered out the final price.[46] Not until 2002 did *Consumer Reports* get explicit about bargaining techniques, and even then it was quick to recommend non-negotiating alternatives for its readers.[47]

Customers eager—or at least willing—to duke it out in the closing room could follow the lead of Denny Armstrong, a Kansas City area auto salesman turned car broker who wrote one of the first of a genre of lurid exposés that not only described the system but also provided detailed instructions on how to win the fight. Writing under the pen name "Joe Car" in 1977, Armstrong's self-published typescript *I'm a Legal Hold Up Man; I'm a Car Salesman* was both an account of the tricks of the trade and an advertisement for his business that promised to get any car for $150 over invoice.[48] Armstrong's book was followed the next year by another with an equally unrestrained title, *Getting Screwed.*[49] In 1981 they were joined by L. J. Brun's *How to Beat the Car Dealer at His Own Game*, which was also privately published. Brun's book abandoned any pretense at ethical restraint and recommended that the customer match the salesman lie for lie. For example, he not only explained how to solicit competing bids from several dealers, but he instructed the buyer to tell the lowest bidder that he had another offer for a hundred dollars less.[50]

The vast majority of how-to-buy titles after 1970 adopted this confrontational tone.[51] These pieces offered the same suggestions that had been first set in print by Denny Armstrong and were later popularized by Remar Sutton, who wrote the first how-to-bargaining guide for a mainstream press in 1982.[52] Sutton's book, *Don't Get Taken Every Time*, opens with a fictional scenario in which a couple buy a car, thinking they have gotten a good deal, but then explains how they were taken advantage of by the salesman. Over its four hundred pages, the book describes how the retail automobile business works and suggests strategies for dealing with its sales techniques. It is an excellent book, better written than most.[53] Would-be car buyers could shell out Viking's MSRP of fourteen dollars for Sutton's SUV-sized tome (one-price to all) and get extensive detail, or they could save themselves 80 percent by picking up Michael Royce's subcompact *Beat the Car Salesman* at the supermarket checkout stand for two and a half bucks.[54] Both give the same advice: do your homework; comparison shop; bargain hard.

The broad advice on strategy was generally consistent, but for buyers who wanted step-by-step tactical instructions, it could sometimes be contradictory, and nothing was as inconsistent as the advice on when was the best time to buy a car. The assiduous reader could find quite definitive statements both that cars should be bought at the beginning of the model year and on weekends when the dealers were busy and that the end of the model year and during the week when business was slow was the best time. They were told to shop early in the day and to walk in at closing time. Shop in good weather said one; shop in bad weather said another. And finally, they were told that it did not matter when they shopped, as long as they knew how to haggle. For the record, however, the consensus was that slow periods of the day, week, and year were probably better than other times.[55]

By the last decade of the twentieth century, the concept that the retail price of new cars should be bargained for had become more or less conventional wisdom. A 1994 how-to book on negotiating for all kinds of products was titled *How to Outnegotiate Anyone (Even a Car Dealer!)*. The parenthetical phrase emphasized that the author thought his techniques were so good that readers would learn to best even the superstars of hard-nosed marketplace haggling.[56] Magazines whose target audiences were as varied as African-American women, stay-at-home wives, working-class men, and members of the lower-middle class and the upper-middle class all ran similar articles on how to play hardball in the world of lowballs and highballs.[57]

Brokers

Before the arrival of the Saturn and its smattering of copycat one-price dealers, car buyers who refused to participate in the bargaining game had only one alternative to overpaying: to use a third party, an agent, to do the negotiating and buying for them. Some early car owners employed their chauffeurs in that capacity, although as mentioned earlier, chauffeurs, like grooms before them, often took kickbacks or demanded bribes from dealers. In any event, chauffeurs became increasingly rare after 1912.

Brokers, who would match a buyer with a seller of secondhand cars and facilitate the negotiating, appeared on the scene very early. In 1910 a consignment dealer in New York City had a lot on West 44th Street where he displayed cars with the sellers' posted prices. Buyers could examine the cars at the Manhattan Storage Company and then submit a counteroffer, which the broker would present to the owner. "Frequently, when hard pushed for cash, [the seller] accepts several hundred dollars less than the consigned price," he said. The broker's fee was 5 percent.[58] Variants on the consignment-broker used-car lot continued on and off for the following century. In 1980 there were several attempts to establish such brokerages on a larger scale, and at least one, National Autofinder, franchised its approach.[59] Yet the system was never sufficiently widespread to challenge trade-ins and their sale on new-car lots or independent used-car dealers who bought and resold vehicles.

New-car brokers also appeared before World War I, and they promised to provide cars for less than list price. A man calling himself an "automobile broker" set up shop in 1908 in New York's Algonquin Hotel, where he said he would sell a variety of makes and models, claiming to have "many bargains."[60] In 1914 another enterprising New Yorker, also calling himself a broker, offered to get any car on the market at a discount.[61] New-car brokers like these constituted a gray market that got its automobiles from franchised dealers at less than list price and resold them at a small markup. For buyers who did not want to bargain, or, in the earlier period, for buyers who did not know they could negotiate prices with the new-car dealer, buying through a broker could mean a significant saving.

Sellers calling themselves brokers continued to operate on the edges of the retail automobile business, though they never had much impact on the basic negotiating model. Supply may have been a limiting factor. Factories sold only to franchised dealers, and dealers who wholesaled their cars to brokers risked the ire of the factory and their fellow franchisees. One group of "brokers" who emerged during strong sellers' markets were, in fact, gray marketers. They sold scarce cars at above, not below, list price—at least if they had an ounce of business sense. In 1947 one particularly inept broker was arrested because he took deposits to deliver new autos at list price but wound up paying dealers thousands of dollars over list to get the promised cars. He then found himself short of the money needed to fulfill his remaining contracts.[62] Manufacturers, franchised dealers, and some states sued at various times to stop brokers, but those situations usually involved brokers who sold below, not above, market price.[63]

In the 1980s, however, as part of the general realignments prompted by the women's movement, there was a flurry of interest in using intermediaries to negotiate deals. Buyers who did not live near a dealer trying out one of the short-lived experiments in no-haggle selling could hire a broker who would find the car they were interested in at a price that was below the MSRP. Broker customers appear to have been disproportionately female. Stories about them appeared in women's magazines and always emphasized how buying through a broker eliminated the hassle of bargaining.[64] Because the broker had to charge a commission and the dealer who sold the broker the car also needed to make a profit, buyers who used a broker might have been able to get a better price if they had been willing to do the hard bargaining themselves. Nevertheless, broker clients thought the slight additional cost was worth not having to go through the hell of "the system." A northern Virginia professor called her previous buying experience "very painful," as she and a male "shopping buddy" went from dealer to dealer, haggling at each stop and never being sure if they could get a better price somewhere else. So in 1993 she was happy to pay a fee to have a broker collect the bids for her and, she believed, get a better price than she could have gotten by herself.[65]

Seeking a way to capture the non-negotiating segment of the market from the brokers, dealers established special arrangements with membership discount stores like Costco and Sam's Club, large employers, credit unions, the American Automobile Association, and other affinity groups. These agreements provided members with discount prices for new cars that were supposedly not available to the public. By the mid-1990s, there was an extensive variety of such pseudo-insider deals. Sometimes the brokers promised the "fleet price" (the price paid by large-volume buyers). Other times they would charge a specific amount, like $100, above the invoice price. Still others offered to beat any deal the buyer had found elsewhere. As this last promise indicates, these no-haggle discounts were often no more than a way to lure customers into the showroom. The prices were seldom lower than, and often not as low as, could be negotiated by a knowledgeable walk-in. As one sales manager noted, "With a good trade and some financing, it's a pretty normal deal."[66] If the buyers were averse to bargaining, they could get a decent price; however, they still had to sell their current car, and for that, there was no way to avoid a round of negotiating. Where they had previously given away profit on the trade-in and made it back on the list price, dealers were now giving away profit on the list price but making it back on the trade-in. It did not matter which end of the balloon was squeezed; the volume remained the same.

Cars and Masculinity

The masculinized culture of car selling would have been harder to maintain if cars themselves had not resisted being neutered in the marketplace. The steadily increasing role of women in auto sales has toned down auto gender, but the male bias remains. About fifteen years ago Joseph Corn, an historian of technology, breathed a sigh of relief that academics had finally moved beyond the use of Freudian symbolism to describe the meaning of automobiles and had begun to use more contemporary interpretive tropes.[67] He was no doubt happy to leave behind the kind of heavy-handed sexual innuendo with which John Keats opens *The Insolent Chariots*, his 1958 attack on American automobiles. Keats spins out a three-page metaphor in which the libidinous male driver with "an adolescent tightening in the groin" is seduced into a marriage with the automobile that he lives to regret.[68] Musing about the termination of the Edsel, the comedian Mort Sahl expressed his own distain for the ubiquitous sexualization of cars by noting that critics said it failed because its vulviform grill was too female. Sahl said he personally thought it was because the Edsel cost more than a Pontiac and was not as good a car.[69] (Sometimes a car is just a cigar.) It is not, however, retrograde to observe the extent to which car owners and car sellers have historically understood their vehicles to be sexualized. To do so is not the imposition of an observer's psychoanalytic bias but a simple exposition of the quite conscious meaning that men attributed to automobiles.

Automobiles inherited the double-gendered symbolic role that horses had held. As possessions, they were feminized, but as representations, they were masculinized. Once owned, men's cars, like men's horses and wives, were symbols of their wealth and status, so choosing the right one was particularly important. There were more nice girls than nice cars, so choosing a wife was harder, observed Robert Slofs in 1909, but there were enough attractive choices in both categories "to quite bewilder anyone who approaches the array of them for the first time with serious intentions." Having chosen one of each, the fortunate young man he was writing about was able to spin "along the level New Jersey roads with the exhilaration that can be felt only by a man in love with a girl and an automobile at the same time."[70]

The obvious love affair between men and motors struck early car buffs as particularly droll. "Who gives this automobile away?" asks the minister at the front of the congregation in a 1912 cartoon. The salesman responds that considering "our well-known guarantee, the low price asked, decreased vibration, rich black body, sweet running qualities, increased power, and unsurpassed flexibility. . . . for all intents and purposes, I am giving her away." The groom then vows to love, honor, and repair his flower-bedecked bride, so the minister pronounces them "One." The salesman's allusion to the great bargain the buyer was getting ("giving her away"), and the buyer's promise to be only temporarily faithful ("till the secondhand dealer do you part"), mocked both the sales system and social meaning of a new car.[71] (See fig. 5.)

If cars were possessions, whether or not they were female, then controlling them was an essential masculine skill. Early car salesmen were advised to get the male prospect into the driver's seat where he would get "the pleasure of knowing that the machine beneath him will respond to his touch. There is a sort of enchantment in being able to control so easily a thing so powerful."[72] However, suppose he could not control it? When the husband in a 1910 short story found he could not drive the car he had just purchased, he decided to sell it back to the dealer even though he would lose half of his $2000 investment. His wife, however, refused to allow him to be defeated by a machine. She insisted he go to the garage where he bought it and have somebody teach him to drive. At the end of the story he gives her credit for finding her nerve when his failed.[73] It may have taken the woman to give this man the courage to drive, but in the end it was he, not she, who did the driving.

A few years earlier, in 1904, when the writer Louise Closser Hale and her husband took a motor trip through Europe, the sex of the car became a rather more pointed issue. The proposed trip was a difficult enough undertaking that Mrs. Hale playfully predicted that the car would lead to a divorce. Louise Hale viewed the car as a competitor for her husband's attentions and began to refer to it as "Girlie." When her husband heard this appellation, rather than being amused by his wife's pet name, he became highly indignant because that would make him a girlie man. "'My beautiful big car,' he kept groaning over and over. 'My beautiful big car a Girlie! Oh, Lord! A Girlie!'" Not wanting to undermine her husband's masculine self-esteem, she agreed not to feminize the car. To her the auto was a silly little plaything; to him it was an emblem of self.[74] It was, after all, a "big" car, and size most definitely mattered. Explaining how to use a car to enhance one's reputation with passengers, a 1915 article suggested that the driver "give passing cars a lightening look of critical superiority. . . . If the car is smaller than yours, emphasize the fact; if larger, don't see it."[75]

Historian Virginia Scharff has pointed out that almost every innovation designed to make a car more convenient to drive was coded as feminine in the discourse of automobility. Moreover, she notes, despite the increasing presence of women in the driver's seat, society has "tenaciously preserved those attributes of the automobile regarded as masculine." Beginning with electric starters and continuing through seat belts and speed limits, innovations that made cars easier to drive or safer were dismissed as an insult to the driver's manhood.[76] Detroit designed cars for men even when they were sold to women because, as a female Ford marketing executive explained in 1981, "Masculine cars will appeal to women, but feminine cars usually will not appeal to men."[77] Men were not attracted to a car's safety or convenience; they wanted a display of bright plumage. A young clerk arrested for embezzling in 1909 explained to the judge that he stole the money to buy a new car, even though he already owned one. "Why were you not satisfied with your first machine?" the judge asked. The financially and grammatically challenged youth replied, "Because it did not look as well as the others. It did not have as many lamps."[78]

Men's close identification with their cars created opportunities to take advantage of the masculine desire for speed and power.[79] Manufacturers, of course, often adopted aggressive names and advertising images for their cars.[80] It was not a car; it was the virile antithesis of killjoy bourgeois responsibility. An article on the "psychology of a sale" in 1920 suggested that the salesman should make the idea of owning a car drive everything else out of the prospect's head: "The about-to-be-ravaged bank account, the heart-rending burden of up-keep, the mortgage on the house, last year's unpaid coal bill—all must be forgotten."[81] Used-car buyers tended to be younger and less frequently married than new-car customers, so secondhand car sellers too could tap into the desire to be the alpha male on the road.[82] A used-car salesman in 1914 boasted of how he transformed a run-of-the-mill sedan into an ersatz "racing car" by stripping off various body parts and painting it bright red with yellow racing numbers. To sell the automotive sizzle rather than the mechanical steak there had to be sizzle, which the seller achieved by installing an oversize exhaust pipe coated in oil that produced both a satisfying roar and a cloud of smoke. He also added a speedometer calibrated to read high so that the rich young man who was buying the car thought he was going much faster than he was.[83]

By the same token, salesmen were reminded that even when men were trading in their cars, they thought of their vehicles as extensions of themselves and bridled at negative comments. During the negotiations over the value of the trade-in, a salesman's natural inclination was to explain that a low allowance was due to the various shortcomings in a customer's current vehicle; it was old, had high mileage, was in poor mechanical or cosmetic condition, was not in high demand, and so forth. To the extent that the customer identified with his car, each of these observations became a criticism not only of the car but also of the owner. Denigrating a customer was always a bad sales tactic, and car salesmen were warned that criticizing a customer's trade-in would be taken as a personal insult and a challenge, causing him to fight even harder for victory in the negotiating arena.[84]

While buyers focused on the meaning of the car, sellers focused on the meaning of the buyers. In her study of automobile retailing, Helene Lawson cataloged the sales staff's "aggressive and violent" language that routinely veered between physical and sexual conquest.[85] Salesmen often depicted themselves as hunting for the prey that was their customers, even as their customers were hunting for Mustangs, Impalas, and Barracudas.[86] The "top gun" salesman at a Bethesda, Maryland, dealership said he lived for the "home-run deals." Going on to explain what he meant, he switched from sport to hunting imagery: "The trick is to go for the jugular and ask the top figure."[87]

Fighting to maintain his masculine integrity in his uneven battle with the professional salesman, there was a strong temptation for car buyers to assume an unwarranted air of confidence about matters automotive. Like their forefathers who pretended to know more about horses than they did, amateur car experts were an easy mark.[88] Salesmen took advantage of the gendered meaning of the sales process by challenging the prospect's manliness. If he hesitated to commit to the sale or expressed doubt, the salesman was advised to "try to awaken a spark of manhood in him" and force him to decide by saying, "I'm going to leave this office for a few minutes, and when I return I would like to know what your decision is," and then walking out. If the prospect said he wanted to think it over, the salesman should ask, "Are you the kind of man who needs your wife's, or your credit union's permission to buy a new car?"[89]

For the salesman, the customer, not the car, was the trophy, and the conquest was framed in the locker-room language of sexual domination.[90] A favorite car salesman's joke tells of the beautiful woman who was included as part of the deal on a new car. She would stay with the car for the first twenty-four hours. The delighted buyer asks her to participate in a series of increasingly intimate activities. Each time she responds, "Of course, that's part of the deal." Finally, he leans over and whispers the ultimate request. At which point she turns and says, "Absolutely not. You got that when you bought the car."[91]

Women as Buyers and Sellers

The paucity of female drivers before World War I was more than a transposition of the cultural meaning of horses onto cars. It is hard to argue that the continuity between the culturally gendered male horse and the masculine automobile was inevitable when so many women participated in the bicycle craze that linked the era of horses to the era of horsepower. Bicycles may have been perceived as more difficult for women to ride, but automobiles, like horses, were even farther outside the female comfort zone, perhaps because they both were powerful forces that needed to be controlled. Louise Hale recounted an incident in her 1904 trans-European motor tour when her husband suddenly shoved her aside as she was trying to crank-start the engine. She was upset both by the rough treatment and by what she heard as a muttered threat to break her arm if she ever did it again. He restored her emotional equanimity by describing "the funny way crank handles have of flying back and breaking the arms of the inexperienced unless they are grabbed away most unceremoniously." Though she was not allowed to start the car, Hale was mollified by her duties as "the Drop-per of the Sprag, the Official Timekeeper, the Watchdog of the Odometer, and the Royal Pathfinder."[92] (A sprag was a pointed rod dropped and dragged on steep hills to prevent the car from rolling backward if it stalled.) Except for the sprag drop, these were all essentially secretarial skills.

The woman's role in early motoring was primarily as a passenger, and that is how the vast majority of early advertisements depicted them. When Edith Wharton motored through the Northeast gathering background for her novels, neither she nor her husband drove. Well-bred people like the Whartons did not drive themselves, either in carriages or cars—that was the job of coachmen and chauffeurs. Nevertheless, automobile manufacturers did not automatically as-sume that only men would drive their products. A 1907 Winton ad featured a head-on illustration of a determined woman gripping a steering wheel.[93] A few years later the aggressively named Chalmers Torpedo, a small two-passenger roadster, presented itself as "an ideal car for a lady" because it was "so easy to handle and control."[94] In the same hopeful vein, Heald College, a vocational school in San Francisco, offered driving and maintenance lessons in 1909 to "car-owners and prospective car-owners (ladies and gentlemen)."[95]

A small number of women accepted the challenge of driving these early auto-mobiles. Some of the most adventurous of them drove coast-to-coast at a time when doing so was a stunt worthy of newspaper coverage. A male mechanic usu-ally accompanied them, but that was also true for many early male cross-country drivers.[96] Historian Martin Wachs notes that driving a car was an assertive act for a woman, which was why suffragists made a point of having women drive the speakers to their rallies.[97] Virginia Scharff and Georgine Clarsen have both ar-gued persuasively that scholars have been too quick to dismiss the role of women as drivers in the pre-electric-starter era.[98] Although their studies restore female visibility to the world of early motoring, they also confirm male hegemony both in the cultural discourse and in cultural practice. Driving women were admired more than they were emulated.

Just as women took up the bicycle once the safety bicycle made it practical for them (and for most men), women were more willing to drive once cars were invented that did not require them to be mechanically inclined speed-demons. Electric cars, which started instantly, ran quietly and slowly, and were light and easy to steer, found an appreciative market among early women drivers. "The electric . . . is a woman's car," a car salesman's manual explained in 1915. It was not practical for over-the-road travel, but was used exclusively by "society" for getting about in town. Remember, said the book's author, "a woman is more in-terested in the cushions, lights, upholstery and finish than she is in the motor. Practically all electric cars are enclosed cars, and these points should be played up well."[99] Unfortunately for the electric car companies and for women drivers, internal combustion engines were sufficiently superior to electric motors that they dominated the market despite the problems involved in starting, driving, repairing, and maintaining them.

Once electric starters had replaced hand cranks, and enclosed bodies had be-come the norm rather than the exception, manufacturers began to market more aggressively for women, but not always *to* them. The 1912 Cole, for example, introduced itself in an imagined dialogue with the male buyer. The ad copy quotes the man as saying, "When I find a gasoline motor car my wife can start every time from the driver's seat by simply pressing an electric button—I'll buy it then and there."[100] Husbands did buy cars with electric starters for their wives. "Look for the man in the Moon car," urged a 1916 advertisement, "and the woman too." The woman pictured was not a passenger but the driver "who drives him to the station [and] meets his returning train." Even before World War I, women had assumed the task of chauffeur for their commuting husbands, and on the weekend the couple who owned the Moon would "quarrel about the seat behind the steering-wheel" because "their Moon is more like a fascinating pet than a family conveyance."[101]

After World War I, women drivers became commonplace as even low-priced Fords came equipped with electric starters. Along with electric headlights, eas-ier steering and shifting, and increased mechanical dependability, cars in the 1920s were less demanding for any person to drive.[102] Had that Jordan Playboy pictured in the frontispiece been an electric car, the woman driver might have purchased the car herself. There is some indication that women bought as well as drove electrics, but not at high speed on unpaved Wyoming roads.[103] Ned Jor-dan's daughter had been the inspiration for the lively young woman behind the wheel of the Playboy. Did she buy the car herself, or, as in the Chalmers ad, was it bought for her by her father or some other male? For virtually the entire twen-tieth century, automobile marketers assumed the latter. Women may have been the presumptive buyers of almost all other consumer goods, but not of cars.[104]

Women were not, however, irrelevant to automobile retailing. From the teens of the twentieth century onward, marketers assumed that women would have a say in most sales. Instructions to salesmen invariably reminded them that cars were a family purchase and that wives would both veto cars (and salesmen) they did not like and lobby for those that they did.[105] Children, especially sons, were also brought into the equation, because they were assumed to be knowledgeable early-adopters of new technology. "The man who is ashamed to admit to himself that he made a wrong selection in a motor will confide weak points to an inquisitive boy. The boy is apt to be a storehouse of information on makes and models," wrote an author giving advice to car salesmen in 1916.[106] Up through the 1930s, when salesmen were supposed to go canvassing house to house, the initial sales pitch might well be to a wife who was home during the day. If she could be persuaded that the car was right for her, she would influence her husband to make the actual purchase.[107]

The auto industry psychoanalyst who first asked, "What do women want—in a car?" was no more successful than Freud himself in finding an answer. Manufacturers regularly announced that they had conducted this or that study to find what women preferred. Then they introduced this or that feature that was supposed to appeal to female buyers. These studies and features usually focused on color, ease of operation, and comfort. Size, power, speed, and mechanical innovation continued to be male-oriented selling points.[108] The almost universal assumption that men and women looked for different qualities in a car created a dilemma not only in the manufacturing and the marketing departments but on the sales floor as well. Emphasizing the masculine might diminish the feminine and vice versa. In the mid-1920s this emphasis on appearance became something of a problem for Ford, whose Model T was almost twenty years old and distinctly unstylish. The company acknowledged this problem when its marketing manual told salesmen to compare their car to a watch: it was an expensive movement in a silver case, not a cheap movement in a gold case.[109]

By asking which the customer would prefer, a good watch or a good-looking watch, Ford was appealing to the presumed male propensity to focus on the technical elements of a car. However, all too often neither the wife nor her husband knew anything about automobile mechanics. A check-list article for new-car buyers in 1917 described such a couple thus: "He takes his wife on his arm, and the pair of mechanical imbeciles paddle off down automobile row to pass judgment on something about which they know rather less than nothing at all."[110] They might well have been the pair depicted in a 1915 cartoon. The salesman speaks to the wife, who is accompanied by a timid-looking husband: "I appeal to you as a woman of taste and judgment; the static lag of the motor is as the square of radius impulse." She responds, "Oh, of course!"[111] The cartoon does double duty by having the technologically ignorant wife agree with a line of pseudo-mechanical nonsense and by having her husband, who as a man should know better, stand mutely at her side. Whatever their real degree of mutual ignorance, salesmen were usually advised to sell differently to each half of a couple.

Ultimately, the new "emphasis on women" might not amount to anything more than advice to "greet all lady prospects cordially [and] be courteous, well-groomed and understanding."[112] Such basic advice was necessary because before the 1970s, women buyers were relatively rare, and salesman usually dismissed them. A female reporter who went to Macy's in 1939, when it briefly experimented with selling the tiny new Crosley, was pointedly ignored by salesmen, who rushed up to any man who appeared even vaguely interested. On the other hand, when she went to a local New York Ford dealer, the salesman treated her promptly and politely, and assumed she was both knowledgeable about automobiles and would be doing the buying herself.[113] The Ford salesman's attentiveness was unusual in 1939—and in 1999 when another female reporter walked into a showroom. The salesman who showed her a car said, "Well, I guess we're really not going to do any business today. Your husband will have to come back to drive it." Shocked that thirty years after the women's movement a salesman could still make such sexist assumptions, she firmly informed him that she was buying the car for herself and by herself. Despite her assurances, he later repeated, "But we're not going to talk numbers, right? I'm sure your husband will have to come back and do that."[114]

The women's movement of the 1970s may have increased industry awareness of women as a distinct market segment, but the message often failed to percolate down to the showroom floor. In 1978 a J. D. Powers marketing consultant told a Department of Transportation hearing that women believed they were treated differently from men. Women buyers thought they were quoted higher prices, got fast-talk rather than clear answers to their questions, and were ignored, especially if they were shopping with a male companion.[115] Every time industry leaders described their efforts to welcome women as customers, the press would run another story of boorish salesmen offending female shoppers.[116] Even the syndicated etiquette columnist Judith Martin ("Miss Manners") was moved to comment on a positive car buying experience in 1996 because it was in such contrast with the shabby way she had previously been "hustled and insulted" by car salesmen.[117]

To some extent, women's continuing complaints about objectionable treatment from salesmen derives from the difference between men and women when buying cars. What women perceived as discriminatory treatment may have been, in some cases, an evenhanded application of an historically gendered system. Women who bought cars were playing an established game. If they were ignored, it was because they were not considered serious buyers. Male looky-loos, flakes, and be-backs were also given short shrift. If women were brow-beaten or taken advantage of, it was not only because they were women but also because *everybody* was brow-beaten and taken advantage of whenever possible. For cultural reasons, women were less likely to fight back and more likely to be uncomfortable with a system so at odds with the conventional retail experience.

Bargaining was not anathema to women so much as it was alien. While vacationing in Nova Scotia in 1930, Patience Eden was overcome with the desire to own a little blue roadster with red wheels (à la Nancy Drew). Although she knew she could buy one for less back home in Connecticut, "a man acquainted with the guile and wisdom of the breed suggested that, in order to make a sale, an agent could sometimes be induced to whittle down his commission." Convinced she could bargain as well as any man, Eden summoned a salesman to her home, where he sold her a coupe, not a roadster, without whittling down the price at all.[118]

Negotiating women remained rare but not unheard of, and in 1966 Ford salesmen were told they could sometimes clinch a deal with a woman buyer by adding a little boot at the end of the negotiating, which worked because of the "feminine compulsion to 'get something extra.'"[119] When Paula Ganzi Licata went shopping for a new car in 2003, she encountered the standard catalogue of salesmen's slights: they assumed she knew nothing about cars; they talked to her husband even when she asked the questions; they high-pressured her, and so forth. She, however, was the bargainer in her family. As her husband stood by and recommended compromise, she offered no quarter. She wanted to "eviscerate" the salesman, and she took delight in recounting the final insult. The dealer had made an error in her favor on the signed contract and asked her to allow him to correct it. She refused; "A deal's a deal," she said, even when the deal was in fact not the deal to which she had agreed.[120]

Ganzi Licata's story was newsworthy because it inverted the gender stereotypes (woman bites dog). As a rule, American women disliked bargaining even more than men did, and both sides in the sales transaction sought to take advantage of this fact. When they were not being accused of ignoring women car shoppers, salesmen were charged with taking advantage of women's reluctance to negotiate.[121] In reporting that the proportion of women who bought their own cars had risen to 13 percent in 1978, the *Wall Street Journal* quoted a sales-man who said women were more profitable because "they won't haggle over price if you can assure them they'll get good service."[122] Hard evidence on this point is mixed, but academic studies indicate that women may not, in fact, have paid more for cars than men, even if they thought they did.[123] Whether or not they were taken advantage of, women preferred to avoid the game, and they could sometimes use that fact to get better prices. By not challenging the sales-man but instead appealing to his presumed expertise, some female shoppers have done quite well.[124] In other words, women shoppers could occasionally take advantage of a chivalrous salesman who believed women deserved kinder treatment than men.

Chivalry, however, was not a quality that abounded on the showroom floor, and the woman who counted on it was simply announcing her status as a bare-foot pilgrim and praying that the salesman extended dispensations to the faith-ful. Women car shoppers regularly received two pieces of advice: One, learn how to bargain; and two, take a man with you to do the bargaining. From *Better Homes and Gardens* to *Seventeen*, the recommendations were the same. Do what men do. Do your homework so you know what you want. Shop at more than one store. Do not be embarrassed or intimidated by the haggling process. Hold your ground, because if you don't, you will pay more than a man would. Finally, if you are not sure of yourself, shop with a man whom you can use to back you up.[125] Even though only 13 percent of women bought their own cars in 1978, more than half of them were accompanied by a male family member or friend. The men may have provided advice on other matters, but the main reason women brought them along was to help in the bargaining.[126]

The concept of a "bargaining buddy" or "purchase pal" turned up quite fre-quently in the how-to literature and appears to have been widespread among women—as well as among men suffering from showroom performance anxi-ety.[127] The advice could be quite specific, for example, giving each partner a par-ticular role in the retail psychodrama. While many women buyers might have abdicated the bargaining role completely, those who followed the scripts would usually have the friend play "bad cop" to their own "good cop." The friend (the buyer's equivalent of the sales manager in the back room) would continually turn down the seller's offers and find fault with the car in order to keep the sales team off-balance and on the defensive.[128]

According to J. D. Powers, by 2006 almost half of all cars sold were sold to women. Presumably, that means that women's names appeared on the registration.[129] It is much less clear who actually did the car buying. Several surveys by the finance company Capital One indicate that three-quarters or more of women who planned to buy a car said they would bring along a man to help them. The women did not feel they needed a man to help them choose a car, but they did need someone to help them do the bargaining. "It's troubling to see that women still do not feel empowered to manage the car-buying process on their own," commented a Capital One spokesperson.[130] Troubling, perhaps, but not surprising; a woman walking into a dealership was invading alien territory, and it made sense to take along somebody who was supposed to know how to speak the native language. Women who did not want to joust brought along a knight.

Sometimes, albeit rarely, the seller turned out to be a woman. Helene Lawson, a sociologist who did an extensive analysis of automobile saleswomen, concluded that virtually all male car sellers are what she calls "tough guys." As a type, tough guys are competitive hunters who view their customers as opponents or prey that have to be defeated or killed.[131] The urge to kill rather than cooperate spills over into male relationships with each other even when it works to their disadvantage. A California firm that brokered exchanges among dealers so that they could locate available cars for customers in the 1970s found that it had to use women intermediaries. Male brokers could not deal with the constant sniping and petty cheating that salesmen in one store tried to put over on their cross-town rivals. Women, on the other hand, could defuse the tension and get the exchanges done more smoothly.[132] If women could soothe the savage beasts at the wholesale level, it seemed reasonable that there might be a role for women sales staff at retail, where they would be less offensive to female customers and non-combative men.

Women drivers were rare in the early days of automobiles, and women sellers were rarer. There are almost no references to automobile saleswomen before World War II.[133] Florence Emdee was one of the exceptions. In 1914, the twenty-four-year-old music teacher and self-taught auto mechanic sold cars in Lafayette, Indiana. She made her first sale after demonstrating to the buyer's twelve-year-old daughter how easy it was to drive. Emdee refused to increase her trade-in allowance offer when the buyer tried to negotiate a better deal and was able answer all the questions he asked about the technical aspects of the car. The other car sellers in Lafayette accepted Emdee without "a ripple of disturbance," presumably because she played the game by their rules.[134]

Playing the boys' game by the boys' rules was the norm until the 1970s, but saleswomen had to be careful not to play too hard. Lois Light agreed to sell

Chevrolets in Charleston, West Virginia, in the 1950s. When she first asked the staff to help her learn about the cars, they sent her on the proverbial search for a left-handed monkey wrench. In this case, the fellows on the floor explained she could tell which model had six cylinders and which had eight by looking up the tailpipe. Whether because she was simply a green recruit or because she was a female green recruit, the existing staff made it clear she would have to earn her place in the showroom. She went home and read everything about cars she could get her hands on, and in three weeks she knew so much that the men were coming to her for technical information. Light gave away her own commissions to quiet the men's fears that she would steal their customers. When her male colleagues were off the floor and their "be-backs" actually returned, she completed the sale but gave the commission to the original salesman. On the other hand, by being more sympathetic to prospects, she could sometimes score when the others refused to play. For example, when the men scorned a poorly dressed customer as a looker but not a buyer, she approached him, and he bought a brand new car for cash and "didn't ask for a discount or anything."[135]

It occurred to more than one dealer that women customers might be more comfortable dealing, not with a salesman, but with a saleswoman. Published reports say that peers and employers viewed such "salesgirls" positively. As in the case above, the women were more willing than men to work with "unqualified" customers, a trait that led some dealers to dismiss them because they "couldn't distinguish the buyers from the talkers."[136] Despite positive press stories about female success on the sales floor, there is little evidence of long-term participation by women in car sales.[137]

In the mid-1980s, just before the fixed-price Saturn appeared on the market, dealers began to hire more saleswomen. The number of women sales personnel appears to have increased over the next twenty years, but it never reached 10 percent of the total except at Saturn, which at one point had almost 20 percent female sales staffers.[138] The careers of most saleswomen were short, even by the standards of an industry that turned over sales agents faster than manufacturers introduced new models. Those women who did well and stayed in the profession for any length of time usually attributed their success to their empathy with women customers and to their low-key style that worked with some men as well.[139] They succeeded, in other words, not by being better than men at their own game, but by playing a somewhat different game. Some admitted that their success was due to their willingness to take a smaller commission on each sale, that is, to give away more than men did.[140] The proportion of women customers increased much faster than the proportion of women sales agents.

Even as larger numbers of women moved into traditionally male high-commission selling, cars sales remained dominated by men because aggressive bargaining had become an alien process to most American women. Whether they were inside sales clerks or outside sales representatives, non-car sales people sold value—a good product at a good price—and women were comfortable with that principle. Automobile sellers, however, sold the deal, and the deal had to be negotiated.

More than a century of single-price retailing had eliminated bargaining as part of the retail process for customers of both genders under most circumstances, but the tradition of horse trading had preserved it for men as they bought and sold cars. A process that was part of the retail experience of all people in other societies became the domain of men in twentieth-century America. Most women participated in it only reluctantly and resentfully as buyers and almost not at all as sellers.

Still Horse Trading in the Internet Age

In a bargaining situation, knowledge is power. If one side knows that the other is "highly motivated," then the price can be adjusted accordingly. Knowing the other party's desires, concerns, and financial resources provides the bargainer an edge in deciding whether to accept a given offer or hold out for a better one. The one thing that neither side wants is for the other to know what their best offer will be. For the buyer, the purely financial elements in that calculus are based on personal factors like savings, income, ability to borrow, current debt, and current expenses. In car bargaining the buyers were always at a disadvantage, because the salesmen felt free to ask about any or all of these factors. Getting this data was part of the qualifying process that the sales staff used to determine which cars they might be able to sell this particular person, based on the prospect's capacity to pay.

The customers, however, were in no position to ask the sellers about *their* financial condition and thereby determine how motivated they were to make a sale. Nor could the customers know about the dealers' economic particulars, not the least of which would be what the dealers paid the manufacturers for the cars—the wholesale price. The Studebaker Company described their costs and dealer markups to the public in 1916, but their frankness was not followed up by others—or for that matter, even by themselves.[1] As a rule, sellers do not tell buyers what their goods cost them or how much they are marking them up, although in some atypical instances, such as real estate and stock shares, that information is a matter of public record. Because prices were negotiable and car dealers were always claiming that they were selling for just a few dollars over wholesale, the dealers' cost was a datum point that mattered to auto sales.

The Dealer's Cost

No businesses had ever routinely published their wholesale prices, and automobile retailers were not about to break that pattern. From time to time individual dealers did offer to show their invoices to customers as part of a particular promotional campaign, but these attempts were either short-lived advertising gimmicks or met with concerted industry opposition.[2] Just before the hearings that would lead to the Monroney Act, Ford dealer O. Z. Hall of Birmingham anticipated the law by displaying Photostats of his factory invoices along with posted prices that represented a low markup. Neither the factory nor his competitors were pleased by this breach of retail protocol, and they successfully pressured the firm to end its experiment in commercial transparency.[3]

Industry attempts to stop the public from knowing dealer costs were ultimately doomed to failure by the industry's own history of negotiating prices. Before World War II, posted list prices for autos meant that most negotiation took place over trade-in allowances, thus maintaining the semblance of price normalcy for new cars. That changed between 1946 and 1959, when companies stopped posting list prices, and the entire industry pricing system (for both new and used cars) reverted to a preindustrial practice of price haggling. When the Monroney price stickers became standard, the postwar system of bargaining ensured that the sticker price would not be the selling price. Except in rare instances, the sticker became the ceiling not the floor in negotiations. The floor was what the car cost the dealer, and the most determined consumers wanted to bargain up from the bottom, not down from the top.

The easiest way to find out what the dealer had paid for a car was to ask to see the invoice, and there were customers who would do just that. There were also dealers willing to comply, and even more dealers who were willing to show customers what they claimed were the invoices but that were actually forgeries concocted to make the wholesale price appear higher.[4] Even if the dealers were unwilling to show it, buyers were advised to ask to see the invoice, because the request would mark them as savvy shoppers.[5] Asking to see the invoice took a lot more brass than most people had. In many cases they were asking for information that the dealer denied to the salesmen themselves out of fear that they would use the information to clinch sales at an unacceptably low price.[6]

Industry representatives were understandably annoyed at the growing assumption among consumers that they had a right to know what the car cost the dealer. "If I buy a suit, or my wife buys a dress, does the department store have to disclose what it paid for the garment so I can decide if I think the margin is fair or not?" asked Marc Stertz, the publisher of *Automotive Executive*.[7] Stertz refrained from mentioning that neither he nor his wife expected to dicker over the price of their clothes as they presumably did when they bought their cars. Knowing the wholesale price of their clothes would have made no difference to what they paid. Knowing the wholesale price of their cars would have given them a real advantage when bargaining in the automotive marketplace.[8]

Consumers did not have to depend on the willingness of dealers to disclose their costs. By the early 1960s formulas were widely available that allowed buyers to approximate the wholesale price of new cars by working backward from the sticker.[9] Third-party sources went the formulas one better by providing specific dealer wholesale prices for a fee. Car/Puter was the first such firm in 1972, but it found that pressure from auto advertisers forced many newspapers to reject ads for its price disclosures and its related broker services.[10] Then, in 1983, *Consumer Reports* began offering a similar service, which it could do with impunity because the magazine did not accept any advertising.[11] The jig was up. Salesmen had to assume that an increasing number of prospects would come armed with knowledge of the dealer's cost. *Consumer Reports* was followed by other fee-based services, and then by print, and finally by Internet sources that would provide the information for free.[12] The historical moment had arrived for the barefoot pilgrim to become a steel-shod warrior. The new-car market had been transformed from an opaque, almost preindustrial environment where prices were established on an ad hoc basis, to a market of limpid transparency where every customer could know exactly what the product cost the seller and offer to pay accordingly.

Few doubted that the Internet and its World Wide Web were a revolution; fewer were sure just what was being revolutionized. Information distribution, certainly, but to what end? In the field of auto retailing, observers thought, this new medium had the power to do what no other technological, social, or political force had done before it, and that was to change the way personal transportation was bought and sold. It was no longer necessary to pay nine dollars apiece to *Consumer Reports* for the wholesale price of each model a consumer might be interested in and wait for it to show up in the mail. Anybody could go on line and find out what the dealer paid—for free and immediately. Once that information became common knowledge, the reasoning went, the impossibly old-fashioned process of haggling over price would be so anachronistic that even the retail automobile industry would have to enter the late-nineteenth century (now that it was almost the twenty-first) and begin to post its prices and sell to all comers for the same amount. There would be no more dickering and bickering, no more greeters, qualifiers, and turn-overs to manager closers. The customer—man or woman, rookie or veteran, white or black—would know what the car cost the dealer as well as exactly what it would cost every customer and could order one on line to have it delivered directly to the house. It would be the automotive equivalent of the self-service supermarket checkout. Or more accurately, it would be the equivalent of buying a car from Amazon.com.

The idea of a "robot" salesman had first appeared in 1954. Touted as "a machine that sells automobiles," it was in fact a machine that got the customer's name, telephone number, and car preference, thus generating a hot lead for a salesman to come calling.[13] It was no more than a marketing gimmick in a gimmicky era. Similar gadgets appeared from time to time in the following three decades. Robot advocates boasted that they could do everything a salesman could do except give the customer a test drive and negotiate the price.[14] Those were pretty significant exceptions from "everything," and the admission that negotiating the price was something that had to be done before one could purchase a car was an unwarrantedly casual reference to the core anomaly of automobile retailing. (See fig. 6.)

The computer's real potential for altering car sales lay in the possibility of finding the best deal online and then buying online without having to go *mano a mano* with a salesman. That possibility emerged in the mid-1990s with the creation of the World Wide Web and the availability of efficient Internet search engines to find things on it. At first, dealers perceived the Net as a catalog and an advertising medium, a more efficient version of the shopping mall robot gizmos.[15] However, the Internet was already ahead of them. In the fall of 1995 reporter Ed Henry described how he bought a new Jeep without ever talking to a live person until he picked up the car. The process was clumsy and involved paying separate fees for some of the information, but he was able to research the cars, get feedback from reviewers and other owners, discover the dealers' cost, find a dealer who had the model he wanted at a price he was willing to pay, and confirm an order with a deposit—all online.[16] It was, said Harvard professor Jeffrey Rayport, the "disintermediation" of the industry—a B-school buzzword for the death of the salesman.[17]

For about five years, from 1995 to 2000, industry pundits and participants predicted the end of "auto retailing as we know it." Some thought that meant dealers would start to offer fairer prices, haggle less, and emphasize "professional treatment of customers."[18] Others were more apocalyptic. In 1996, *Fortune* magazine predicted that because of computers, superstores, and brokers, "traditional car dealers—among the most hated business people in America" were about to be put "on the endangered species list." J. D. Power III, the head of the eponymous consulting firm, concurred that car dealers would become as rare as travel agents and that those who survived the great shakeout "will be able to do business like normal merchants rather than like sharks fighting over the same piece of flesh."[19]

No such change occurred. Instead, three previously established forms of car buying became a bit more clearly defined. First, untutored buyers who might not make more than the most perfunctory effort at negotiating would continue to be milked dry by predatory salesmen and the occasional saleswoman. They would be charged list price for the car and its factory-installed accessories. They would be sold a "pack" of unnecessary and over-priced dealer add-ons. They would get less for their trade-in than it was worth and pay more for financing their car with the dealer than they would have with an outside lender. They would be the classic "barefoot pilgrims," disproportionately poor, black, or female, who would become trophies to be bragged about in the salesmen's break-room. Second, knowledgeable buyers would come into the showroom armed with more information than they had ever had before, including the wholesale cost of the car and each of its accessories. However, all the forearming and forewarning would not change the fundamental process: they would still have to fight with the tag-team of sales staffers to get the best possible deal on the new car and the trade-in. Finally, there would be those who were knowledgeable but reluctant to commit the time and emotional energy necessary to bargain for the very best deal. They would use the Internet to find a good (if not the best) price and arrange all the particulars online, showing up only to hand over the check and drive off the car—and sometimes even that would be delivered to their door.[20] But then, there was still the issue of what to do about their present car. . . .

At first, dealers worried out loud that the manufacturers would revert to their old threat of setting up competing retail outlets, but now the outlets would be online and would not involve substantial investments in brick and mortar.[21] Some factory executives may have dreamed about doing so, but manufacturers took no significant steps toward direct selling. Instead they used the Internet to set up advertising sites that directed customers to the traditional retail outlets.[22]

Buyers who used the Internet to check on prices became a major concern of dealers and salesmen in the late 1990s. The buyers showed up with printouts, some of which included the always mysterious "holdback," the roughly 4 percent of the factory price that was rebated to the dealership at the end of the year. Although the holdback did not appear on the Monroney sticker, and was not factored into the salesmen's compensation, it represented real profit for the dealer and actually allowed a car to be sold below invoice while still providing the dealer with a profit—albeit a thin one.[23] These informed shoppers, noted a Washington State dealer, "don't want a rapport with the salesman; all they care about is price, price, price. They want to get down to business, buy their car, and get out."[24] The number of sites that would provide the invoice prices proliferated in the late 1990s, and although many offered a referral service, most of the people who used them just wanted the price information so they could do their own bargaining.[25] For a brief period the trend was so strong that the National Automobile Dealers Association joined the stampede by setting up its own Web site that contained all the requisite information—including the holdback, a service that did not sit well with its members and was soon dropped.[26]

By the year 2000, dealers were recognizing that they had to respond to the growth in Internet customers by setting up their own Web sites that would provide specific price information online.[27] But whether the prospects got their numbers from a third-party site, NADA's site, or the dealer's own site, many still wanted to talk to a sales representative to consummate the deal. Customer John Hyater explained why he would not buy online in 1997: "It's the thrill of the game. It's a challenge, you know. Maybe it just goes back to all that old testosterone laden genes in the past, you know, going out and hunting for something and bagging it and bringing it home."[28] For customers like Hyater, a car was not bought—it was won.

The one relatively new wrinkle in the retail sales scene was the appearance of so-called "third party" sellers. On the one hand, these firms were nothing more than the latest version of brokers, who had functioned on the fringes of the auto market for generations. On the other, they were able to move from the periphery toward the center because they were easily accessible online and they provided a convenient way to get comparative price information. Information sites like Kelley Blue Book and Edmunds, which were Internet extensions of preexisting companies, experimented first by selling their data online, and then by giving it away free but earning money from online advertising. A company called Auto-By-Tel (later Autobytel.com), however, evolved the form that would become the Internet model.

Autobytel was founded in 1995 by Peter Ellis, a failed California and Arizona car dealer. Ellis's idea was to give auto customers as much information as they wanted for as many models as they wanted for free. Although it was part of the original cohort of Internet retailers (the Amazon.com generation), Autobytel could not duplicate Amazon's business model because it had no way to acquire and deliver the product.[29] Nevertheless, the firm generated the kind of extravagant predictions that accompanied so many Internet startups of that period. Ellis claimed that his company would do away with price haggling and poor service. It was going to lower dealer costs and transform sales staffers into salaried professionals instead of a cigarette-smoking lowlifes who would "mug the customer's wallet" and "gull the customer into thinking they're getting a great deal" on an overpriced car. Ellis, said one writer, was doing nothing less than "burning down the house."[30] Visitors to Autobytel who were interested in a car could fill out a form that would be forwarded to one of the 2,700 dealers who affiliated themselves with the firm. In a day or two, the customers would receive a specific no-haggle quote, and all they needed to do was go to the dealership to pay and drive home with their new car. To be listed on the Web site, the dealers paid Autobytel a sign-up fee, an annual fee, and monthly fees based on the number of brands they sold.[31]

For the buyer who knew that prices could be negotiated but did not like to negotiate, buying through a service like Autobytel seemed to make sense. For one thing, it allowed buyers to believe that they had gotten a good deal: "Usually when you leave the lot, you feel like the next guy who arrives is going to get a better price than you. This is the only time I've left the lot feeling good," said a New York financial consultant. Through Autobytel he paid $4000 less than his local dealer, with whom he had a long-term personal relationship, had asked for.[32] The system looked like it was working, and other firms jumped onto the bandwagon. By 2000 there were a dozen sites that acted as intermediaries for purchasing a car. Some merely put buyers in touch with sellers; some allowed the buyer to make a firm transaction online; and at least one, CarsDirect, would deliver the new car to the purchaser's house.[33]

Like so many other retail concepts that faded with the end of the dot-com boom in 2000–2001, car-buying sites lost their fearsome aspect. Some retailers worked out arrangements with the third-party sites to supply their customers with cars. In theory, they could recoup the fees the Web sites charged by spending less on advertising and sales help, although the correlation was so indirect that nobody could pin down the costs one way or the other. Other dealers developed their own retail Web sites, often in collaboration with the manufacturers, which worked well enough to dampen worries about the end of automotive retail outlets.[34] When Ford tried to centralize Internet pricing, in effect creating a national one-price policy for its cars, the dealers balked and the project died an early death.[35] Dealers and customers may have said they did not like haggling, but when the time came to do the deed, both sides appear to have preferred face-to-face negotiation. Although the vast majority of buyers—estimates range up to 80 percent—do their preparatory information-gathering online, relatively few of them buy there. A car, it seems, continues to be a prize as well as a purchase.[36]

Many of the most prominent car-buying sites consolidated after 2000, and those that survived provided reluctant bargainers with a relatively painless way to get a pretty good deal on a car.[37] Women in particular found the absence of adversarial bargaining on the Internet a more congenial way to buy, and several studies have shown that the Internet is a reasonable alternative for anybody who dislikes haggling.[38] There was, however, no assurance that the dealers to which the online sites referred their customers would be the cheapest, or even cheap. In 2002, *Consumer Reports* found that buyers did better by aggressive face-to-face bargaining than they could do online, but the online services did get them better prices than either telephone negotiation or buying through a big-box discount store.[39] Buyers might *think* they had gotten the same price as any other person, but if they wanted the best possible price they had to comparison shop among sites, and even that price could often be further negotiated with the dealer whose name came up.[40]

For both individuals and firms dealing in secondhand cars, the Internet provided an improved form of classified advertising, but aside from the immediacy of electronic information and the convenience of being able to post a picture along with the description, the transaction between the buyer and seller was no different than it had been in 1895 when men were swapping horses. Used-car buyers (and private sellers) could easily check the suggested wholesale and retail prices for their vehicles at Edmunds or Kelley Blue Book online, but that was simply a more efficient way to gather data they could have gleaned from the classified ad section of their local newspaper. Buyers could search on Web sites that featured used cars, some run by local newspapers who were losing advertising revenue to the Web and some by national firms like Autobytel or Microsoft's CarPoint, but when it came time to buy, they had to show up to look the car over, give it a test drive, and dicker face-to-face in a way that would have been familiar to their great-great-grandfathers.[41]

Make Me an Offer!

The historical model established by horse trading provided an alternative that helped keep auto dealing from following the lead of other consumer retailing into a single-posted-price retail model. The horses ran roughshod through history, trampling all obstacles that threatened to alter their path. The bicycle craze of the 1890s challenged male dominance of personal transportation and its accompanying trading system, but it fizzled out before it could shift the paradigm. Electric cars never became popular enough to give women a firm footing in the new-car market, and when used cars became an issue after 1909, trade-ins resurrected the male tradition of transportation negotiation. Somewhere west of Laramie a flapper may have driven her car recklessly across the prairie in 1923, but the culture of the horseman racing by her side still dominated the car-sales system. The Depression only deepened the pattern of what was then called "wild trading," and it took government intervention through the NRA to put on the brakes in 1933. Then it took the Supreme Court only two years to release them.

Intoxicated by the colossal demand after World War II, car buyers and sellers created their own gray market to circumvent manufacturers' list prices. The shady retail practices of the postwar sellers' market continued into the 1950s, entrenching ever more deeply the pattern of establishing the price of each sale through adversarial negotiation. Public outrage at some of the most aggressive dealer practices, and dealer outrage at some of the most aggressive manufacturer practices, led to federal intervention in the form of the Monroney Act with its requirement of a window sticker that listed the MSRP. Rather than changing the historically established pattern of price negotiation, the Monroney Act gave it a unique legislative basis. Alone among all consumer goods, automobiles had to carry their list price; and given the tradition of price negotiation, that became a point of negotiation, not a standard sales price. The women's movement roiled the waters a bit, but the challenges of the single-price Saturn and of more women buying and selling cars were insufficient to alter selling patterns that had become so normative that it was easier to change the way women shopped, when they were shopping for cars, than it was to change the way cars were sold.

Just as the tradition of bargaining over the price of automobiles survived the challenge of the Internet, so did the standard one-price model for retailing all other manufactured products. Analysts regularly announced the imminent demise of the posted-price paradigm, but no serious change has taken place.[42] Web sites like NexTag, Priceline, and eBay have all experimented with auction/bidding approaches to selling, but none has altered the consumers' preference for comparing posted prices and buying with the knowledge that they paid the same as every other person buying from the same source at the same time. Cars alone have withstood the pressure to conform to the single-price retailing norm. The pundits who predicted that the Internet would change the way retailers price both regular goods and automobiles have so far been wrong. The democratic, equalitarian, female model dominates everywhere in retail except on the showroom floor, which retains its masculine style even in the relatively rare instances when women are doing both the buying and selling.

The persistence of bargaining in automobile retail history can be attributed to a number of factors, none of which by itself would have been enough to keep the sale of new cars out of the single-price retail mainstream. Furthermore, almost all of the reasons for automotive exceptionalism could be addressed by the industry. Mechanically, cars remain very large and complex machines. Although the amount of dealer preparation that needs to be done has declined steadily since the days when some cars were shipped partially disassembled, automobiles still need to be given a pre-delivery going over by dealer employees. There is no reason, however, why this could not be done in regional preparation centers where the vehicles could also be stored until they were sold and prepped for delivery. Dealers like to emphasize that they are needed to provide warranty service for cars, but again, there is no reason why this could not be done by authorized factory service centers that did not double as retailers. The whole test-drive ritual could be handled by showroom demonstrators, which was the pattern throughout most of automotive history and which is what happens in any case when a car is special-ordered.

Neither the size nor the relative cost of a new car is an insurmountable obstacle to selling cars like other manufactured goods—at the same posted price to all customers. What was historically called "the used-car problem" does, however, inject an inherently unpredictable element into the transaction. But why should that transaction be subsumed into the sale of the new car? The manufacturers' use of exclusive retail franchises allowed them to put pressure on their dealers to sell more units than the factory-established list price could generate. Dealers who cut MSRP to meet factory demands risked losing their franchises, but horse trading had established an alternative model. By swapping the old car plus a cash difference for the new car dealers preserved the illusion of a list price while continuing to do what men had always done. Haggling over the price of a car became part of the meaning of the car, just as it had been part of the meaning of owning a horse. To stop swapping and haggling would require that a large number of people agree to simultaneously give up a method of doing business that is deeply embedded in the culture of conventional automobile retailing. Such a system of car sales is not unimaginable; it is just unlikely. Nothing, not depression, war, car shortages and surpluses, or radically new retail technology has been able to bring it about.

What has been called path dependence is surely an apt description of the stickiness of the car-buying process. However, the stickiness does not arise from the continuation of some past technological decision but comes from the culturally constructed meaning of manhood and the things men ride. The path that car buyers take was an animal track before it was a superhighway. The peculiar folkways of horse trading, with its tradition of male contestation, survived the transition from horse to bicycle to car because it was the sociocultural path of least resistance. Horses, and then cars, were bought and controlled by men who viewed them as extensions of themselves and who incorporated that identification into the process of acquiring them. Even when women entered the picture, first as drivers then as buyers, their historically different style of buying was not enough to change the route. Men and women buyers still walk the path to the showroom floor where a sales staffer will eventually start the bargaining process by saying, "Make me an offer!"

Notes

INTRODUCTION: The Cowboy and the Flapper

1. Peter N. Stearns, ed., *American Behavioral History: An Introduction* (New York: New York University Press, 2005).
2. Paul A. David, *History Matters: Essays on Economic Growth, Technology, and Demographic Change*, ed. Timothy W. Guinnane and William A. Sundstrom (Stanford, CA: Stanford University Press, 2004).

ONE: Horse Trading

1. "Tricks of Horse Traders," *New York Times*, 1 December 1889, 20.
2. Counselor at Law, "A Horse Bought and a Lawyer Sold," *Saturday Evening Post*, 27 July 1861, 4.
3. Quoted in "What Horses Think of Men," *Harper's New Monthly Magazine*, October 1850, 594; Frederick Taylor, *Recollections of a Horse Dealer* (London: Ward and Lock, 1861), 8.
4. "The Broadway Rounder, No. V, Gotham on Wheels," *National Police Gazette* (New York), 28 June 1884, 6.
5. M. Abendstern, "The Professor's Story," *Atlantic Monthly*, November 1860, 614.
6. Thorstein Veblen, *The Theory of the Leisure Class* (New York: Dover, 1994 [1899]), 87; see also "How to Buy a Horse," *American Turf Register and Sporting Magazine*, December 1839, 660; Irving Bacheller, *Eben Holden: A Tale of the North Country* (Boston: Lothrop Publishing, 1900), 227–35.
7. George E. Waring, "Vix," *Atlantic Monthly*, June 1868, 736.
8. Frederick Marryat, *Diary in America*. 1839, chapter 18; retrieved 21/06/2004 from Athelstane E-Texts, www.athelstane.co.uk/marryat/diaramer/diaramer.htm.
9. William M. Brewer, "A Horse Swapping Convention," *Cosmopolitan*, October 1899, 584.
10. "Living in the Country," *Putnam's Monthly Magazine*, October 1855, 392.
11. "Tricks of Horse Traders," 20.
12. Ben K. Green, *Some More Horse Tradin'* (New York: Alfred A. Knopf, 1972), 154–55; Edward Noyes Westcott, *David Harum: A Story of American Life* (New York: D. Appleton, 1899), 263–66.
13. Franklin Clarkin, "Thirty Cents," *McClure's Magazine*, April 1902, 493–98.
14. "Humorous Papers: Anecdotes of Horse Dealing," *Cincinnati Mirror and Western Gazette of Literature*, 13 August 1836, 229.

15. Henry Childs Merwin, "The Horse Market," *Century Illustrated Magazine*, March 1895, 691, 700.

16. "Horse-Keeping and Horse-Dealing," *Cornhill Magazine* (London) 1861, 619.

17. Cicero, *The Letters to His Friends*, trans. W. Glynn William (Cambridge, MA: Harvard University Press, 1952), 28; Francis Henry Lascelles, *Horse Warranty: On the Purchase and Sale of Horses with Hints as to Methods of Procedure in Cases of Dispute* (London: Reeves & Turner, 1877), 91.

18. William Henry Herbert, *The Spider and the Fly or, Tricks, Traps, and Pitfalls of City Life* (New York: C. Miller & Co., 1873), 7–9.

19. "A. Lincoln. Attorney and Counselor at Law," *An American Time Capsule: Three Centuries of Broadsides and Other Printed Ephemera*, 1864, Library of Congress; retrieved 8/10/2005 from http://memory.loc.gov/cgi-bin/.

20. "A Rare Case," *Saturday Evening Post*, 9 June 1866, 6; "The Incendiary," *Lady's Book*, July 1831, 11.

21. "Old Horse Revelations," *Brooklyn Eagle*, 19 March 1894, 10; see also George Stephen, *The Adventures of a Gentleman in Search of a Horse* (Philadelphia: Carey, Lea & Blanchard, 1836), 15.

22. "The Frenchman and the Clerical Horse Dealer," *New York Telescope*, 24 February 1827, 155; Fritz Reuter, "Seed Time and Harvest," *Littell's Living Age*, 4 March 1871, 599–616; S. J. Gibson, "Hell of No Use," *Evangelical Magazine and Gospel Advocate*, 15 April 1842, 117, 616; Roger L. Welsch, "Straight From the Horse Trader's Mouth," *Kansas Quarterly* 13, no. 2 (1981): 27–34; Ben K. Green, *Horse Tradin'* (New York: Knopf, 1967), 254.

23. For example, see "American Humor from Eliza Cook's Journal," *Eclectic Magazine of Foreign Literature*, June 1855, 268.

24. S. H. Hammond and L. W. Mansfield, *Country Margins and Rambles of a Journalist* (New York: J. C. Derby, 1855), 241.

25. Lulu Gray Noble, "A Story of Our Magazine," *Our Young Folks: An Illustrated Magazine for Boys and Girls*, January 1870, 20.

26. "An Alibi," *Harper's New Monthly Magazine*, September 1856, 516.

27. "Jerry Guttridge: Or an Idler's Nature Changed," *The Knickerbocker*, May 1839, 418–27; Edward P. Pressey, "The Mistress of the Old Grey Schoolhouse," *New England Magazine*, February 1900, 704.

28. A. P. Montague, "True Stories of Old Virginia," *New Peterson Magazine*, September 1893, 943.

29. J. K., "As a Tree Falleth, So It Lies," *The Friend: A Religious and Literary Journal*, 19 May 1900, 349; see also "Editor's Easy Chair," *Harper's New Monthly Magazine*, September 1868, 575.

30. Merwin, "The Horse Market," 204.

31. "His Match at Last," *Puck*, 20 September 1911, 3.

32. "Zingaro, A Gang of Gypsies Visit the City," *Brooklyn Eagle*, 11 October 1873, 2; "A Gypsy Camp," *New York Times*, 14 July 1875, 2.

33. "The Gypsy Race," *Saturday Evening Post*, 17 May 1884, 14; Brewer, "Horse Swapping," 584; Riley M. Fletcher Berry, "The American Gypsy," *Frank Leslie's Popular Monthly*, March 1902, 18–30.

34. John Rhett Rushing, "Horsetrading: An East Texas Study in Establishing Context" (MA thesis, Western Kentucky University, 1991), 33; Margaret E. Derry, *Horses in Society:*

A Story of Animal Breeding and Marketing Culture, 1800–1920 (Toronto, ON: University of Toronto Press, 2006); C. C. Buel, "At the Old Bull's Head," *Scribner's Monthly*, January 1879, 427; Fred Pfening, "William P. Hall," *Missouri Historical Review* 62 (1968): 286–313.

35. "A New England Quilting Match," *The Artist: A Monthly Lady's Book*, May 1843, 130; Mabel Percy, "The Tin-Peddler," *Saturday Evening Post*, 2 August 1873, 4.

36. "Let Me Tell You About This Mule," in *Foxfire 8*, ed. Eliot Wigginton and Margie Bennett (New York: Doubleday, 1984), 505; Welsch, "Straight From the Horse Trader's Mouth," 11.

37. Charles P. Sawyer, "How to Buy a Horse," *Country Life in America*, May 1906, 720.

38. F. M. Ware, "How to Know the Horse You Buy," *Outing* 1906, 505–508; "Where Not to Buy Horses," *New York Times*, 13 March 1881, 5; J. Irvine Lupton, *Horses: Sound and Unsound, with the Law Relating to Sales and Warranty* (New York: William R. Jenkins, 1893), 116–17.

39. Buel, "At the Old Bull's Head," 428.

40. "Horse Market Scenes," *Brooklyn Eagle*, 12 December 1886, 11.

41. Porte Crayon, "Old Time Militia Masters," *Harper's New Monthly Magazine*, July 1878, 215; "Hanging of Rev. Enos G. Dudley," *Liberator*, 1 January 1849, 87.

42. A. E. Winship, "Are the Massachusetts Country Towns Degenerating?" *New England Magazine*, August 1900, 658; see also Westcott, *David Harum*, 294–95.

43. "News Notes from the Wide Field," *American Missionary*, March 1891, 106.

44. "Horse Swapping in Georgia," *Brooklyn Eagle*, 21 August 1896, 3.

45. "Editor's Drawer," *Harper's New Monthly Magazine*, May 1858, 853–54.

46. Edmund Kirke, "A Merchant's Story," *Continental Monthly*, December 1862, 719.

47. J. T. Trowbridge, "Mr. Blazay's Experience," *Harper's New Monthly Magazine*, July 1863, 212.

48. Frank DeFriece, "The Abingdon Jockey Lot," in *The Historical Society of Washington County, Va.*, Publication Series II, vol. 18 (1981), 25–30.

49. "One of the Horses," *New England Farmer*, November 1854, 529.

50. Brewer, "Horse Swapping," 584.

51. Terrence A. Mizell, "Getting Snookered in the Horse Business," *Tennessee Folklore Society Bulletin* 44, no. 4 (1978): 197.

52. Morton Sedley, "The Horse Trade," *Brooklyn Eagle*, 10 November 1849, 1.

53. "Gossip and Note Book," *Potter's American Monthly*, February 1877, 158.

54. Paul Leicester Ford, "Thomas Jefferson in Undress," *Scribner's Magazine*, October 1892, 513.

55. Rushing, "Horsetrading," 13, 56 ; Welsch, "Straight From the Horse Trader's Mouth," 25–26.

56. Welsch, "Straight From the Horse Trader's Mouth," 103–105; Green, *Horse Tradin',* 6–8.

57. Judd F. Sylvester, "Hoss Tradin'," *Saturday Evening Post*, 6 January 1934, 12.

58. Green, *Horse Tradin'*, 10–13.

59. Myra Queen, "Horse Trading," in *Foxfire 4*, ed. Eliot Wigginton (Garden City, NY: Anchor Press, 1977), 234–36.

60. Rushing, "Horsetrading," 40–47.

61. Augustus B. Longstreet, *Georgia Scenes, Characters, Incidents, Etc. in the First Half Century of the Republic* (Savannah, GA: Beehive Press, 1992 [1835]), 16–17.

62. "Let Me Tell You About This Mule," 507.

63. Green, *Horse Tradin'*, 60; Green, *Some More Horse Tradin'*, 32, 284–85; Welsch, "Straight From the Horse Trader's Mouth," 5.

64. "The Horse Dealer," *Literary Journal and Weekly Register of Science and the Arts*, 7 December 1833, 216; James Michael Morrissey, *Reflections of a Tractor Salesman* (Plymouth, IN: Privately printed, c. 1990), 17; Welsch, "Straight From the Horse Trader's Mouth," 166–67.

65. Page Holmes, "An Analysis of Horsetrading Narratives" (MA thesis, University of North Carolina, Chapel Hill), 1972.

66. "Selections from New Publications," *New York Mirror*, 18 March 1837, 302; "A Dunkard's Honor," *Brooklyn Eagle*, 22 March 1887, 2.

67. "The Horse Dealer," 216.

68. Fanny Barrow, "Monsignore Capel," *The Galaxy*, November 1870, 683; Westcott, *David Harum*, 160–16.

69. "As to Christian and Other Novels," *Brooklyn Eagle*, 11 March 1901, 4.

70. "Pot-Pourri," *Potter's American Monthly*, July 1882, 107.

71. Longstreet, *Georgia Scenes*, 28.

72. "He Sold Josiah," *Brooklyn Eagle*, 23 June 1888, 5; see also a case discussed in Paula J. Dalley, "The Law of Deceit, 1790–1860: Continuity Amidst Change," *American Journal of Legal History* 39 (1995): 425.

73. "Circuit Court," *Brooklyn Eagle*, 13 January 1849, 3; "Meadowbrook Club Men Who Do not Speak Now," *Brooklyn Eagle*, 22 September 1901, 24; "Horse Trade Adjusted," *Brooklyn Eagle*, 24 September 1901, 17.

74. Westcott, *David Harum*, 9.

75. Deane C. Davis, "Nothing but the Truth," *Blair and Ketchum's Country Journal*, March 1979, 35.

76. Green, "Horse Tradin'," 13; see also George S. Brooks, "Horse Dealing Is Different," *Saturday Evening Post*, 19 November 1932; Welsch, "Straight From the Horse Trader's Mouth," 168–76.

77. "Local Miscellany, Mock Auction of Horse Sales," *New York Times*, 15 October 1876, 12; "Swindlers Balked," *New York Times*, 9 November 1878, 8.

78. "The Buying of Horses," *New York Times*, 6 September 1885, 10; Waring, "Vix," 733; Stephen, *Adventures*, 37.

79. Lascelles, *Horse Warranty*, 24.

80. "Old Horse Revelations"; Merwin, "The Horse Market," 694; Leroy Judson Daniels, *Tales of an Old Horse Trader* (Manchester, NH: Carcanet Press, 1989), 129.

81. John Houston Merrill, ed., *The American and English Encyclopaedia of Law* (Northport, NY: Edward Thompson Co., 1889), 761–66.

82. Merwin, "The Horse Market," 698.

83. Peter Howden, *Horse Warranty: A Plain and Comprehensive Guide to the Various Points to Be Noted* (London: Robert Hardwicke, 1862), 16.

84. William Burdon, *Ten Minutes Advice to Every Gentleman Going to Purchase a Horse Out of a Dealer, Jockey, or Groom's Stables* (Philadelphia: W. Aikman, 1775), 12; Herbert, *Spider and the Fly*, 38.

85. "Lawrence, On the Age of a Horse," *American Farmer*, 16 April 1824, 28; R. A. Sturdevant, "Telling a Horse's Age by His Teeth," *Country Life*, 1 May 1911, 59; Taylor, *Recollections of a Horse Dealer*, 32–33; Henry William Herbert, *Hints to Horse-Keepers: A Complete Manual for Horsemen* (New York: Orange Judd & Co., 1859), 101, 115–20.

86. Herbert, *Spider and the Fly*, 42; Queen, "Horse Trading," 216.

87. Ibid., 216, 244.

88. Taylor, *Recollections of a Horse Dealer*, 25; Herbert, *Spider and the Fly*, 33.

89. Queen, "Horse Trading," 218, 244.

90. Frank Townene Barton, *The Horse: Its Selection and Purchase* (London: Hurst and Blackett, 1907), 142.

91. Queen, "Horse Trading," 229, 233; "How to Buy a Horse," 651; Taylor, *Recollections of a Horse Dealer*, 34–35.

92. "Tricks of Horse Jockeys," *National Police Gazette*, 16 May 1885, 14; Welsch, "Straight from the Horse Trader's Mouth," 4, 125–31; Conrad, *Horse Trader*, 16–17, 10–72, 46–49, 63–68.

93. "Tricks of Horse Jockeys," 14.

94. Paul B. Rasor, "The History of Warranties of Quality in the Sale of Goods: Contract or Tort? A Case Study in Full Circles," *Washburn Law Journal* 21 (1982): 182–85.

95. Marcus D. Hanover, *A Practical Treatise on the Law of Horses, Embracing the Law of Bargain, Sale, and Warranty of Horses and Other Live Stock* (Cincinnati: Robert Clarke & Co., 1875), 150, 167; David S. Garland, ed., *The American and English Encyclopedia of Law* (Northport, NY: Edward Thompson Co., 1900), 756.

96. Henry Hewit Oliphant, *The Law Concerning Horses, Racing, Wagers, and Gaming* (Philadelphia: T. & J. W. Johnson, 1847), 86. American experts cited English law as precedent, as in Hanover, *A Practical Treatise on the Law of Horses*, 102.

97. William Fearnley, *Lectures on the Examination of Horses as to Soundness* (London: Bailliere, Tindall, and Cox, 1878), 167.

98. "On Horse Dealing," *The Athenaeum*, 1 August 1825, 362; Howden, *Horse Warranty*, 4; Lascelles, *Horse Warranty*, 10.

99. Hanover, *A Practical Treatise on the Law of Horses*, 109.

100. Stephen, *Adventures*, 127–29, 232; see also Garland, *American and English Encyclopedia of Law*, 751–56.

101. Oliphant, *Law Concerning Horses*, 45–46.

102. Hanover, *A Practical Treatise on the Law of Horses*, 143–44.

103. Robert S. Surtees, *The Horseman's Manual: Being a Treatise on the Soundness, the Law of Warranty, and Generally on the Laws Relating to Horses* (New York: W. R. H. Treadway, 1832), 47.

104. Counselor at Law, "Horse Bought," 4.

T W O : Retailing

1. Robert Jennings, *The Horse and His Diseases* (Philadelphia, PA: John E. Potter, 1860), 384; Henry Jeremy, *The Laws Relating to Horses* (London: J. & W. T. Clarke, 1825), 4, 17–19, 94–95; Marcus D. Hanover, *A Practical Treatise on the Law of Horses Embracing the Law of Bargain, Sale, and Warranty of Horses and Other Live Stock* (Cincinnati: Robert Clarke & Co., 1875), 153–69; D. Ross Stewart, *The Law of Horses* (Edinburgh: William Green & Sons, 1892), 44–48.

2. Gerard D. Eftink, "Implied Warranties in Livestock Sales: Case History and Recent Developments," *Agricultural Law Journal* 4 (1980): 209–10.

3. Kevin M. Teeven, *A History of the Anglo-American Common Law of Contract* (New York: Greenwood Press, 1990), 136.

4. Henry Hewit Oliphant, *The Law Concerning Horses, Racing, Wagers, and Gaming* (Philadelphia: T. & J. W. Johnson, 1847), 86–87; Teeven, *History of the Anglo-American Common Law of Contract*, 136.

5. "Warranty on the Sale of Horses," *American Turf Register and Sporting Magazine*, July 1842.

6. Oliphant, *Law Concerning Horses*, 80; Francis Henry Lascelles, *Horse Warranty: On the Purchase and Sale of Horses with Hints as to Methods of Procedure in Cases of Dispute* (London: Reeves & Turner, 1877), 2–3; William Fearnley, *Lectures on the Examination of Horses as to Soundness* (London: Bailliere, Tindall, and Cox, 1878), 116; Paula J. Dalley, "The Law of Deceit, 1790–1860: Continuity Amidst Change," *American Journal of Legal History* 39 (1995): 420.

7. Walton H. Hamilton, "The Ancient Maxim Caveat Emptor," *Yale Law Journal* 40, no. 8 (June 1931): 1163.

8. Morton J. Horwitz, "The Historical Foundations of Modern Contract Law," *Harvard Law Review* 87, no. 4 (March 1974): 917–19, 945–47.

9. Lawrence M. Friedman, *Contract Law in America: A Social and Economic Case Study* (Madison: University of Wisconsin Press, 1965), 103.

10. Paul B. Rasor, "The History of Warranties of Quality in the Sale of Goods: Contract or Tort? A Case Study in Full Circles," *Washburn Law Journal* 21 (1982): 189–93.

11. Teeven, *History of the Anglo-American Common Law of Contract*, 140.

12. William Whiting, *The Year of David Harum in Homer New York*, retrieved at www .Homerny.org/Webpages2/VillageofHomer/Harum; Arthur Turner Vance, *The Real David Harum* (New York: Baker and Taylor, 1900), 32.

13. John Ward Regan, "The Carriage Trade in Gilded Age America" (Ph.D. diss., State University of New York at Stony Brook, 2000); Joanne Abel Goldman, "From Carriage Shop to Carriage Factory," in *19th Century American Carriages: The Manufacture, Decoration and Use* (Stony Brook, NY: The Museums at Stony Brook, 1987), 9–33.

14. United States Department of Commerce, *Historical Statistics of the United States, Colonial Times to 1970, Part 2* (Washington, DC: Government Printing Office, 1975), 696; Regan, "The Carriage Trade in Gilded Age America," 63.

15. United States Department of Commerce, *Historical Statistics*, 716.

16. George Stephen, *The Adventures of a Gentleman in Search of a Horse* (Philadelphia: Carey, Lea & Blanchard, 1836), 212; Henry William Herbert, *Hints to Horse-Keepers: A Complete Manual for Horsemen* (New York: Orange Judd & Co., 1859), 374–76.

17. Goldman, "From Carriage Shop to Carriage Factory," 16–17, 20, 25; Regan, "The Carriage Trade in Gilded Age America," 194.

18. Edith Wharton, *The Age of Innocence* (Mineola, NY: Dover, 1997 [1920]), 54.

19. F. M. Ware, "How to Know the Horse You Buy," *Outing* 1906, 507; see, for example, Classified Advertisements, *Brooklyn Eagle*, 28 April 1888, 5.

20. T. S. Arthur, "What Will People Say?" *Ladies' Magazine of Literature, Fashion and Fine Arts*, March 1844, 122–27; ERS, "Hard Times!" *Ladies' Companion*, March 1840, 237–40; Boston Pearl, "No! No! No! I Won't," *Baltimore Monument*, 29 October 1836, 30.

21. Robert A. Smith, *A Social History of the Bicycle: Its Early Life and Times in America* (New York: American Heritage Press, 1972), 6–7.

22. Quilibet, "A Query," *Galaxy*, January 1873, 129.

23. Smith, *Social History of the Bicycle*, 14–18.

24. Ibid., 19.

25. "The Point of View: The Role of the Bicycle," *Scribner's Magazine*, June 1896, 783.

26. Ellen Gruber Garvey, *The Adman in the Parlor: Magazines and the Gendering of Consumer Culture, 1880s to 1910s* (New York: Oxford University Press, 1996), 106–34; Isaac B. Potter, "The Bicycle Outlook," *The Century*, September 1896, 785–91; Smith, *Social History of the Bicycle*, 21–30.

27. Smith, *Social History of the Bicycle*, 9–10.

28. "Rush to Buy Bicycles," *New York Times*, 15 September 1896, 9.

29. Smith, *Social History of the Bicycle*, 26–29, 36–38.

30. "American Bicycle Co." [Advertisement], *Outing, A Journal of Recreation*, May 1883, xi.

31. "Fastest Bicycle on Earth" [Advertisement], *Current Literature*, April 1892, xxv.

32. Smith, *Social History of the Bicycle*, 36–37; "10 Days Free Trial," *McClure's Magazine*, April 1912, 73.

33. *Journal of George Fox*, chapter 8, "A Visit to Oliver Cromwell," 1653; retrieved 16/11/2005 from www.strecorsoc.org/gfox/ch08.html. For a similar claim from a horse trader, see John F. Judy, *Help Yourself—and I Will Help You* (Lafayette, IN: Home Journal Printing Co., 1899), 7.

34. "Original Tales," *New York Mirror*, 16 June 1838, 401; J. R. Dolan, *The Yankee Peddlers of Early America* (New York: Bramhall House, 1964), 229.

35. Joseph T. Rainer, "The 'Sharper' Image: Yankee Peddlers, Southern Consumers, and the Market Revolution," *Business and Economic History* 26, no. 1 (1997): 38.

36. Dolan, *Yankee Peddlers of Early America*, 232–33.

37. James D. Norris, "One Price Policy Among Antebellum Country Stores," *Business History Review* 36, no. 4 (1962): 455; Richard S. Tedlow, "Nineteenth Century Retailing and the Rise of the Department Store," in *Management Past and Present*, ed. Alfred D. Chandler, Thomas K. McCraw, and Richard S. Tedlow (South-Western College Publishing, 1983), 3–6; David Monod, *Store Wars: Shopkeepers and the Culture of Mass Marketing 1890–1939* (Toronto: University of Toronto Press, 1996), 21.

38. ERS, "Hard Times!" 238; Boris Emmet and John E. Jeuck, *Catalogues and Counters: A History of Sears, Roebuck and Company* (Chicago: University of Chicago Press, 1950), 17.

39. Robert Hendrickson, *The Grand Emporiums: The Illustrated History of America's Great Department Stores* (New York: Hill and Day, 1979), 27; Harry E. Resseguie, "Alexander Turney Stewart and the Development of the Department Store, 1833–1876," *Business History Review* 39, no. 3 (1965): 310–11.

40. Walter J. Primeaux Jr., "The Effect of Consumer Knowledge and Bargaining Strength on Final Selling Price: A Case Study," *Journal of Business* 43 (1970): 419–26; Glenn Lovell, "Shoppers Are Ready to Haggle," *San Jose Mercury News*, 21 January 2005, A1; Kristen Gerencher, "Haggling for Bargains," *San Jose Mercury News*, 4 May 2003, F3; Linda Epenshade, "How to Haggle Like the Pros," *Intelligencer Journal* (Lancaster, PA), 11 July 2002, B4; Terry Pristin and Marianne Rohrlich, "The Latest in Luxury: Haggling," *New York Times*, 16 October 2002, 1; Joseph P. Vaccaro and Derek W. F. Coward, "Selling and Sales Management in Action: Managerial and Legal Implications of Price Haggling: A Sales Manager's Dilemma," *Journal of Personal Selling and Sales Management* 13, no. 3 (1993): 79–86.

41. David Jaffee, "Peddlers of Progress and the Transformation of the Rural North, 1760–1860," *Journal of American History* 78, no. 2 (September 1991): 529.

42. Hendrickson, *Grand Emporiums*, 14.

43. Monod, *Store Wars*, 44–45.

44. Lloyd Wendt and Herman Kogan, *Give the Lady What She Wants: The Story of Marshall Field & Company* (Chicago: Rand McNally, 1952); William Leach, *Land of Desire: Merchants, Power, and the Rise of a New American Culture* (New York: Pantheon, 1993); Elaine S. Abelson, *When Ladies Go A-Thieving: Middle-Class Shoplifters in the Victorian Department Store* (New York: Oxford University Press, 1989).

45. Mark A. Swiencicki, "Consuming Brotherhood: Men's Culture, Style and Recreation as Consumer Culture, 1880–1930," *Journal of Social History* 31, no. 4 (Summer 1998): 774–808.

46. *Golden Book of the Wanamaker Stores* ([Philadelphia: Wanamaker Stores], 1911), 144–45.

47. "Wanamaker's Work," *Current Opinion*, 1 February 1923, 139.

48. Stephen N. Elias, *Alexander T. Stewart: The Forgotten Merchant Prince* (Westport, CT: Praeger, 1992), 18–19; Wendt and Kogan, *Give the Lady What She Wants*, 18–22.

49. Norris, "One Price Policy," 455–56.

50. Bill Lancaster, *The Department Store: A Social History* (London: Leicester University Press, 1995), 16–17.

51. Ralph M. Hower, *History of Macy's of New York 1858–1919* (Cambridge, MA: Harvard University Press, 1946), 26–29, 53–54.

52. Lizabeth Cohen, "Encountering Mass Culture at the Grassroots: The Experience of Chicago Workers in the 1920s," *American Quarterly* 41, no. 1 (1989): 23; Ted Ownby, *American Dreams in Mississippi: Consumers, Poverty, and Culture 1830–1998* (Chapel Hill: University of North Carolina Press, 1999), 72–73, 96.

53. For cultural meanings of bargaining, see Nancy R. Buchan, Rachel T. A. Croson, and Eric J. Johnson, "When Do Fair Beliefs Influence Bargaining Behavior? Experimental Bargaining in Japan and the United States," *Journal of Consumer Research* 31 (June 2004).

54. Betty Smith, *A Tree Grows in Brooklyn* (New York: Harper Collins, 1943), 389–91.

55. Andrew Heinze, "Jewish Women and the Making of an American Home," in *The Gender and Consumer Culture Reader*, ed. Jennifer Scanlon (New York: New York University Press, 2000), 24.

56. Federal Trade Commission, *Report on Motor Vehicle Industry*, 76 Cong., 1 sess., 5 June 1939.

57. Hendrickson, *Grand Emporiums*, 27.

58. Wendt and Kogan, *Give the Lady What She Wants*, 34; Robert W. Twyman, *History of Marshall Field & Co., 1852–1906* (Philadelphia: University of Pennsylvania Press, 1954), 3; Hower, *History of Macy's*, 26, 53–54.

59. Wendt and Kogan, *Give the Lady What She Wants*, 75; Twyman, *History of Marshall Field*, 128.

60. *Golden Book of the Wanamaker Stores*, 55–56, 151–57.

61. Susan Strasser, *Satisfaction Guaranteed: The Making of the American Mass Market* (New York: Pantheon Books, 1989), 29–57.

62. Garvey, *Adman in the Parlor*.

THREE: Cars

1. "The Horse and the Bicycle," *Scientific American*, 20 July 1895, 43; Isaac B. Potter, "The Bicycle Outlook," *The Century*, September 1896, 786; Robert A. Smith, *A Social*

History of the Bicycle: Its Early Life and Times in America (New York: American Heritage Press, 1972), 51.

2. James M. Rubenstein, *Making and Selling Cars: Innovation and Change in the US Automobile Industry* (Baltimore: Johns Hopkins University Press, 2001), 251–54; Walter A. Friedman, *Birth of a Salesman: The Transformation of Selling in America* (Cambridge, MA: Harvard University Press, 2004).

3. Richard S. Tedlow, *New and Improved: The Story of Mass Marketing in America* (Boston: Harvard Business School Press, 1996), 112–36.

4. James J. Flink, *America Adopts the Automobile, 1895–1910* (Cambridge, MA: MIT Press, 1970); idem, *The Automobile Age* (Cambridge: MIT Press, 1988).

5. Classified Advertisements, *New York Times*, 9 April 1899, 19; Stephen L. McIntyre, "The Repair Man Will Gyp You: Mechanics, Managers, and Customers in the Automobile Repair Industry, 1896–1940" (Ph.D. diss., University of Missouri-Columbia, 1995), 41–42.

6. Henry Childs Merwin, "The Horse Market," *Century Illustrated Magazine*, March 1895, 693; "How the Trick Is Worked," *Brooklyn Eagle*, 27 April 1902, 10; Wilf P. Pond, "Fraud in Horse Dealing," *Outing*, April 1905, 102.

7. McIntyre, "Repair Man," 41–42.

8. H. P. Burchell, "The Value of Last Year's Automobile," *Outing*, April 1904, 124.

9. Day Allen Willey, "Who Can Afford an Automobile?" *Good Housekeeping*, May 1909, 476; "Are Automobiles Expensive?" *New York Times Magazine*, 21 February 1909, 12.

10. "Startling Automobile Bargains" [Display Ad], *New York Times*, 13 December 1908, 34.

11. McIntyre, "Repair Man," 119–20; see also "A Chip Off the Old Block," *Puck*, 2 January 1915, 17.

12. Rubenstein, *Making and Selling Cars*, 253.

13. "The Untold News" [Display Ad], *New York Times*, 7 December 1900, 4.

14. "Our New Automobile Salesroom Now Open" [Display Ad], *New York Times*, 15 April 1905, 4; "The Untold News" [Display Ad]. The last advertisement for a car in a Wanamaker ad was 1905: "What It Costs to Run a Ford Car" [Display Ad], *New York Times*, 18 April 1905.

15. Boris Emmet and John E. Jeuck, *Catalogues and Counters: A History of Sears, Roebuck and Company* (Chicago: University of Chicago Press, 1950), 108–109; "Sears Motor Buggy, Model P," *University of Illinois Library Collections*; retrieved 22/11/05 from images .library.uiuc.edu:8081/cdm4/.

16. Henry L. Dominguez, *The Ford Agency: A Pictorial History* (Osceola, WI: Motorbooks International, 1981), 14–20; Thomas A. Dicke, *Franchising in America: The Development of a Business Method, 1840–1980* (Chapel Hill: University of North Carolina Press, 1992), 61–68; Rubenstein, *Making and Selling*, 265–66.

17. John H. Eagal, "The Reminiscences of Mr. John H. Eagal Sr., July 1953," 37–38, Benson Ford Research Center, record group 65, box 17. (Hereafter abbreviated as Ford Research Center.)

18. Henry Norman, "Can I Afford an Automobile?" *World's Work*, June 1903, 3504.

19. See McIntyre, "Repair Man."

20. For examples, see Senate Subcommittee of the Committee on Interstate and Foreign Commerce, *Automobile Marketing Practices*, 84 Cong., 2 sess., January–March 1956; Martin H. Bury, "Why Is an Automobile Dealer?" *N.A.D.A. Magazine*, October 1951, 24.

21. Thomas G. Marx, "The Development of the Franchise Distribution System in the U.S. Automobile Industry," *Business History Review* 59 (Autumn 1985): 465–66.

22. "Curry Comb or Polish," in *The Ford Dealer Story* (Dearborn, MI: Ford Motor Co., 1953), 58; Art Spinella et al., *America's Auto Dealer: The Master Merchandisers* (Van Nuys, CA: Freed-Crown, 1978), 19.

23. Dicke, *Franchising in America*, 63–68; Charles Mason Hewitt Jr., "Automobile Franchise Agreements" (Ph.D. diss., School of Business, Indiana University, 1955), 32–39.

24. Marx, "Development of the Franchise," 469–71; Hewitt, "Automobile Franchise Agreements," 69; Rubenstein, *Making and Selling*, 267–69.

25. "Business Bulletin," *Wall Street Journal*, 23 May 1957, 1; "New System for Selling Cars?" *Business Week*, 24 August 1957, 105.

26. The New Super-Dealers," *Business Week*, 2 June 1986, 60–63.

27. "Sues Auto Makers on Resale Contract," *New York Times*, 5 March 1916, 4–5; House Subcommittee of the Committee on Interstate and Foreign Commerce, *Automobile Marketing Legislation*, 84 Cong., 1 sess., July 6, 1955–May 2, 1956; Senate Subcommittee, *Automobile Marketing Practices*, 7; "Are Supermarkets for Autos Next?" *Business Week*, 2 May 1966, 33.

28. James Surowiecki, "The Financial Page: Dealer's Choice," *New Yorker*, 4 September 2006, 42.

29. Walton Hamilton, *Price and Price Policies* (New York: McGraw-Hill, 1938), 69.

30. Ralph C. Epstein, *The Automobile Industry: Its Economic and Commercial Development* (Chicago: A. W. Shaw, 1928), 135–36.

31. Hewitt, "Automobile Franchise Agreements," 220; Federal Trade Commission, *Report*, 1069.

32. J. Schiott, "Automobile Industry Needs: 1. New Car Price Maintenance. 2. Stabilized Used Car Values," *N.A.D.A. Bulletin*, June 1939, 2–4; Theodore H. Smith, *The Marketing of Used Automobiles* (Columbus, OH: Bureau of Business Research, Ohio State University, 1941), 246; William N. Leonard and Marvin Glenn Weber, "Automakers and Dealers: A Study of Criminogenic Market Forces," in *White-Collar Crime: Offenses in Business, Politics, and the Professions* (New York: Free Press, 1977), 137.

33. Jesse Rainsford Sprague, "Confessions of a Ford Dealer," *Harper's*, June 1927, 27–29.

34. Lois Cohorst, *High Mileage: Behind Every Successful Car Dealer is a Woman With Jumper Cables and a Tow Rope* (Hillsboro, KS: Hearth Publishing, 1995), 88.

35. E. R. Taylor, "The Swinging Pendulum," N.A.D.A. convention news release, 30 January 1960, National Automobile Dealer Association, McClean, Va.

36. Hewitt, "Automobile Franchise Agreements," 43.

37. A haphazard but representative selection of ads can be found in Q. David Bowers, *Early American Car Advertisements* (New York: Bonanza Books, 1966); "Automobile Topics of Interest," *New York Times*, 29 June 1902, 15.

38. Burchell, "The Value of Last Year's Automobile," 123; "Automobile Topics of Interest," *New York Times*, 17 May 1903, 14.

39. "Winton" [Classified Ad], *New York Times*, 23 March 1903, 10.

40. "Times Square Automobile Company" [Display Ad], *New York Times*, 29 November 1908, s: 3.

41. "The Fallacy of Buying a Discount Automobile" [Display Ad], *New York Times*, 6 November 1912, 16; Jacob H. Newmark, *Automobile Salesmanship* (Detroit, MI: Automobile Publishing Co., 1915), 98–99.

42. Dominguez, *Ford Agency*, 16.

43. Commercial Manager, Detroit, Branch Managers, "Branch Letter #8," 20 December, 1911; Secretary Ford Motor Company, Columbus, OH, Branch Managers, "Secretary, Ford Motor Company," 31 October, 1913, both in Benson Ford Research Center: box 1, ACC 509 (hereafter Ford Research Center).

44. No Price Cutting," *Ford Sales Bulletin*, 5 April 1913, 2; "I Can't Do That Bill," *Ford Sales Bulletin*, 12 April 1913, 8.

45. "Caveat Emptor," *Ford Sales Bulletin*, 31 May 1913, 40.

46. "No Premiums Necessary with Fords," *Ford Sales Bulletin*, 24 January 1914, 175.

47. "Price Cutting," *Ford Sales Bulletin*, 9 May 1914, 235.

48. "The New Prices—Buyers to Share in the Profits," *Ford Sales Bulletin*, 15 August 1914, 289; Manager of Sales Ford Motor Company, Detroit, "From a Report Just Received . . . ," 10 March, 1915, Ford Research Center, box 2, ACC 509.

49. Joseph C. Ingraham, "Rambler is Offering Savings Bond Bonus," *New York Times*, 16 December 1960, 1.

50. William D. Smith, "Auto Stockpiles Reach High Level," *New York Times*, 3 July 1966, 59; William K. Stevens, "General Motors to Rebate $200–$500 on Small Cars," *New York Times*, 21 January 1975, 69.

51. Detroit's Rebate War," *Marketing and Media Decisions*, October 1979, 62.

52. Jonathan J. Bean, *Beyond the Broker State: Federal Policies Toward Small Business, 1936–1961* (Chapel Hill: University of North Carolina Press, 1996), 68.

53. Ward MacCauley, "The Maintained Price," *Forum*, November 1914, 738.

54. Ibid., 740.

55. House Committee on Interstate and Foreign Commerce, *To Prevent Discrimination in Prices and to Provide for Publicity of Prices to Dealers and to the Public*, 63 Cong., 2 sess., 27 February 1914–9 January 1915.

56. House Committee, *To Prevent Discrimination*, 5–10; Bean, *Beyond the Broker State*, 69.

57. Schiott, *Automobile Industry*, 150.

58. Paul H. Nystrom, *Automobile Selling: A Manual for Dealers* (New York: Motor Magazine 1919), 117.

59. Fordex Editorial Staff, *The Model T Specialist* (Detroit, MI: Sales Equipment Company, 1926), 175; Paul G. Hoffman and James H. Greene, *Marketing Used Cars* (New York: Harper and Brothers, 1929), 43.

60. Paul W. Seiler, "Price Courage Rids a Business of Bad Selling Tactics," *Magazine of Business*, May 1929, 511.

61. *Selling Chevrolets: A Book of Information for Chevrolet Retail Salesmen* (Detroit, MI: Chevrolet Motor Co., 1930), 155–56.

62. *100 Car Salesmen: Final Recapitulation* (Chicago Branch, 1935), 8, Ford Research Center, 449.

63. Helpful Hints for the Sales Manager: "Chiseling," *N.A.D.A. Bulletin*, November 1937, 14.

64. "The Ten Little Chiselers," *N.A.D.A. Bulletin*, August 1937, 10.

65. Bean, *Beyond the Broker State*, 72.

66. House Subcommittee of the Committee on Interstate and Foreign Commerce, *Automobile Labeling*, 85 Cong., 2 sess., 28 May 1958.

67. Bean, *Beyond the Broker State*, 32–35, 73–75.

68. Independent Business Protected Under Robinson-Patman Law," *N.A.D.A. Bul-*

letin, February 1937, 5; "What is Meant by Fair Trade Legislation," *N.A.D.A. Bulletin*, February 1937, 3.

69. Philip M. Klutznick, "Nebraska Dealer Licensing Law Survives Three Years Operation," *N.A.D.A. Bulletin*, December 1940, 6.

70. Federal Trade Commission, *Report*, 138; "Ten Objectives Sought for Dealers," *N.A.D.A. Bulletin*, 10 June 1935, 3; F. W. A. Vesper, "Dealers' Objectives in Relationship with the Automobile Manufacturers," *N.A.D.A. Bulletin*, 10 June 1935, 5–15.

71. "Wisconsin Pioneers!" *N.A.D.A. Bulletin*, July 1936, 4; see also "Pennsylvania License Bill Aims at Control of Used Car Allowance," *N.A.D.A. Bulletin*, May 1937; "Oregon Enacts Anti-Price Discrimination Law," *N.A.D.A. Bulletin*, April 1937, 10.

72. "Richberg Appointed Special N.A.D.A. Counsel," *N.A.D.A. Bulletin*, May 1940, 6; "Auto Dealers Bar Bill for FTC Rule," *New York Times*, 2 April 1940, 46.

73. Bean, *Beyond the Broker State*, 67–87; Stephen Labaton, "Supreme Court Lifts Ban on Minimum Retail Pricing," *New York Times*, 29 June 2007, 1.

74. Senate Subcommittee, *Automobile Marketing Practices*, 738.

75. Ibid., 38, 84.

76. Bowers, *Early American Car Advertisements*, 126.

77. Peter Roberts, *Any Color So Long as It's Black: The First Fifty Years of Automobile Advertising* (New York: William Morrow, 1976), 26.

78. Federal Trade Commission, *Report*, 111; "Suggested Trade Practice Rules for the Automotive Industry," *Automotive Industries*, 30 April 1938, 591; "F. O. B. Advertising," *N.A.D.A. Bulletin*, May 1936, 4.

79. Based on a sampling of *Time* magazine and the *San Jose (CA) Mercury* newspaper, 1924 to 1959.

80. Martin H. Bury, *The Automobile Dealer* (Philadelphia: Philpenn Publishing, 1958), 24–26; House Subcommittee, *Automobile Marketing*, 40; Charles A. Snyder, "Playing by the Rules," *Automotive Executive*, May 1992, 70.

81. Senate Automobile Marketing Subcommittee of the Committee on Interstate and Foreign Commerce, *Automobile Price Labeling*, 85 Cong., 2 sess., 21–24 April 1958.

82. "Hot Cars," *Forbes*, 21 May 1984, 12; Jerry Knight and Benjamin Weiser, "Fuel-Efficient Cars Demanding Premium Prices," *Washington Post*, 10 July 1979, D6; Jerry Flint, "How to Bargain for a New Car," *Readers Digest*, May 1986, 149–51.

83. William Jeanes, "Eye on the Road: Sticker Shock vs. Sucker Shock," *Car and Driver*, October 1988, 9.

84. "Business Bulletin," *Wall Street Journal*, 23 May 1957, 1.

85. Liz Pinto, "One Price Only," *Automotive News*, 14 January 1991, 3.

86. William C. Miller, "No Salesman System Works—Maybe," *Automotive News*, 23 August 1976, 16; Richard Klein, "The House Deals—and Everyone's Happy," *Ford Dealer Magazine*, January–February 1968, 12–16.

87. Richard A. Wright, "Case Study: How to Make Money, Lose Friends," *Automotive News*, 5 September 1983, 1, 8.

88. For an attempt at a theoretical explanation for this see, Preyas S. Desai and Devavrat Purohit, "Let Me Talk to My Manager: Haggling in a Competitive Environment," *Marketing Science* 23, no. 2 (2004).

89. Mark Rechtin, "Saturn Rises, Ranks No. 1 in Pleasing New-Car Buyers," *Automotive News*, 19 June 1995, 8; Jean Halliday, "The Way to a Man's Heart Is Through His Saturn?" *Automotive News*, 1 September 1997, 1.

90. "Funding Customer Satisfaction Efforts," *Automotive Executive*, September 1994, 30.

91. Julie Cantwell, "Saturn Regains No. 1 Rank in Power Satisfaction Study," *Automotive News*, 14 August 2000, 48.

92. Chandler Phillips, "Confessions of a Car Salesman," 2004, part 8: Parting Shots, Edmunds.Com. Retrieved 12/9/2004 from www.edmunds.com/advice/buying/articles/42962/.

93. Thom Rae, "Price-Point Brings in Buyers," *Dealer World* [Ford] May 1991, 30–31; Dom Del Prete, "The 'Wheeler' Dealer," *Dealer World* [Ford], September 1989, 15–17; Neal Templin, "Ford Expands One Price Plan for Its Escorts," *Wall Street Journal*, 12 March 1992, 1; Douglas Lavin, "U.S. Launches Antitrust Probe of Auto Dealers," *Wall Street Journal*, 11 October 1994, 3; Neal Templin and Joseph B. White, "Autos: Ford Motor Ventures Into Value Pricing," *Wall Street Journal*, 18 September 1991, 1.

94. Michelle Krebs, "Moving Out the Cars with a 'No-Dicker Sticker,'" *New York Times*, 11 October 1992, 12; see also David Woodruff, "What's This—Car Dealers with Souls?" *Business Week*, 6 April 1992.

95. Steven D. Kaye, "The No-Dicker Sticker," *U.S. News and World Report*, 27 April 1992, 74–76; Marti Benedetti, "One Price, Many Rewards," *Dealer World* [Ford], May 1993, 35–36; Lisa Doll, "No Hassles in Los Gatos," *Dealer World* [Ford], March 1994, 11–12.

96. Dick Strauss, "One-Price: Revolution or Evolution?" *Automotive Executive*, October 1992, 8.

97. Mary Anne Shreve, "Revolving Floor," *Automotive Executive*, September 1996, 27; Marc H. Stertz, "Random Access," *Automotive Executive*, October 1994, 3.

98. Thomas Moore, "Car Marketers Try the Soft Sell Approach," *Fortune*, 12 May 1986, 71; Kevin Reid, "Full Disclosure," *Dealer World* [Ford], May 1996, 31–33.

99. Arlena Sawyers, "One Pricers Stress 'Cultural' Changes," *Automotive News*, 26 September 1994, 1.

100. Robert Simison, "Automobiles," *Wall Street Journal*, 18 February 1994, 1.

101. Jake Kelderman, "Is Value-Pricing Valid?" *Automotive Executive*, September 1993, 23; Bill Dodge, "Learning from History," *Automotive Executive*, September 1994, 11. A useful typology of dealerships can be found in Helene M. Lawson, *Ladies on the Lot: Women, Car Sales, and the Pursuit of the American Dream* (Lanham, MD: Rowman & Littlefield, 2000), 24–30.

102. Skip Kaltenheuser, "At Car Dealers, a No Haggle Policy Sets Off a Battle," *New York Times*, 29 August 1999, 4; Keith Bradsher, "Sticker Shock: Car Buyers Miss Haggling Ritual," *New York Times*, 13 June 1996, 1, 23; Kurt Allen Weiss, *Have I Got a Deal for You! How to Buy or Lease Any Car Without Getting Run Over* (Franklin Lakes, NJ: Career Press, 1997), 23; Gabriella Stern and Rebecca Blumenstein, "GM Expected to Expand No Haggle Prices," *Wall Street Journal*, 24 April 1996, 3.

103. Bradsher, "Sticker Shock," 23; Jenny King, "One Price Sellers Find a Niche in Some Markets," *Automotive News*, 27 January 1997, 42.

104. Keith Bradsher, "Don't Trust Car Dealers? Here's a New Deal," *New York Times*, 24 January 1999, 1.

105. Joseph B. White and Fara Warner, "Car Makers May Try to Alter Pricing Practices," *Wall Street Journal*, 24 January 2000, 4; Karen Lundegaard, "Putting on the Brakes," *Wall Street Journal*, 23 October 2000, 6.

FOUR: Used Cars

1. George A. Akerlof, *Banquet Speech.* 10 December 2001, Nobel Foundation, re-trieved 16/8/2005 from http://nobelprize.org/economics/laureates/2001/akerlof-speech.html; Roger L. Welsch, "Straight From the Horse Trader's Mouth," *Kansas Quarterly* 13, no. 2 (1981): 6–7.

2. Gallaway, "The Farmers' Failing" [Cartoon], *Puck,* 7 December 1910, 16.

3. Henry L. Dominguez, *The Ford Agency: A Pictorial History* (Osceola, WI: Motorbooks International, 1981), 86.

4. William R. Ferris Jr., "Ray Lum: Muletrader," *North Carolina Folklore Journal* 21 (1973): 118; Gail Barnes and Pam Nix, "I Swapped That Dog Even for That Ole T-Model," in *Foxfire 5,* ed. Eliot Wigginton, vol. 5 (Garden City, NY: Anchor Press/Doubleday, 1979), 42–43; Edwin Muller, "Roving the South with the Irish Horse Traders," *Reader's Digest,* July 1941, 61; Clyde W. Johnson, "To Trade Autos—What Have You?" *Nation's Business,* March 1937, 70–72; "Half Century of Change Surveyed," *Automotive News,* 4 December 1978, 33.

5. Carl E. Feather, "Go See Willard: Selling Farm Machinery in Preston County," *Goldenseal,* Spring 1995, 35: James Michael Morrissey, *Reflections of a Tractor Salesman* (Plymouth, IN: Author, ca. 1990), 98.

6. Theodore H. Smith, *The Marketing of Used Automobiles* (Columbus, OH: Bureau of Business Research, Ohio State University, 1941), 160.

7. "Announcing a Sale of Used Automobiles" [Display Ad], *New York Times,* 10 December 1916, 5.

8. Paul G. Hoffman and James H. Greene, *Marketing Used Cars* (New York: Harper and Brothers, 1929), 76–78, 129.

9. Suzanne Seixas, "Warranted Deals on Used Wheels," *Money,* May 1980, 126; Alexander R. Hammer, "Rent-a-Cars Also Sell," *New York Times,* 28 February 1971, 12; "Hertz Announces" [Display Ad], *New York Times,* 2 April 1972, 26.

10. Lora Hines, "Short Circuiting the Dealer," *Automotive Executive,* December 1993, 20–21.

11. Douglas Lavin, "Cars Are Sold Like Stereos by Circuit City," *Wall Street Journal,* 8 June 1994, 1; Neal Templin, "Superstores Aim to Dominate Used Car Sales," *Wall Street Journal,* 17 June 1996, 1.

12. Steven D. Kaye, "Goodbye to Haggling: It Also Means Goodbye to Steals," *U.S. News & World Report,* 20 October 1997, 57; James M. Rubenstein, *Making and Selling Cars: Innovation and Change in the U.S. Automobile Industry* (Baltimore: Johns Hopkins University Press, 2001), 278–83.

13. Jesse Birnbaum, "No Need to Kick the Tires," *Time,* 19 February 1996, 50.

14. Bradford Wernle, "Republic Gobbles up Rival Driver's Mart," *Automotive News,* 27 April 1998, 1.

15. Daniel McGinn, "A Cream Puff or a Lemon?" *Newsweek,* 10 March 1997, 48.

16. Mary Anne Shreve, "Super Influence," *Automotive Executive,* March 1997.

17. Matt Nauman, "Opening the Big Box Again," *San Jose Mercury News,* 7 June 2002, i: 1–2.

18. "The Automobile: A Few Suggestions That Will Bear Closer Investigation, the

Long and Short of It" [trade catalog], New York, Smith & Mabley, 1905; "The Simple Way," [trade catalog] New York, C. A. Duerr & Company, 1903.

19. Samuel H. Williamson, *What Is the Relative Value?* Economic History Services, retrieved 29/12/2005 from www.eh.net/hmit/compare; Henry Norman, "Can I Afford an Automobile?" *World's Work*, June 1903, 3503.

20. Ibid.

21. "For Sale-Automobiles" [Classified Ads], *Brooklyn Eagle*, 15 December 1901, 32.

22. "Automobiles" [Classified Ad], *New York Times*, 13 November 1903, 10.

23. "Automobile Notes," *Scientific American*, 1 March 1902, 135.

24. "Automobiles" [Display Ad], *New York Times*, 30 August 1903; emphasis added.

25. "Little Used Stearns Cars" [Display Ad] *New York Times*, 2 November 1908, 5; "Times Square Automobile Company" [Display Ad], *New York Times*, 29 November 1908, 3; "Little Used Cars at Low Prices," *New York Times*, 25 October 1908, 2.

26. H. P. Burchell, "The Value of Last Year's Automobile," *Outing*, April 1904, 123.

27. "Several 1906 Rainier Cars" [Display Ad], *New York Times*, 18 January 1907, 18; "Thomas Used Car Department" [Display Ad], *New York Times*, 30 January 1909, 7. For trade-in, see "Automobile Notes"; Smith, *Marketing of Used Automobiles*, 2–3, 5.

28. John Reed Scott, "Mrs. Randolph's Nerve," *Lippincott's Magazine*, December 1910, 708–18; "The Automobile Exchange," *New York Times*, 29 August 1909, 5; E. S. Partridge, "Selling Used Cars," *New York Times*, 24 July 1910, 8.

29. "Every Used Car a Bargain" [Display Ad], *New York Times*, 24 May 1914, 14.

30. C. L. Edholm, "Selling the Second-Hand Car," *Lippincott's Magazine*, August 1914, 211.

31. Pamela Walker Laird, "The Car Without a Single Weakness: Early Automobile Advertising," *Technology and Culture* 37, no. 4 (1996): 800; Jacob H. Newmark, *Automobile Salesmanship* (Detroit, MI: Automobile Publishing Co., 1915), 90–91.

32. "A Business Proposition for Car Owners" [Display Ad], *New York Times*, 22 November 1917, 9.

33. Charles Coolidge Parlin and Fred Bremier, *The Passenger Car Industry: Report of a Survey* (Philadelphia: Curtis Publishing Company, 1932), 76.

34. "Second-Hand Sirens," *Business Review*, April 1959, 3; Charles Mason Hewitt Jr., "Automobile Franchise Agreements" (Ph.D. diss., School of Business, Indiana University, 1955), 39–40, 99–105.

35. "Second Hand Cars Worry Dealers," *New York Times*, 1 December 1912, 16.

36. "Solve Problem of Second Hand Cars," *New York Times*, 2 April 1911, 8.

37. Richard S. Tedlow, *New and Improved: The Story of Mass Marketing in America* (Boston: Harvard Business School Press, 1996), 154–58; Smith, *Marketing of Used Automobiles*, 7; J. Schiott, "Automobile Industry Needs: 1. New Car Price Maintenance. 2. Stabilized Used Car Values," *N.A.D.A. Bulletin*, June 1939, 150.

38. F. Hopkinson Smith, "In Which Our Landlord Becomes Both Entertaining and Instructive," in *The Arm Chair at the Inn* (New York: Charles Scribner's Sons, 1912); "Price Cutting Root of Most Automotive Retailing Problems," *N.A.D.A. Bulletin*, July 1938, 1.

39. John H. Eagal, "The Reminiscences of Mr. John H. Eagal, Sr., July 1953," Ford Research Center, record group 65, box 17; Detroit, to Louisville Ford Motor Company, 27 September 1912, Ford Research Center: box 1, ACC 509.

40. *How to Run a Retail Automobile Business at a Profit* (Chicago: A. W. Shaw Company, 1917), 33.

41. Federal Trade Commission, *Report on Motor Vehicle Industry*, Rep. No. 76–House Document No. 468 (1939), 234; see also Parlin and Bremier, *Passenger Car Industry*, 76.

42. Federal Trade Commission, *Report*, 240.

43. Don C. Prentiss, *Ford Products and Their Sale* (Detroit, MI: Franklin Press, 1923), 495.

44. Fordex Editorial Staff, *The Model T Specialist* (Detroit, MI: Sales Equipment Company, 1926).

45. Tedlow, *New and Improved*, 163.

46. Federal Trade Commission, *Report*, 215, 218–19, 1069; Walter A. Friedman, *Birth of a Salesman: The Transformation of Selling in America* (Cambridge, MA: Harvard University Press, 2004), 220.

47. Senate Subcommittee of the Committee on Interstate and Foreign Commerce, *Automobile Marketing Practices*, Part 1, 84 Cong., 2 sess., January–March 1956, 189; H. Bertram Lewis, "It's Nonsense to Argue That Over Allowances Create Profits," *N.A.D.A. Bulletin*, August 1940, 4.

48. "Motor Industry Fails to Find Panacea for Dealers' Ills," *Business Week*, 24 June 1931, 11.

49. Chicago Automobile Trade Association, *Automobile Selling by Practical Salesmen* (Chicago: Chicago Automobile Trace Association, 1924), 63, 69; *Ford Sales Manual*, Ford Research Center, 175, 1926; *Selling Chevrolets: A Book of Information for Chevrolet Retail Salesmen* (Detroit, MI: Chevrolet Motor Co., 1930), 91; Prentiss, *Ford Products*, 502.

50. Schiott, "Automobile Industry Needs."

51. Federal Trade Commission, *Report*, 113; Paul H. Nystrom, *Automobile Selling: A Manual for Dealers* (New York: Motor Magazine 1919), 120–23.

52. Fordex Editorial Staff, *Model T Specialist*.

53. Prentiss, *Ford Products*, 496–97; "Used Cars Ruining Deals," *Literary Digest*, 14 July 1923, 59–61.

54. A. R. Pinci, "The Used-Car Puzzle Can Be Solved," *Nation's Business*, November 1930, 35ff.

55. "High Lights of 1934 Dealer Operations," *N.A.D.A. Bulletin*, 25 June 1935, 11.

56. Paul G. Hoffman and James H. Greene, *Marketing Used Cars* (New York: Harper and Brothers, 1929), 8 (illustration).

57. "What Dealers Think," *N.A.D.A. Bulletin*, July 1936, 9.

58. James O. Spearing, "At the Wheel," *New York Times*, 9 March 1930, 152.

59. Spearing, "At the Wheel"; "Junking Program Might Aid Industry," *New York Times*, 2 November 1930, N118.

60. John T. Vogel, "Aiding the New Deal," *New York Times*, 23 July 1933, 8; Walton Hamilton, *Price and Price Policies* (New York: McGraw-Hill, 1938), 73.

61. "Industry Junking Plan a Necessity!" *N.A.D.A. Bulletin*, February 1938, 4; "Plan Would Junk Worn Out Used Cars Systematically," *N.A.D.A. Bulletin*, February 1938, 6; "Dealers Endorse Industry Junking Plan," *N.A.D.A. Bulletin*, March 1938, 10.

62. "Used Cars Move Apace as Milwaukee Stages Spectacular Sales Drive," *Sales Management*, 15 March 1938, 30–31.

63. Howard J. Cook, "Inevitable Change Coming in Automobile Retailing," *N.A.D.A. Bulletin*, April 1937, 8.

64. "Solve Problem of Second Hand Cars."

65. "Trading Second Hand Cars," *New York Times*, 5 January 1911, 12; "Second Hand Autos," *New York Times*, 25 December 1910, 8.

66. "Second Hand Cars Worry Dealers."

67. Hoffman and Greene, *Marketing*, 2–4.

68. Smith, *Marketing of Used Automobiles*, 106–107.

69. Ibid., 55.

70. "Manufacturers Endorse NADA Guide," *N.A.D.A. Bulletin*, 25 August 1935, 1.

71. Smith, *Marketing of Used Automobiles*, 107–12; Federal Trade Commission, *Report*, 365–66; "How Muskegon Controls Wild Trading," *N.A.D.A. Bulletin*, March 1938, 6.

72. Federal Trade Commission, *Report*, 374.

73. The History of Kelley Blue Book, Kelley Blue Book/Home, retrieved 1/3/2006 from www.kbb.com/kb/ki.dll/ke.kb.

74. Federal Trade Commission, *Report*, 374.

75. "Beware of Old 'Shock' Appraisal System," *N.A.D.A. Bulletin*, 10 February 1935, 4; Hoffman and Greene, *Marketing*, 58; "The Code and Competition," *N.A.D.A. Bulletin*, 25 June 1934, 2.

76. Smith, *Marketing of Used Automobiles*, 10; see also Sidney Fine, *The Automobile Under the Blue Eagle: Labor, Management, and the Automobile Manufacturing Code* (Ann Arbor: University of Michigan Press, 1963), 133–39.

77. "Selling Cars by Code," *Business Week*, 16 December 1933, 11–12; Federal Trade Commission, *Report*, 366.

78. "Motor Dealers Code," *Business Week*, 16 September 1933, 7; "Selling Cars by Code."

79. Federal Trade Commission, *Report*, 1070; *The Model A Specialist: Devoted to the Advancement of the Model A Salesman*, vol. 3, "The Model A by Comparison" (Detroit, MI: Sales Equipment Company, 1930), 175.

80. "Sales Control," Edgewater Branch, Ford Motor Company, Ford Research Center, 449, 9, 1936

81. Smith, *Marketing of Used Automobiles*, 123.

82. "A New Era in Factory-Dealer Relations," *N.A.D.A. Bulletin*, 10 March 1934, 3.

83. Ibid.

84. F. W. A. Vesper, "Auto Dealer Code Protects Public," *N.A.D.A. Bulletin*, 25 March 1934, 6; "The Dealer Down the Street," *N.A.D.A. Bulletin*, 10 June 1934, 2.

85. "Sales Code Is Weighed," *New York Times*, 20 August 1933, 6.

86. "Used Car Menace Being Recognized," *N.A.D.A. Bulletin*, 10 July 1935, 7; Federal Trade Commission, *Report*, 337–38.

87. Federal Trade Commission, *Report*, 399.

88. "The Used Car Problem Is Still with Us," *N.A.D.A. Bulletin*, 25 September 1934, 1; Smith, *Marketing of Used Automobiles*, 133.

89. Federal Trade Commission, *Report*, 368, 376.

90. Federal Trade Commission, *Report*, 405–06; "Auto Dealers Want Price Laws," *Business Week*, 6 February 1937, 7.

91. Hewitt, "Automobile Franchise Agreements," 149–50; Federal Trade Commission, *Report*, 249.

92. Federal Trade Commission, *Report*, 366.

93. Ibid., 384.

94. Ibid., 370.

95. Ibid., 390–92.

96. William C. Callahan, "Output Gain in Quarter," *New York Times*, 15 February 1940, 128; William Ullman, "Auto Trade Before FTC," *New York Times*, 17 March 1940, 146; "Auto Dealers Bar Bill for FTC Rule," *New York Times*, 2 April 1940, 46; Art Spinella et al., *America's Auto Dealer: The Master Merchandisers* (Van Nuys, CA: Freed-Crown, 1978), 65.

97. "Ceilings on Autos," *Business Week*, 17 June 1944, 32–35.

98. "OPA Warns Dealers on New Car Sales," *New York Times*, 17 May 1943, 21.

99. John Desmond, "Used Car Market Hits Peak," *New York Times*, 5 September 1943, 10.

100. "History of Kelley Blue Book"; Kenyon Lee, "Gold Rush Days for the Used Car," *New York Times*, 31 October 1943, 12; "Ceiling Threat," *Business Week*, 19 February 1944, 90–91.

101. "OPA Moves to Curb Used Auto Frauds," *New York Times*, 23 June 1944, 21; "Used Car Ceilings Begin Tomorrow," *New York Times*, 10 July 1944, 38; James J. Nagle, "Big Black Market Cited in Used Cars," *New York Times*, 20 August 1944, 5; "OPA Investigates 21,000 Car Sales," *New York Times*, 12 February 1944, 26.

102. Thomas Byrnes, *Selling Sense* (Dearborn, MI: Ford Motor Co, 1954), 28–29.

103. Elmo Roper, "A Report from 1952 Ford and Chevrolet Owners on Their New Cars and Dealers," Vol. II, 1952, record group 695, box 3, Ford Research Center; Elmo Roper, "A Report from 1952 Ford and Chevrolet Owners on Their New Cars and Dealers," Vol. I, 1952, record group 695, box 3, Ford Research Center.

104. "Use Buyer Cunning, Auto Dealers Hear," *New York Times*, 8 December 1958, 16.

105. Richard Munro, *How to Sell Cars: A Complete Manual on Selling New and Used Cars and Trucks* (Toronto: General Publishing Co., 1962), 44; C. E. Groves, *How to Buy Automobiles* (New York: Information Inc., 1970), 24; Julie Candler, "How to Deal with a New-Car Dealer," *Mechanix Illustrated*, October 1983, 94.

106. Debra Sherman, "Ex-Car Dealer Tells All," *Ms.*, November 1988, 70.

107. Joy Browne, *The Used-Car Game: A Sociology of the Bargain* (Lexington, MA: Lexington Books, 1973), 40–43, 50–51; Helene M. Lawson, "Service Values-Profit Goals: The Divided Selves of Car Sales Women" (Ph.D. diss., Loyola University of Chicago, 1991), 122; James Bennet, "A Charm School for Car Salesmen," *New York Times*, 29 March 1995, 1; Benjamin Cheever, "How to Sell Cars," *New Yorker*, 1 May 2000, 144.

108. W. Dayton Wegefarth, "Professional Advice," *Lippincott's Magazine*, March 1909, 408.

109. For example, see, Helene M. Lawson, *Ladies on the Lot: Women, Car Sales, and the Pursuit of the American Dream* (Lanham, MD: Rowman & Littlefield, 2000), 32–33.

110. Newmark, *Automobile Salesmanship*, 100.

111. Automobile Trade Association, *Automobile Selling by Practical Salesmen*, 11–13.

112. Bruce Throckmorton, "Boundary Roles and Occupational Integration: An Examination of the Automobile Salesman" (Ph.D. diss., University of Washington, 1973), 34.

113. Browne, *Used-Car Game*, 12.

114. "The Dealer Down the Street"; Martin H. Bury, *The Automobile Dealer* (Philadelphia: Philpenn Publishing, 1958), 164–65.

115. Munro, *How to Sell*, 8; Leo Levine, "Honest Dishonesty, or Do Unto Others as They Do Unto You," *Motor Trend*, February 1969, 67; J. Michel White, *Buying Your Next*

Car: How to Stick It to the Dealers Before the Dealer Can Stick It to You (Tucson, AZ: Harbinger House, 1993), 37.

116. Darrell Parrish, *The Car Buyer's Art . . . How to Beat the Salesman at His Own Game* (Bellflower, CA: Book Express, 1992), 143.

117. "Sell Your Car Yourself and Get More," *Changing Times,* June 1971, 32; "Sell Your Car the Way a Dealer Would," *Changing Times,* February 1977, 11–12.

118. R. P. Stevenson, "Upping Your Car's Value," *Popular Science,* September 1950, 207–11.

119. Mike Willingham, *The New Car Dealer's Secret Agenda: An Insider's View of Dealer Strategies, Salesman's Tactics, the Finance Office Trick and Ploys, and How You Can Be in Charge of Negotiations* (Melbourne, FL: National Negotiating Services, 1992), 21.

120. Marc H. Stertz, "Odds & Ends," *Automotive Executive,* September 1995, 3; Levine, "Honest Dishonesty."

121. Levine, "Honest Dishonesty."

122. "Autos: Every Car Must Go!" [Display Ad], *New York Times,* 19 May 1907, 10; see also "Announcing Series Eight Cole" [Display Ad], *New York Times,* 23 September 1912.

123. "Challenge Sale! Good Automobiles" [Display Ad], *New York Times,* 5 April 1904, 7.

124. "Novel Used Car Trick," *New York Times,* 11 July 1915, 10; Fred J. Wagner, "Let the Buyer Beware When It Comes to Used Car Deals," *House Beautiful,* October 1915, 14; "Auto Prices Dropped" [Display Ad], *New York Times,* 23 August 1907, 8.

125. "Widow Must Sell Fine Car at Terrible Sacrifice," *Literary Digest,* 10 April 1920, 104–109.

126. "Looks and Runs Like New: Reminiscences of an Old-Time Secondhand Car Dealer," *Saturday Evening Post,* 18 April 1925, 162.

127. Colwell, "Advice on Buying," 32.

128. Nystrom, *Automobile Selling: A Manual for Dealers,* 109; "The Truthful Tale of Gettby Who Sold Old Cars," *Literary Digest,* 22 May 1920, 109–11; Ralph Baker, "Watch Your Step," *Review of Reviews,* August 1935, 25.

129. Ryland P. Madison, "The Automobile," *Country Life,* 15 March 1912, 47–58; see also Douglas Robinson, "Clinics for Ailing Autos Use Latest Equipment," *New York Times,* 31 March 1968, 27; Michael Lamm, "How to Become a Smiling Used Car Buyer," *Popular Mechanics,* June 1970, 70.

130. Ralph Blumenthal, "8 Used Car Dealers Are Charged with Deceptive Trade Practices," *New York Times,* 17 January 1980, 11.

131. C. H. Claudy, "New or Second Hand?" *Country Life in America,* September 1914, 96–99; Martin Bunn, "Traps to Avoid in Buying a Used Car," *Popular Science Monthly,* October 1934, 68–69; idem, "Gus Drives a Bargain," *Popular Science,* February 1942, 142–44; Robert J. Bohaty, "Somebody Wants Your Car," *American Magazine,* October 1953, 83; Elliott Arnold, "The Misused-Car Market," *Reader's Digest,* November 1936, 107–08; Carl Isica, "The Fine Art of Used Car Buying," *Motor Trend,* September 1964, 66–69; Duane L. Gregg, "A Close Look at Used Car Buying," *Better Homes and Gardens,* May 1969, 44–47; idem, "How to Get the Most from Your Car at Trade-in Time," *Better Homes and Gardens,* September 1970, 12.

132. L. J. Brum, *How to Beat the Car Dealer at His Own Game: Buying a New or Used Car* (San Jose, CA: B-M Consumer Publications, 1981), 33.

133. Willingham, *New Car Dealer's Secret*, 46; Lamm, "How to Become," 85.

134. Isica, "Fine Art," 66; Diana Bartley, "How to Buy a Used Car," *Esquire*, March 1968, 117–18.

135. Warren Weith, "A Good Car is Hard to Find. So's an Honest Man," *Car and Driver*, July 1976, 20; see also Robert J. Gottlieb, "Classic Comments: A Not So Simple Case of Larceny," *Motor Trend*, March 1977.

136. Gregory Hill, *How to Sell Your Car for More Than It's Worth* (Rosemead, CA: Gregory Publications, 1977), 15.

137. Ibid., 91.

138. Ibid., 81.

139. Bunn, "Gus Drives a Bargain."

140. Wagner, "Let the Buyer Beware."

141. "Looks and Runs," 166–68.

142. Cliff Knoble, *Automobile Selling Sense: A Book on the Merchandising of Motor Cars, Prepared in the Good Interest of Distributor, Dealer, and Salesman* (New York: Prentice-Hall, 1923), 181.

143. R. N. McGraw, "We Sold 1350 Used Cars in 1936," *N.A.D.A. Bulletin*, March 1937, 3.

144. O. G. Bechtel, "Hints to Motor Car Buyers and Sellers," *New York Times*, 7 January 1912, 13.

145. "Looks and Runs," 22.

146. C. H. Claudy, "Buying the Second Car First," *Country Life in America*, September 1915, 72–76; "Used Car Dealers—See How They Operate," *Changing Times*, September 1972, 10.

147. "Truthful Tale"; Baker, "Watch Your Step"; Arnold, "Misused-Car"; Bohaty, "Somebody Wants"; "Queens Studying 'New Car' Racket," *New York Times*, 20 July 1962, 27.

148. E. D. Fales Jr., "Can We Stamp Out Speedometer Rigging?" *Popular Science*, January 1961, 60.

149. Robert J. Cole, "Personal Finance," *New York Times*, 1 March 1973, 57; John D. Morris, "Automobile Sellers Are Now Required to Certify Mileage," *New York Times*, 2 March 1973, 70; Fales, "Can We Stamp Out."

150. Charles W. Bishop, "Proposed Fair Trade Practice Rules for the Automobile Industry," *N.A.D.A. Bulletin*, March 1939, 13.

151. Bury, *Automobile Dealer*, 48–49.

152. Fales, "Can We Stamp Out"; Gene Ritzinger, "Selling Old Autos," *Wall Street Journal*, 20 June 1962, 1; Sam Crowther and Irwin Winehouse, *Highway Robbery* (New York: Stein and Day, 1966), 41, 50.

153. "Buying a Used Car? I'll Cheat You If You Don't Watch Out," *Popular Science*, December 1967, 76–78; "Does the Odometer Lie? If It Does You May Never Know," *Consumer Reports*, April 1985, 186–87.

154. James E. Scripture, "Odometer Rollback Schemes," *FBI Law Enforcement Bulletin* 59 (August 1990): 8–12.

155. "Car Odometer Designed to Prevent Tampering," *New York Times*, 21 January 1976, 94.

156. Joseph F. Sullivan, "U.S. Finds Used Car Odometer Frauds in Jersey," *New York Times*, 12 November 1976, 13; "Odometer Fraud Cited," *New York Times*, 18 January

1977, 67; "7 Car Dealers Admit Odometer Tampering," *New York Times*, 18 February 1977, 21; "Auto Fraud Is Charged," *New York Times*, 9 June 1977, 27; "Eight Car Dealers Fined for Rolling Back Meters," *New York Times*, 15 July 1977, 19; "Fraud Charged to Auto Dealer," *New York Times*, 6 April 1977, 24; Arnold H. Lubasch, "3 Auto Dealers in Bronx Indicted on Charges of Altering Odometers," *New York Times*, 18 April 1978, 32; "Odometer Fraud Charged," *New York Times*, 1 July 1978, 43.

157. "Odometer Fraud up, Federal Officials Say," *New York Times*, 3 September 1996, 9; Cathy Nikkel, "Odometer Fraud Heats Up," *Motor Trend*, November 1996, 32; Arlena Sawyers, "The Twisted History of a Used Lexus RX 300," *Automotive News*, 18 April 2005, 49.

158. Micheline Maynard, "Playing Used Car Detective, Online," *New York Times*, 29 July 2002, 10; Sawyers, "The Twisted History."

F I V E : The Triumph of the Price Pack

1. Paul M. Millians, "The Dealer and His Public," *Commercial and Financial Chronicle*, 12 September 1946, 1385.

2. C. E. Groves, *How to Buy Automobiles* (New York: Information Incorporated, 1970), 114–15; Art Spinella et al., *America's Auto Dealer: The Master Merchandisers* (Van Nuys, CA: Freed-Crown, 1978), 67.

3. Charles Grutzner, "OPA Centers Drive on New Auto Fraud," *New York Times*, 25 June 1946, 23.

4. C. P. Trussell, "New Car Buyers Held Stung $450,000 in 7 Months," *New York Times*, 11 November 1948, 1; C. P. Trussell, "Buyers in 30 States Hit New Car Deals," *New York Times*, 18 November 1948, 31.

5. OPA Bans Rentals with Auto Tie-Ins," *New York Times*, 15 November 1946, 14.

6. "New Car Delay, Dealer Discount, Black Market Told Public in Ads," *N.A.D.A. Magazine*, June 1946, 7–8; "How Dealer Associations Are Meeting a Public Relations Problem," *N.A.D.A. Magazine*, September 1946, 29; "Public Relations Program of Dealers Expanding Throughout Nation," *N.A.D.A. Magazine*, October 1946, 7.

7. "OPA Order Hailed by Auto Dealers," *New York Times*, 14 August 1946, 18.

8. "Used Car Racket," *Life*, 16 June 1947, 95–96; William S. Dutton, "Don't Shoot Your Car Dealer," *Saturday Evening Post*, 4 December 1948, 32–33.

9. Dutton, "Don't Shoot," 32.

10. "Resale Racket Under Fire," *Business Week*, 26 July 1947.

11. "Gray Market Wins," *Business Week*, 16 September 1950, 65–66; John D. Morris, "24 Ford Agencies Lose Franchises," *New York Times*, 16 December 1948, 46.

12. "Will Automobile Retailing Come to This?" *N.A.D.A. Bulletin*, July 1936, 2; Federal Trade Commission, *Report on Motor Vehicle Industry*, Rep. No. 76–House Document No. 468 (1939), 121.

13. Don Wharton, "So You Want a New Car," *Reader's Digest*, August 1947, 61; "The Used Car Deal," *Fortune*, September 1948, 132.

14. "Gray Market"; Morris, "24 Ford Agencies."

15. "Detroit Hot Potato," *Business Week*, 22 November 1947, 49–50; "Car Price Gouge Fought," *Business Week*, 16 August 1947, 21.

16. Trussell, "Buyers in 30 States"; J. R. Davis, "Pitfalls of Seller's Market in the Automobile Industry," *Commercial and Financial Chronicle*, 16 September 1948, 1097;

W. G. Patton, "Complaints of Unfair Dealer Practices Plague Auto Producers," *Iron Age*, 20 November 1947, 122–28.

17. George Melloan, "Chevy Factory Tagged at $2,220 Shows up at Dealers Near $3,100," *Wall Street Journal*, 11 November 1957, 18; "On Motor Row," *Wall Street Journal*, 18 March 1957, 1; House Subcommittee of the Committee on Interstate and Foreign Commerce, *Automobile Labeling*, 85 Cong., 2 sess., 28 May 1958, 4.

18. Senate Subcommittee of the Committee on Interstate and Foreign Commerce, *Automobile Marketing Practices*, 84 Cong., 2 sess., January–March 1956, 624, 635; Senate Automobile Marketing Subcommittee of the Committee on Interstate and Foreign Commerce, *Automobile Price Labeling*, 85 Cong., 2 sess., 21–24 April 1958, 23.

19. Ray Goldman, "Does It Pay to Buy a Car Costing Less Than $500?" *Illustrated World*, September 1917, 99–101; Waldemar Kaempffert, "The Average Man and His Perfect Automobile," *McClure's*, February 1917, 27; Bryan Baker, "How I Handle a Prospect with a Used Car to Trade," in *Automobile Selling by Practical Salesmen* (Chicago: Chicago Automobile Trace Association, 1924), 58.

20. "Ford Sales Manual," 1926, Ford Research Center, record group 175.

21. "Retail Organization / Sales of Accessories," 31 December, 1928, Detroit Sales Department, Ford Research Center, record group 509, box 5.

22. Service department, "Sale of Accessories 6–1–33," 1933, Detroit, Ford Research Center, record group 509, box 5.

23. Federal Trade Commission, *Report*, 49–51, 111, 248; Theodore H. Smith, *The Marketing of Used Automobiles* (Columbus, OH: Bureau of Business Research, Ohio State University, 1941), 114–15.

24. "Dealers Sensitive," *Business Week*, 24 August 1946, 24; "They Call It Optional," *Fortune*, December 1947, 138–39.

25. "Here is Just What You've Been Looking for," *NADA Magazine*, January 1947, n.p.; "Dealers' Public Relations Challenged," *NADA Magazine*, April 1947, 14.

26. "Recommendations to Tell Your Story," *NADA Magazine*, July 1947, 6; "The Truth About the Current Automobile Situation," *NADA Magazine*, February 1949, n.p.; Trussell, "New Car Buyers Held Stung $450,000 in 7 Months."

27. Martin H. Bury, *The Automobile Dealer* (Philadelphia: Philpenn Publishing, 1958), 27.

28. Nowland and Company, "Automobile Bootlegging: Pilot Study of Consumer Motives," ca. 1956, Ford Research Center, record group 695, box 6.

29. Senate Subcommittee, *Automobile Marketing*, Part 1, 206, 224, 733.

30. Ibid., Part 1, 436; Anthony Lewis, "U.S. Opens Inquiry Into Price Fixing by Auto Dealers," *New York Times*, 12 April 1958, 1.

31. Senate Automobile Marketing Subcommittee of the Committee on Interstate and Foreign Commerce, *Automobile Price Labeling*, 85 Cong., 2 sess., 21–24 April 1958, 7.

32. Donald MacDonald, "How to Buy a New Car," *American Home*, December 1959, 96–100.

33. Joe Car [Denny Armstrong], *I'm a Legal Hold Up Man, I'm a Car Salesman* (Shawnee Mission, KA: Joe Car, 1977), 24; "Toyota Distributor Accused of 'Bait and Switch' Tactics," *Automotive News*, 9 June 1980, 4; L. J. Brum, *How to Beat the Car Dealer at His Own Game: Buying a New or Used Car* (San Jose, CA: B-M Consumer Publications, 1981), 14–15; Jerry Flint, "How to Bargain for a New Car," *Readers Digest*, May 1986, 149–51; "Car Buying Without Fear," *U.S. News and World Report*, 12 October 1987, 76.

34. Helen Kahn, "County Charges Chain Dealer Deceived Buyers," *Automotive News*, 29 February 1988, 58.

35. "The Future of the Auto Industry," *Automobile Executive*, July 1993, 26.

36. "Dealership Financial Trends," *Automotive Executive*, August 1994, 51.

37. Annelena Lobb, "Six Dirty Secrets of Car Sales," *CNN/Money*, 10 January 2003, CNN; retrieved 15/1/03 from http://cnnmoney.printthis.

38. Ted Orme, "Aftermarket / Accessories," *Automotive Executive*, August 1985, 37–41.

39. Leonard Felman, "Chemicals & Protectants," *Automobile Executive*, July 1985, 21.

40. C. B. Robertson, *How to Deal on an Automobile* (Lyons, CO: Blue Mountain Publishing, 1990), 53; Felman, "Chemicals & Protectants"; Tom Nitch, "Appearance Maintenance," *Automotive Executive*, March 1985, 29–37; Kurt Allen Weiss, *Have I Got a Deal for You! How to Buy or Lease any Car Without Getting Run Over* (Franklin Lakes, NJ: Career Press, 1997), 140.

41. Lendol Calder, *Financing the American Dream: A Cultural History of Consumer Credit* (Princeton, NJ: Princeton University Press, 1999), 17.

42. Jas. S. Holmes Jr., "Marketing Automobiles," *Cycle and Automobile Trade Journal*, 1 January 1901, 24–25.

43. Spinella, *America's Auto Dealer*, 31.

44. Day Allen Willey, "Who Can Afford an Automobile?" *Good Housekeeping*, May 1909, 476.

45. Calder, *Financing the American Dream*, 186–88.

46. Ibid., 192–95; Smith, *Marketing of Used Automobiles*, 177–79; Ralph C. Epstein, *The Automobile Industry: Its Economic and Commercial Development* (Chicago: A. W. Shaw, 1928), 116–19.

47. Walter A. Friedman, *Birth of a Salesman: The Transformation of Selling in America* (Cambridge, MA: Harvard University Press, 2004), 196–97; Donald Rea Hanson, "Downtown: Buying on Installment," *Forum*, 1 January 1926, 34; see also Martha L. Olney, *Buy Now, Pay Later: Advertising, Credit, and Consumer Durables in the 1920s* (Chapel Hill: University of North Carolina Press, 1989), 118–20.

48. Calder, *Financing the American Dream*, 31.

49. Ibid., 191–99.

50. Norman G. Shidle, "Telling the Public What It Costs," *Automotive Industries*, 12 November 1923, 807–809.

51. Charles F. Ronayne, "Is Installment Buying Sound?" *Forum and Century*, September 1937, 114–16; "G.M. III: How to Sell Automobiles," *Fortune*, February 1939, 106; Federal Trade Commission, *Report*, 221.

52. William Longgood, "Watch Out for Those Gyp Car Deals!" *Saturday Evening Post*, 29 October 1955, 27; Albert Q. Maisel, "The Art of Buying a New Car," *Reader's Digest*, November 1957, 48–51.

53. Nowland and Company, "Bootlegging."

54. Senate Subcommittee, *Automobile Marketing Practices*, Part 1, 235.

55. Nowland and Company, "Bootlegging."

56. "Trading-in the Old Way," *Economist*, 26 October 1985, 85–86.

57. H. J. Maidenberg, "Personal Finance: Discovering Why New-Car Salesmen Are Frightened by the Sight of Cash," *New York Times*, 20 April 1967, 61; Groves, *How to Buy Automobiles*, 46–50; Car, *I'm a Legal Hold Up Man*, 10.

58. Dennis Rockstroh, "Beware Financing Car Through Dealerships," *San Jose*

Mercury News, 30 April 2006, b: 3; idem, "New Law Helps Clarify Dealership Financing," *San Jose Mercury News*, 9 May 2006, b: 3.

59. Monica Langley, "Cut Rate Loans on Some Cars Are No Bargain," *Wall Street Journal*, 20 August 1986, 17; William M. Graves Jr., "Selling Your Way to F&I Success," *Automotive Executive*, August 1984, 33–34; "F&I: Only for Those Interested in Making Money," *Automotive Executive*, September 1981, 34; Ed Henry, "How Buyers Win the Haggle and Lose the War," *Kiplinger's Personal Finance Magazine*, October 1997, 101–105.

60. John Keats, *The Insolent Chariots* (Greenwich, CT: Fawcett Publications, 1958), 140.

61. Ibid., 86–113.

62. Leon Mandel, *Driven: The American Four-Wheeled Love Affair* (New York: Stein and Day, 1977), 125–33; John K. Teahen Jr., "Let's Make a Deal," *Automotive News*, 16 September 1983, 278–79; Chandler Phillips, "Confessions of a Car Salesman," 2004, part 8: parting shots, Edmunds.Com; retrieved 12/9/2004 from www.edmunds.com/advice/buying/articles/42962/, 45.

63. James J. Flink, *The Automobile Age* (Cambridge: MIT Press, 1988), 281–82.

64. J. Eustace Wolfington, ""The Customer," "Thinking Through," *N.A.D.A. Magazine*, February 1951, 42, 46.

65. James A. Ayers, "Bunk, Bosh, and Bother," *N.A.D.A. Magazine*, February 1951, 46.

66. Elson G. Sims, "Key to Success—Profit Control," National Automobile Dealers Association, *1957 NADA Convention and Exhibition Publicity*, vol. II, News Release, 30 January, 1957, San Francisco, National Automobile Dealers Association, McClean, Va.

67. Ibid.

68. Bert Pierce, "Car Dealers Ethics Assailed by McKay," *New York Times*, 14 January 1954, 54.

69. William C. Hamilton, "What's Wrong?" *NADA Magazine*, November 1954, 20–25.

70. John A. Williamson, "A Price Is a Price Is a Price," *NADA Magazine*, July 1957, 14–16.

71. "Car Merchandising Using New Concept," *New York Times*, 11 September 1955, 1; Frederick Bell, "The Moorish Market," *NADA Magazine*, September 1954, 15.

72. "Used Car Business: A Comeback," *Business Week*, 3 April 1954, 104–106.

73. House Subcommittee of the Committee on Interstate and Foreign Commerce, *Automobile Marketing Legislation*, 84 Cong., 1 sess., 6 July 1955–2 May 1956, 23.

74. Nowland and Company, "Bootlegging"; Senate Subcommittee of the Committee on Interstate and Foreign Commerce, *The Automobile Labeling Bill, Report to Accompany S. 3500*, 85 Cong., 2 sess., 13 May 1958, 13; Senate Subcommittee, *Automobile Marketing Practices*, Part 1, 14.

75. Nowland and Company, "Bootlegging."

76. "A Basic Change in Auto Selling," *Business Week*, 3 March 1956, 104–105; A. S. Mike Monroney, "Free Markets for Free Men" [speech transcript], in *1956 Nada Convention and Exhibition Publicity*, vol. 16 (Washington D.C.: NADA Convention News Center: press release, 31 January 1956), 12, National Automobile Dealers Association, McClean, Va.; Senate Subcommittee, *Automobile Marketing Practices*, Part 1, 501.

77. Keats, *Insolent Chariots*, 101; Senate Subcommittee, *Automobile Marketing Practices*, Part 1, 287, 313, 727.

78. Senate Subcommittee, *Automobile Marketing Practices*, Part 1, 306–09.

79. Martin H. Bury, "With the Right Program You Can Forget the Used Car Problem," *NADA Magazine*, July 1950, 14–15; Jane Wilcox, "How A Sailor Sells Cars," *Ad-*

vertising and Selling, May 1946, 80; Sam Crowther and Irwin Winehouse, *Highway Robbery* (New York: Stein and Day, 1966), 38–39.

80. C. P. Edwards, "The Used Car Racket," *Popular Mechanics*, January 1933, 26–29.

81. Senate Subcommittee of the Committee on Interstate and Foreign Commerce, *The Automobile Marketing Practices Study*, 84 Cong., 19 January 1956.

82. Foster Hailey, "Car Dealers Seek to Check Losses," *New York Times*, 6 October 1954, 26; "Senators Will Study Auto Sales Practices," *New York Times*, 26 December 1955, 1.

83. David C. Corbin, President, City Chevrolet, Akron, Ohio, "How to Clean up False and Misleading Advertising on the Local Level," (Washington DC: NADA Convention News Center: press release, 31 January 1956), National Automobile Dealers Association, McClean, Va.

84. "Auto Dealers, BBB to Fight False Ads," *Editor and Publisher*, 28 January 1956, 20; Keats, *Insolent Chariots*, 100.

85. Frank H. Yarnall, "It's Still a Great Industry" (Washington DC: NADA Convention News Center: press release, 30 January 1956), National Automobile Dealers Association, McClean, Va.

86. House Subcommittee, *Automobile Labeling*, 7–9.

87. Joseph C. Ingraham, "Automobiles: Ethics," *New York Times*, 1 September 1957, 21–23; "Phony Car Deals Reported on Rise," *New York Times*, 14 November 1957, 67.

88. Senate Subcommittee, *Automobile Marketing Practices*, Part 1, 994.

89. "New Price Laws Bring Change to Auto Pitch," *Sponsor*, 4 July 1959, 32–33.

90. Joseph B. Paul, "The Apples at the Bottom of the Barrel," *NADA Magazine*, June 1962, 48–49; "Study Finds Men Distrust Most Auto Ads," *Advertising Age*, 15 October 1973, 95.

91. Carl D. Dalke, "Fighting Bad Advertising," *NADA Magazine*, March 1963, 79.

92. Groves, *How to Buy Automobiles*, 63–81.

93. "Cahill, Dealers Vow Truth in Auto Ads," *New York Times*, 13 May 1973, 92; Rudy Johnson, "Used Car Dealers Are Sending in Payments on Fines for False Ads," *New York Times*, 26 January 1977, 19.

94. Joy Browne, *The Used-Car Game: A Sociology of the Bargain* (Lexington, MA: Lexington Books, 1973), 45; Michael deCourcy Hinds, "New York and Other States Cracking Down on Auto Ads," *New York Times*, 19 November 1988, 52.

95. Joseph B. Paul, "Fighting Bad Advertising," *NADA Magazine*, March 1963, 75; David Ogilvy, "What's Wrong with Your Image," *NADA Magazine*, March 1965, 56–57.

96. Federal Trade Commission, *Report*, 1077.

97. Smith, *Marketing of Used Automobiles*, 114.

98. Senate Automobile Marketing Subcommittee, *Automobile Price Labeling*.

99. Ibid., 2–3, 13, 27; Monroney, "Free Markets for Free Men."

100. Senate Committee on Interstate and Foreign Commerce, *The Automobile Labeling Bill, Report to Accompany S. 3500*, 85 Cong., 2 sess., 13 May 1958, 40; "Dealers Endorse Car Price Labels," *New York Times Magazine*, 22 April 1958, 25.

101. Joseph C. Ingraham, "New Car Sales Law to Help the Buyer," *New York Times*, 14 September 1958, 25.

102. Senate Automobile Marketing Subcommittee, *Automobile Price Labeling*, 3, 30; see also Senate Committee on the Judiciary, *Administered Prices: Automobiles*, 85 Cong., 2 sess., 1 November 1958.

103. Ingraham, "New Car Sales Law to Help the Buyer."

104. "Auto Men to Play Down Prices," *Business Week*, 26 July 1958, 19; Bury, *Automobile Dealer*, 22.

105. "42 in Washington Indicted in Plot to Fix Car Prices," *New York Times*, 24 July 1958, 1; "Car Price Fixing Laid to 8 Groups," *New York Times*, 26 March 1959, 32.

106. Joseph C. Ingraham, "U.S. Will Enforce Auto Label Law," *New York Times*, 23 August 1959, 58.

107. Bury, *Automobile Dealer*, 22.

108. Senate Automobile Marketing Subcommittee, *Automobile Price Labeling*, 3.

109. "A Consolidation of Dealer Questions with Answers on Public Law 85–506," *NADA Magazine*, November 1962, 29.

110. "Far-Reaching Effects of the Truth-in-Labeling Law," *NADA Magazine*, October 1959, 15–19; "Everybody Loves Posted Prices," *Business Week*, 20 December 1958, 24–25.

111. "Use Buyer Cunning, Auto Dealers Hear"; for similar dealer belief, see Lois Cohorst, *High Mileage: Behind Every Successful Car Dealer Is a Woman With Jumper Cables and a Tow Rope* (Hillsboro, KS: Hearth Publishing, 1995), 90.

112. "Prices, a Starting Point for Bargaining," *Consumer Reports*, April 1963, 162–63.

113. FTC Plans Probe of Auto Pricing," *Advertising Age*, 26 May 1969, 1; D. N. Williams, "New Car Prices: Ouija Board Please," *Iron Age*, 25 September 1969, 21; "Auto Pricing and Retail Billing Practices Hit in FTC Proposals," *Advertising Age*, 12 October 1970, 2; "Big Three Auto Firms Oppose FTC Proposal on Car Sticker Prices," *Wall Street Journal*, 13 January 1971, 12.

114. "Price Advisory Notice to Appear on GM Models," *Wall Street Journal*, 13 July 1973, 16.

115. Groves, *How to Buy Automobiles*, 121.

116. "Direct Selling Now Challenges Dealer's Place in Motor Industry," *Business Week*, 9 September 1931, 13–14.

117. "Chrysler Dealer Rolling with Idea for Guarantee," *New York Times*, 28 January 1980, 2; "Chrysler Guarantee," *New York Times*, 8 September 1980, 4.

118. Stertz, "Odds & Ends."

119. "Had to Push New Auto," *New York Times*, 30 June 1906, 7.

120. "Bargains in New Automobiles" [display ad], *New York Times*, 22 November 1908, 2.

121. Stephen L. McIntyre, "The Repair Man Will Gyp You: Mechanics, Managers, and Customers in the Automobile Repair Industry, 1896–1940" (Ph.D. diss., University of Missouri-Columbia, 1995), 379–80, 388–89; M. Worth Colwell, "Advice on Buying and Selling a Second-Hand Machine," *House Beautiful*, January 1913, 30–34.

122. George Strobridge, "Value of Service Station to Automobile Buyers," *New York Times*, 6 January 1924, 10.

123. William Ullman, "New Guaranty for Buyer," *New York Times*, 22 November 1931, 148.

124. Teahen, "Let's Make a Deal," 380–82.

125. "Battle of Warranties: How Far Will It Go?" *Steel*, 8 April 1963, 95–96; "Trouble in New Car Warranties?" *Business Week*, 26 November 1960, 55–56; "Detroit Tries a U-Turn on Warranties," *Business Week*, 25 July 1970, 44–45.

126. "Detroit Tries a U-Turn"; Ronald Sullivan, "Warranties Widened by American Motors," *New York Times*, 11 August 1971, 1.

127. Mary B. Kegley and Janine S. Hiller, "Emerging Lemon Car Laws," *American Business Law Journal* (Spring 1986): 87–103; Leonard Sloane, "Seeking Satisfaction If There's No Quick Fix," *New York Times*, 31 July 1994, 1.

128. "John M. Brisben Co., Inc." [Classified Ad], *New York Times*, 18 January 1914, 4; "False Pretense in Selling Second Hand Cars," *Literary Digest*, 20 October 1923, 69.

129. Milton Mayer, "Dissenting Opinion," *Consumer Reports*, May 1950, 207.

130. Paul G. Hoffman and James H. Greene, *Marketing Used Cars* (New York: Harper and Brothers, 1929), 24.

131. Federal Trade Commission, *Report*, 227–28; Ralph Weaver, "How Our 30–Day Guarantee Boosted Used Car Gross," *Ford Dealer Magazine*, September/October 1955, 972.

132. Micheline Maynard, "Why Dealers Are Putting a New Shine on Used Cars," *New York Times*, 15 April 2001, 12.

133. George A. Akerlof, "The Market for 'Lemons' Reconsidered: A Model of the Used Car Market with Asymmetric Information," *Quarterly Journal of Economics* 84, no. 3 (August 1970): 488–500; George A. Akerlof, "Writing the 'The Market for Lemons': A Personal and Interpretive Essay," retrieved 11/14/2003 from http://nobelprize.org.

134. "Used Car Reforms," *Business Week*, 23 February 1935, 8; "Caveat Venditor," *Time*, 16 November 1953, 97–98; "Mileage Must Be Posted on Used Cars Sold Here," *New York Times*, 29 September 1969, 40; Richard Phalon, "Used Car Sellers Face Stiff Rules," *New York Times*, 10 May 1970, 88; Andrew O. Shapiro, "Hoodwinked No More: Tips for the Used-Car Buyer," *New York Times*, 30 October 1978, 104–105.

135. "Unless Excluded or Modified," *Automotive Executive*, January 1980, 34.

136. "Sellers Beware," *The Economist*, 10 January 1976, 54.

137. "Used Car Dealers Face FTC Action to Bar Deception," *New York Times*, 3 January 1976, 1.

138. Helen Kahn, "Sticker on U.C. Condition Moving Near FTC Order," *Automotive News*, 12 June 1978, 1; Helen Kahn and Jake Kelderman, "Used Car Proposals Illegal, Unjustified, Dealers Tell FTC," *Automotive News*, 19 February 1979, 1. For a theoretical confirmation of the NIADA claim, see Michael Metzger, "Cherries, Lemons, and the FTC: Minimum Quality Standards in the Retail Used Automobile Industry," *Economic Inquiry*, January 1983.

139. Minard, "This Cream Puff'"; "FTC Staff Urges More Facts on Used Cars by Dealers, but Omits Repair Disclosures," *Wall Street Journal*, 14 November 1978, 14; Kahn and Kelderman, "Used Car Proposals."

140. A. O. Sulzberger Jr., "New Rule Voted on Disclosures on Used Autos," *New York Times*, 17 May 1980, 3.

141. Russell Baker, "Barnum Lives On," *New York Times*, 29 May 1982, 23; Jeff Angoff, "The Used Car Capital," *New York Times*, 7 December 1981, 27; Michael deCourcy Hinds, "Rule on Used Cars Rejected by Panel," *New York Times*, 11 December 1981, 17; idem, "Used Car Rule: Lesson in Lobbying," *New York Times*, 12 May 1982, 26; "Congress Vetoes FTC Rules on Disclosure of Car Defects," *New York Times*, 27 May 1982, 1.

142. Helen Kahn, "FTC Begins U.C. Educational Drive," *Automotive News*, 17 October 1983, 15; idem, "Next Move on U.C. Rule up to FTC," *Automotive News*, 18 July 1983, 40.

143. Federal Trade Commission, *Trade regulation rule; sale of used motor vehicles* (1988).

six: Bad Guys

1. *How to Run a Retail Automobile Business at a Profit* (Chicago: A. W. Shaw Co., 1917), 29–30, 35; P. M. Braun, "General Letter #51: Payment of Salesmen," 27 February 1926, Ford Research Center, box 3, File: ACC 509; "Commissions Paid Salesmen," Ford Motor Co., 1935, Ford Research Center, box 7, File: 449; William Beltz, "Encourage Your Salesmen to Sell," *NADA Magazine*, July 1955, 18–20; Mary Anne Sarey, "Pay Daze," *Automotive Executive*, February 1998, 34–36; Chandler Phillips, "Confessions of a Car Salesman," 2004, part 8: parting shots, retrieved 12/9/2004 from www.edmunds .com/advice/buying/articles/42962/, 12.

2. Martin H. Bury, *The Automobile Dealer* (Philadelphia: Philpenn Publishing, 1958), 10; C. B. Robertson, *How to Deal on an Automobile* (Lyons, CO: Blue Mountain Publishing, 1990), 33.

3. C. E. Groves, *How to Buy Automobiles* (New York: Information Incorporated, 1970), 124; Steve Finlay, "Salesman's Wife Laments," *Ward's Dealer Business*, 1 July 2003, retrieved 9/10/04 from http://wdb.wardsauto.com/magazinearticle; Phillips, "Confessions of a Car Salesman."

4. Walter A. Friedman, *Birth of a Salesman: The Transformation of Selling in America* (Cambridge, MA: Harvard University Press, 2004), 4–13, 218–24.

5. *Selling Chevrolets: A Book of Information for Chevrolet Retail Salesmen* (Detroit, MI: Chevrolet Motor Co., 1930), 36.

6. "Autos: Joe," *Newsweek*, 2 July 1973, 62–63; Ron Rogers, "The Super Salesmen," *Cars and Trucks*, February 1979, 20–25.

7. "Autos: Joe"; Rogers, "Super Salesmen."

8. Louise Closser Hale, *A Motor Car Divorce* (New York: Dodd, Mead, 1906), 148–51; Harold Whiting Slauson, "The Man Who Sells the Car," *Harper's Weekly*, 3 August 1912, 11–12; "Motor Salesmen to Be Mounted," *New York Times*, 31 March 1912, 10; "Selling Motor Cars Real Business Now," *New York Times*, 12 January 1913, 11.

9. R. G. Kelsey, "Salesman's Duties to His Customers," *New York Times*, 8 January 1911, 2; Homer McKee, "Intensified Sales—the Problem of the Automobile Industry," *Harper's Weekly*, 5 October 1912, 24.

10. "Be an Automobile Salesman" [Display Ad], *McClure's Magazine*, June 1916, 81.

11. Harold M. Parker, "Learning to Sell Autos at School," *Illustrated World*, April 1918, 262; Jacob H. Newmark, *Automobile Salesmanship* (Detroit, MI: Automobile Publishing Co., 1915), 19.

12. W. C. Sills, *Sales Talks: Being a Series of Man-to-Man Articles, Instructive and Inspirational* (New York: Chevrolet Motor Co., 1920).

13. C. D. Paxson, *How to Sell Automobiles* (Cleveland, OH: C. D. Paxson, 1917): 46–47.

14. "Guide to Materials for Dealership Personnel Development," Ford Divisions, Ford Motor Company, 1952, Ford Research Center, Acc 951, 7; George M. Riveire Jr., "Your Salesmen Can Sell More," *NADA Magazine*, May 1954, 34–36; "Techniques That Pay Off in Profit," *NADA Magazine*, March 1962, 32–34; "What Is the Best Approach to Selling?" *NADA Magazine*, July 1969, 28–29; J. Michel White, *Buying Your Next Car: How to Stick It to the Dealers Before the Dealer Can Stick It to You* (Tucson, AZ: Harbinger House, 1993), 17.

15. Kenneth B. Haas, "How to Take the 'Ice' Out of Price" (News Release), National Automobile Dealers Association Convention, Chicago, 1 February 1959; see also John O. Munn, *Automobile Selling: Letters to Salesmen* (Toledo, OH: J. O. Munn Co., 1955), 90.

16. Gerry Donohue, "Good Salesmanship," *Automotive Executive*, May 1987, 38.

17. John Bentley, "Salespeople: Know Thy Product," *Automotive Executive*, July 1985, 38–42; Phillips, "Confessions of a Car Salesman," 34.

18. Helene M. Lawson, *Ladies on the Lot: Women, Car Sales, and the Pursuit of the American Dream* (Lanham, MD: Rowman & Littlefield, 2000), 100; Bentley, "Salespeople: Know Thy Product," 35.

19. Ed Henry, "Confessions of a Car Salesman," *Kiplinger's Personal Finance Magazine*, March 1992, 48–53.

20. Newmark, *Automobile Salesmanship*, 76.

21. John Reed Scott, "Mrs. Randolph's Nerve," *Lippincott's Magazine*, December 1910, 712.

22. Art Hoffman, "Training Salespeople to Succeed," *Dealer World* [Ford], September 1991, 26–27.

23. Paul H. Nystrom, *Automobile Selling: A Manual for Dealers* (New York: Motor, the National Magazine of Motoring, 1919), 31; *Selling Chevrolets*, 60.

24. Flint, "Showroom Strategy," 18; Benjamin Cheever, "How to Sell Cars," *New Yorker*, 1 May 2000, 140.

25. *Chevrolet Presents* [c. 1941] (embedded in *Mystery Science Theatre 3000*, show #505, "Magic Voyage of Sinbad," 1993); Jack Tilles, *Trader Thorne* (Wilding Picture Productions for Ford Motor Company, 1949).

26. Phillips, "Confessions of a Car Salesman," 18; Al Griffin, "Tell It to Them on the Phone," *NADA Magazine*, August 1963, 14–18; Bury, *Automobile Dealer*, 14; Bernard Stengren, "Salesmen Hound GIs at Idlewild," *New York Times*, 9 March 1958, 16; *Salesman! A Close Look at Three Ford Professionals* (Ford Video Network, 1979).

27. Hoffman, "Training Salespeople," 27.

28. Homer Croy, "Buying a Car," *Harper's Weekly*, 6 February 1915, 139.

29. Bury, *Automobile Dealer*, 16; *Selling Chevrolets*, 72; Sam H. White, "What Makes a Good Salesman?" *NADA Magazine*, April 1956, 40–43; Jerry Flint, "Showroom Strategy: Price Labeling Fails to End Deceit in Auto Selling, Salesman Finds," *Wall Street Journal*, 5 May 1959, 1, 18; Friedman, *Birth of a Salesman*, 214.

30. Stengren, "Salesmen Hound GIs."

31. Bury, *Automobile Dealer*, 15; Joseph John Adamek, "A Study of Sales Training Materials and Plans with Recommendations to Improve the Training of Automobile Salesmen" (MS thesis, Northern Illinois University, 1963), 40; "A 16-Point Program for Prospectors," *NADA Magazine*, August 1963, 16–17.

32. Nystrom, *Automobile Selling*, 34–35.

33. K. B. K., "Tricks of the Trade-in," [letter to the editor], *Consumer Reports*, September 1953, 374; Groves, *How to Buy Automobiles*, 79; Phillips, "Confessions of a Car Salesman," 39.

34. "How You Can Make Out as an Auto Salesman," *Kiplinger Magazine*, April 1957, 19; Newmark, *Automobile Salesmanship*, 94.

35. "Untapped Customers," *Wall Street Journal*, 11 April 1958, 5; Joseph Bohn,

"Mystery Shoppers Rate Salespeople," *Automotive News*, 30 July 1984, 14; Mary Anne Shreve, "Showroom Sleuthing," *Automotive Executive*, May 1991, 24–27.

36. Robert Simison, "Softer Sell," *Wall Street Journal*, 11 January 1979, 1; "Questions Answered for Dealers at Convention Clinics," *NADA Magazine*, April 1950, 26, 30.

37. See, for example, "Making the Deal: Old Rules in a New Ball Game," *Consumer Reports*, April 1974, 300.

38. Bury, *Automobile Dealer*, 213.

39. Gregory Hill, *Over the Curb* (Rosemead, CA: Gregory Publications, 1973), 77.

40. Joy Browne, *The Used-Car Game: A Sociology of the Bargain* (Lexington, MA: Lexington Books, 1973), 51; Kevin J. McManus, *The Consumer's Edge: What the Automotive Dealer Doesn't Want You to Know!* (n.p.: 1995), 22.

41. Joseph C. Ingraham, "Automobiles: Ethics," *New York Times*, 1 September 1957, 21–23; Flint, "Showroom Strategy."

42. Ronald G. Shafer, "It's a Deal," *Wall Street Journal*, 13 June 1966, 218; Sam Crowther and Irwin Winehouse, *Highway Robbery* (New York: Stein and Day, 1966), 22–25.

43. Fred M. H. Gregory, "Have I Got a Deal for You," *Motor Trend*, July 1976, 81; Kurt Allen Weiss, *Have I Got a Deal for You! How to Buy or Lease Any Car Without Getting Run Over* (Franklin Lakes, NJ: Career Press, 1997), 83.

44. Manager of Sales Ford Motor Company, To: Chas. Hendy Jr., 8 June 1914, Detroit, Ford Research Center, record group 509, box 2.

45. Newmark, *Automobile Salesmanship*, 77; see also *Selling Chevrolets*, 92–93.

46. Roger Rapoport, "How I Made $193.85 Selling Cars," *Atlantic Monthly*, January 1970, 75–78; Joseph McElliott, "Selling Pianos," *The Bookman*, September 1927, 60–65; Frank I. Dorr, *Hayseed and Sawdust* (Boston: Wormsted, Smith, 1934), 64; Stanley C. Hollander, "Discount Retailing: An Examination of Some Divergences from the One-Price System in American Retailing" (Ph.D. diss., University of Pennsylvania, 1954), 23.

47. "The Care and Handling of Used Car Salesmen," *NADA Magazine*, March 1960, 30–31.

48. Jack Naylon, "Point Program for Selling," *Ford Dealer Magazine*, March–April, 1956, 3; for General Motors, see Adamek, "A Study of Sales Training Materials," 52.

49. Flint, "Showroom Strategy."

50. Richard Klein, "Full Routine System Spurs Sales and Profits," *Ford Dealer Magazine*, Summer 1979.

51. Joe Car [Denny Armstrong], *I'm a Legal Hold Up Man, I'm a Car Salesman* (Shawnee Mission, KA: Joe Car, 1977), 39; Gary Carr, *How to Outsmart the New Car Salesman* (New York: Macmillan, 1987), 71; Henry Luhring, "Automobile Salesmanship at Work: 'The Car Is Yours for Only $25 More,'" *Consumer Reports*, May 1950, 206–207.

52. Hector Olivas, "Dialogue with a Sales Pro," *Ford Dealer Magazine*, March–April, 1969, 8–12.

53. White, "What Makes a Good Salesman?"

54. Robertson, *How to Deal on an Automobile*, 76; Phillips, "Confessions of a Car Salesman," 8.

55. W. P. Mann, *How to Get the Best Buy from Your Car Dealer: An Inside View of What to Watch for in Buying a New or Used Car* (Hicksville, NY: Exposition Press, 1979), 4–5,

34–35; Darrell Parrish, *The Car Buyer's Art . . . How to Beat the Salesman at His Own Game* (Bellflower, CA: Book Express, 1992), 178–81.

56. Groves, *How to Buy Automobiles*, 14–15; Mann, *How to Get the Best Buy*, 40, 48–49.

57. Leo Reilly, *How to Outnegotiate Anyone (Even a Car Dealer!)* (Holbrook, MA: Bob Adams, 1994), 60.

58. Browne, *Used-Car Game*, 12, 33, 68–73.

59. Car, *I'm a Legal Hold Up Man*, 4.

60. Chicago Automobile Trade Association, *Automobile Selling by Practical Salesmen* (Chicago: Chicago Automobile Trace Association, 1924), 64.

61. Jesse Rainsford Sprague, "Confessions of a Ford Dealer," *Harper's*, June 1927, 26–35, 30.

62. See, for example, Joseph P. Turner, "Selling vs. Merchandising," *NADA Magazine*, August 1966, 12–13.

63. Warren Brown, "Keep the Keys and Beat the Dealer's System," *Washington Post*, 1 August 2004, G2.

64. Cheever, "How to Sell," 140; Benjamin Cheever, "Selling Ben Cheever," *Archipelago* (2001), retrieved 23/4/2006 from www.archipelago.org/vol5-3/cheever.htm; see also Paul Gray, "Nice Guys Finish First?" *Time*, 25 July 1994.

65. Robertson, *How to Deal on an Automobile*, 42.

66. Bennett, "A Charm School for Car Salesmen"; Dunk Chen, *Little Known Sources for Getting the Car of Your Dreams at a Fraction of the Market Price* (Medford, OR: DS Publications, 1989), 12.

67. Parrish, *Car Buyer's Art*, 147; Browne, *Used-Car Game*, 10.

68. "Auto Dealer," *Business Week*, 12 October 1957, 65–68.

69. Gary Erichson, *How to Sell Automobiles* (Smithtown, NY: Enlightened Sales Training, 1982), 67.

70. Car, *I'm a Legal Hold Up*, 11; Joseph S. Coyle, "Confessions of a Car Salesman," *Money*, April 1978, 98–99; Hill, *Over the Curb*, 18.

71. *Merchandising Cars and Trucks* (Washington, DC: Northwood Institute for National Automobile Dealers Association, 1967), 108; Car, *I'm a Legal Hold Up Man*, 41.

72. "Pencils Muffled in Coast Car Case," *New York Times*, 12 May 1957, 79; Rapoport, "How I Made," 76.

73. Coyle, "Confessions of a Car Salesman," 13.

74. White, *Buying Your Next Car*, 72–73; Parrish, *Car Buyer's Art*, 79–81.

75. Roald Dahl, *Matilda* (New York: Puffin Books, 1988).

76. James Reston, "Democrats in Doubt," *New York Times*, 12 July 1960, 21.

77. "Franklin Used Cars" [Display Ad], *New York Times*, 8 December 1909, 12.

78. Ray Goldman, "How to Buy a Second Hand Car," *Illustrated World*, January 1918, 742–45.

79. Frank Mitchell, *How to Buy, Keep and Enjoy Your Car* (New York: Arco Publishing, 1950), 6.

80. Lawrence Dietz, "Would You Buy a Used Car from This Man?" *Saturday Evening Post*, 24 August 1968, 56–59; Frederick J. Roth and Christopher A. Roth, "The History of Earl 'Mad Man' Muntz," *Vintage American Sports Cars*, 1 January 2006, www.american sportscars.com/muntz.

81. Dietz , "Would You Buy."

82. Ibid.

83. Paul G. Hoffman and James H. Greene, *Marketing Used Cars* (New York: Harper and Brothers, 1929), 6.

84. Maurice Baum, *Readings in Business Ethics: A Survey of the Principles and Problems of American Business* (Dubuque, IA: W. C. Brown, 1951), 71.

85. Marshall Spiegel, "Used Cars: Wheeling and Dealing," *Senior Scholastic*, 25 April 1968, 40.

86. "The Deals That Keep Used Cars Moving," *Business Week*, 19 September 1953, 88–94; Jenny L. King, "U.C. Dealers Fight Old Problem," *Automotive News*, 9 May 1983, 12.

87. John W. Allen, "Used Car Advertising and Display," 17 February 1953, NADA Convention 1953, San Francisco, National Automobile Dealers Association, McClean, Va.

88. Dave Conrad, "Representing the Final Link to America's Yankee Trader Tradition," *Automotive Executive*, September 1979, 28; Victor Block, "NADA Backs D.C. Used Car Expose," *NADA Magazine*, January 1960, 40–46.

89. Mitchell, "How to Buy," 124.

90. Robert Weber, "I was a used car salesman," *Cartoon Closeup, New Yorker*, 12 January 1987, www.cartoonbank.com.

91. Bruce McCall, "Getting Used to the Used Car Business Again," *Car and Driver*, June 1977, 22–23; see also Browne, *Used-Car Game*, 26–31.

92. William Hamilton, "The Customer," NADA Convention 1951, National Automobile Dealers Association, McClean, Va.; "Dramatic Skit Summary, Merchandising," *NADA Magazine*, February 1952, 68.

93. Hamilton, "The Customer"; "Dramatic Skit Summary, Merchandising," 68; Albert E. Norman, NADA Convention and Exhibition, Publicity, vol. 1, 31, Washington, DC, January 1956, [Press Release], National Automobile Dealers Association, McClean, Va.

94. Lois Cohorst, *High Mileage: Behind Every Successful Car Dealer Is a Woman With Jumper Cables and a Tow Rope* (Hillsboro, KS: Hearth Publishing, 1995), 90; Foster R. Gaylord, *Automotive Industry — a Macro View* (n.p.: Northwood Institute; National Automobile Dealers Association; American Truck Dealers, 1984), 201; Browne, *Used-Car Game*, 40–41.

95. W. H. "Duke" Wilcox, "Automotive Merchandising in the Year 1999," *Automotive Executive*, October 1979, 66–68.

96. Weiss, "Have I Got a Deal," 77; Wolfington, "The Customer, Thinking Through"; "Hit 'Em Where We Live," *Road and Track*, November 1985, 26; Carol A. Leonard, "Prostitution and Changing Social Norms in America" (Ph.D. diss., Syracuse University, 1979); Joan Mooney, "Satisfaction Guaranteed," *Automotive Executive*, October 1987, 26–33. For a more positive spin, see Joan Mooney, "Getting Better All the Time," *Automotive Executive*, June 1999.

97. Erichson, *How to Sell Automobiles*, 68.

98. Associated Press, "Introducing the Robot Car Dealer," *CNN.Com/Technology*, 11 December 2002, retrieved 11/12/02 from www.cnn.com/2002/tech/ptech/12/11/japan.robot.ap/.

99. S. E. Madeline, "Not a Price Ad in Five Years—and Sales Have Tripled," November–December 1965, *Ford Dealer Magazine*; "Florida Auto Dealer Ads Aim to Upgrade Salesman's Image," *Advertising Age*, 8 January 1968, 64.

100. National Automobile Dealers Association, Convention and Exhibition, Publicity, vol. 1, 1955, [Press Release], Chicago, NADA, McClean, Va.

101. "Car Sellers Shun Meeting on Ethics," *New York Times*, 23 June 1961, 14; "Auto Dealers to Get Ethics Code Today in 'House Cleaning,'" *New York Times*, 22 June 1961, 33.

102. Daniel L. Lionel, "8–Page Section Rides on Auto Dealer Code," *Editor and Publisher*, 24 March 1962, 38; see also Richard Munro, *How to Sell Cars: A Complete Manual on Selling New and Used Cars and Trucks* (Toronto: General Publishing Co., 1962), 104–105.

103. William E. Hancock, "The Case for Self-Regulation," *Cars and Trucks*, October 1971, 42–45.

104. Leslie Maria, "Selling Certification," *Automotive Executive*, January 1995, 20–21.

105. Ibid., 20.

106. For example, see Herman Melville, "The Lightening-Rod Man," in *The Piazza Tales* (London: Constable, 1923).

107. Coyle, *Confessions*, 5.

108. Bury, *Automobile Dealer*, 161.

109. Car, *I'm a Legal Hold Up*, 37–38.

110. Rapoport, "How I Made," 75.

111. Groves, *How to Buy Automobiles*, 117. For experimental confirmation of this, see Deborah Larrance et al., "Competence and Incompetence: Assymetric Responses to Women and Men on a Sex-Linked Task," *Personality and Social Psychology Bulletin* 5, no. 3 (1979).

112. Bury, *Automobile Dealer*, 156–57.

113. Munro, "How to Sell," 154–58.

114. Manuel G. Velasquez, *Business Ethics: Concepts and Cases* (Englewood Cliffs, NJ: Prentice Hall, 1982), 235–39.

115. Catherine Saint Louis, "What They Were Thinking," *New York Times Magazine*, 27 August 2000, 26.

116. Marc H. Stertz, "Odds & Ends," *Automotive Executive*, September 1995, 3.

117. Browne, *Used-Car Game*, 35; Phillips, "Confessions of a Car Salesman," 21.

118. Donohue, "Good Salesmanship," 37–38.

119. Browne, *Used-Car Game*, 19, 54; Jeff Gaydos, "How to Curb Sales Staff Turnover," *Dealer World* [Ford], November–December 1991, 12–13; Lawson, *Ladies on the Lot*, 9, 23; James T. Milord and Raymond P. Perry, "Traits and Performance of Automobile Salesmen," *Journal of Social Psychology* 103 (1977): 163–64.

120. Susan Biddle Jaffe, "Creating Your Own Stellar Sellers," *Automotive Executive*, April 1989, 26–28; Gaydos, "How to Curb"; Ivy L. Gilbert, "Service Begets Sales: An Investigation into the Relationship of Automotive Dealership Customer Service Satisfaction with Sales Success" (Ph.D. diss., Western Michigan University, 1986), 55.

121. Browne, *Ladies on the Lot*, 36–39, 40–41.

122. "On Horse Dealing," *The Athenaeum* (Boston), 1 August 1825, 363.

123. Bury, *Automobile Dealer*, 310; Bartley, "How to Buy," 118–19; Browne, *Used-Car Game*, 114–21; Hill, *Over the Curb*, 101–102; Remar Sutton, *Don't Get Taken Every Time: The Insider's Guide to Buying Your Next Car* (New York: Viking, 1982, 2001), 395–98; Robertson, *How to Deal on an Automobile*, 11–16; Parrish, *Car Buyer's Art*, 150–54.

124. Phillips, "Confessions of a Car Salesman," 6.

125. Ibid., 21.

SEVEN: Bargaining and Gender

1. Dennis A. Williams, "Making the Best Deal for New Wheels," *Black Enterprise*, November 1983, 82.

2. John H. Eagal, "The Reminiscences of Mr. John H. Eagal Sr.," Ford Research Center, record group 65, box 17, July 1953.

3. "Advice to the First Car Pest," *Puck*, 2 January 1915, 19.

4. Allen F. Jung, "Price Variations Among Automobile Dealers in Chicago, Illinois," *Journal of Business* 32, no. 4 (October 1959): 315–26; idem, "Price Variations Among Automobile Dealers in Metropolitan Chicago," *Journal of Business* 33 (January 1960): 31–43; E. Scott Maynes, "Variations in Automobile Prices: Lessons for Consumers," *Journal of Business-University of Chicago* 1962, 201–204; "The Voice of the Consumer," *NADA Magazine*, September 1968, 20–24; Robert B. Cialdini, Leonard Bickman, and John T. Cacioppo, "An Example of Consumeristic Social Psychology: Bargaining Tough in the New Car Showroom," *Journal of Applied Sociology* 9, no. 2 (1979): 115–26; David H. Furse, Girish N. Punj, and David W. Stewart, "A Typology of Individual Search Strategies Among Purchasers of New Automobiles," *Journal of Consumer Research*, March 1984, 417–31; Christina J. Taylor and Sharon M. Dawid, "Bargaining for a New Car: The Knowledgeable Versus the Naive Consumer," *Psychological Reports*, August 1986, 284–86.

5. "Ford Sales Manual," 1926, Ford Research Center, record group 175.

6. "Direct Selling Now Challenges Dealer's Place in Motor Industry," *Business Week*, 9 September 1931, 13–14.

7. Charles Coolidge Parlin and Fred Bremier, *The Passenger Car Industry: Report of a Survey* (Philadelphia: Curtis Publishing Company, 1932), 64.

8. Robert Simison, "Softer Sell," *Wall Street Journal* (New York), 11 January 1979, 29.

9. *Merchandising Cars and Trucks* (Washington, DC: Northwood Institute for National Automobile Dealers Association, 1967), 83; Leo Reilly, *How to Outnegotiate Anyone (Even a Car Dealer!)* (Holbrook, Mass.: Bob Adams, 1994), 55-56.

10. Stephen J. Miller, "The Social Base of Sales Behavior," *Social Problems* 12, no. 1 (Summer 1964): 20-22; *Merchandising Cars and Trucks*, 83; Joy Browne, *The Used-Car Game: A Sociology of the Bargain* (Lexington, MA: Lexington Books, 1973), 107, 111; Chandler Phillips, "Confessions of a Car Salesman," 2004, part 8: parting shots, retrieved 12/9/2004 from www.edmunds.com/advice/buying/articles.

11. Theodore H. Smith, *The Marketing of Used Automobiles* (Columbus, OH: Bureau of Business Research, Ohio State University, 1941), 113; see also Senate Automobile Marketing Subcommittee of the Committee on Interstate and Foreign Commerce, *Automobile Price Labeling*, 85 Cong., 2 sess., 21–24 April 1958, 59.

12. Richard S. Tedlow, *New and Improved: The Story of Mass Marketing in America* (Boston: Harvard Business School Press, 1996), 158; see also "How to Buy a New Car," *House and Garden*, September 1959, 133.

13. Senate Automobile Marketing Subcommittee, *Automobile Price Labeling*, 3.

14. Franklin B. Evans, "Correlates of Automobile Shopping Behavior," *Journal of Marketing*, October 1962, 75.

15. Jim Bright, "Success is a Four-Letter Word," *Dealer World* [Ford], June 1985, 8–9; Gregory Hill, *Over the Curb* (Rosemead, CA: Gregory Publications, 1973), 28.

16. Michael Lamm, "The Used Car: Games Salesmen Play," *Motor Trend*, September 1975, 29.

17. Gary Carr, *How to Outsmart the New Car Salesman* (New York: Macmillan, 1987) 75; Phillips, "Confessions of a Car Salesman," 5.

18. Michael Royce, *Beat the Car Salesman* (Boca Raton, FL: American Media Mini Mags, 2002).

19. Carr, *How to Outsmart*, 96; "How to Buy a New Car and Sell Your Old One," *Motor Trend*, May 1975, 45; Herb Adams, "The Tenderfoot's New Car Buying Guide," *Motor Trend*, January 1980, 118–20.

20. Carl Cahill, "Listen, You Salesmen/Listen, Mr. Cahill," *NADA Magazine*, February 1965, 48; see also James B. Treece, "Dealing With a Car Dealer Shouldn't Be So Demeaning," *Business Week*, 12 June 1989, 83.

21. Helen Kahn, "Car Buyers Want More Price Data, Survey Finds," *Automotive News*, 5 May 1986, 26.

22. Brenda M. Eisenhauer, "Haggle Over Car Prices? Yes, Please," *American Demographics*, April 1995, 16–18.

23. Phillips, "Confessions of a Car Salesman," 20.

24. "Hit 'Em Where We Live," 26.

25. Grace Lichtenstein, "Auto Dealers Bitterly Complain Over 'Embezzling Consumers,'" *New York Times*, 11 September 1971, 53.

26. Senate Subcommittee of the Committee on Interstate and Foreign Commerce, *Automobile Marketing Practices*, Part 1, 84 Cong., 2 sess., January–March 1956, 11.

27. "Complaints," Public Relations, Ford Division, 1950–1957, Ford Research Center, record group 669, box 1. For findings of positive customer reactions, see Geoff Sundstrom and Jesse Snyder, "Studies Clash on Sales Competence," *Automotive News*, 19 January 1987, 3; "New Car Buyers Sold by Ads, Dearly Love Their Dealers, Ford Study Shows," *Advertising Age*, 13 October 1958; Glenn Steven Lee, "A Customer Satisfaction Automobile Survey" (MA thesis, California State University, Long Beach, 1990), 31.

28. Dayr Reis, Leticia Pena, and Paulo A. Lopes, "Customer Satisfaction: The Historical Perspective," *Management Decision* 41, no. 2 (2003): 195–98.

29. Susan Strasser, *Satisfaction Guaranteed: The Making of the American Mass Market* (New York: Pantheon Books, 1989); Mary Anne Shreve, "CSI—Pie in the Sky," *Automotive Executive*, October 1998, 26–27.

30. "Danger for the Automobile Buyer" [Display Ad], *New York Times*, 20 April 1917, 22.

31. Don Valentine, "What Sold Me!" *NADA Magazine*, November 1953, 56–57.

32. Senate Subcommittee of the Committee on Interstate and Foreign Commerce, *Automobile Marketing Practices*, 84 Cong., 2 sess., Jan., Feb., Mar. 1956, 28-29.

33. C. E. Groves, *How to Buy Automobiles* (New York: Information Incorporated, 1970), 127-28; J. M. H., "Tips for the New-Car Buyer," *Dun's Review*, September 1974, 105-15; Darrell Parrish, *The Car Buyer's Art: How to Beat the Salesman at His Own Game* (Bellflower, CA: Book Express, 1992), 52.

34. Jung, "Price Variations," 1959; Jung, "Price Variations," 1960; Allen F. Jung, "Finding a Better Deal on a New Car," *Business Horizons*, March–April 1983, 34–36.

35. Lizabeth Cohen, "Encountering Mass Culture at the Grassroots: The Experience of Chicago Workers in the 1920s," *American Quarterly* 41, no. 1 (1989): 23.

36. Ian Ayres and Peter Siegelman, "Race and Gender Discrimination in Bargaining for a New Car," *American Economic Review* 85, no. 3 (1995): 318.

37. Ayres and Siegelman, "Race and Gender"; William E. Schimidt, "White Men Get Better Deals on Cars, Study Finds," *New York Times Magazine*, 13 December 1990, 26; see also Gordon L. Wise, "Differential Pricing and Treatment by New-Car Salesmen: The Effect of the Prospect's Race, Sex, and Dress," *Journal of Business* 47 (April 1974); Gordon L. Wise, Myron K. Cox, and Charles Floto, "Sex and Race Discrimination in the New-Car Showroom: A Fact or Myth?" *Journal of Consumer Affairs* (Winter 1977): 107–13; Kenneth McNeil et al., "Market Discrimination Against the Poor and the Impact of Consumer Disclosure Laws: The Used Car Industry," *Law and Society Review* 13, no. 3 (Spring 1979): 695–720. For discrimination against poor people, see Avelardo Valdez, "Chicano Used-Car Dealers: A Social World in Microcosm," *Urban Life* 13, no. 2–3 (October 1984); Fred C. Akers, "Negro and White Automobile-Buying Behavior: New Evidence," *Journal of Marketing Research* (August 1968): 283–89.

38. Diana B. Henriques, "Review of Nissan Car Loans Finds That Blacks Pay More," *New York Times*, 4 July 2001, 1.

39. Groves, *How to Buy Automobiles*, 91.

40. "How to Shop for a New Car," *Consumer Reports*, May 1955, 222–29.

41. Albert Q. Maisel, "The Art of Buying a New Car," *Reader's Digest*, November 1957, 48–51.

42. Martin H. Bury, *The Automobile Dealer* (Philadelphia: Philpenn Publishing, 1958), 17.

43. Watson Fenimore, "6 Ways to Save Money Buying a New Car," *Popular Science*, October 1960, 86; see also "Smart Way to Buy a Car," *Changing Times*, December 1962, 22; Groves, *How to Buy Automobiles*.

44. "Prices, a Starting Point for Bargaining," *Consumer Reports*, April 1963, 162.

45. "The Art of Buying a New Car," *Consumer Reports*, April 1969, 176.

46. "Dealing with the Dealer," *Consumer Reports*, April 1973, 198–202; "Dealing with the Dealer, 1975: After the Carnival's Over," *Consumer Reports*, April 1975, 220–21.

47. "Deals on Wheels: You Can Drive a Hard Bargain in a Soft Economy," *Consumer Reports*, April 2002, 18–21.

48. Joe Car [Denny Armstrong], *I'm a Legal Hold Up Man, I'm a Car Salesman* (Shawnee Mission, KA: Joe Car, 1977); Joseph S. Coyle, "Confessions of a Car Salesman," *Money*, April 1978, 98-99.

49. Philip F. Tennyson, *Getting Screwed: A Satire of Car Dealer Manipulation* (Portland, OR: Immortality Incorporated, 1978).

50. L. J. Brum, *How to Beat the Car Dealer at His Own Game: Buying a New or Used Car* (San Jose, CA: B-M Consumer Publications, 1981), 23.

51. Parrish, *Car Buyer's Art*; J. Michel White, *Buying Your Next Car: How to Stick It to the Dealer Before the Dealer Can Stick It to You* (Tucson, AZ: Harbinger House, 1993); "Steal a Car," *Men's Health*, October 1999, 61.

52. For example, see Mike Willingham, *The New Car Dealer's Secret Agenda: An Insider's View of Dealer Strategies, Salesman's Tactics, the Finance Office Tricks and Ploys, and How You Can Be In Charge of Negotiations* (Melbourne, FL: National Negotiating Services, 1992); White, *Buying Your Next Car*; Parrish, *The Car Buyer's Art*; Sal Fariello, *The People's Car Book: The One Essential Handbook for People Who Don't Trust Mechanics, Car*

Salesmen, or Car Manufacturers (New York: St. Martin's Press, 1993); Kevin J. McManus, *The Consumer's Edge: What the Automotive Dealer Doesn't Want You to Know!* (np: 1995).

53. Remar Sutton, *Don't Get Taken Every Time: The Insider's Guide to Buying Your Next Car* (New York: Viking, 1982, 2001).

54. Royce, *Beat the Car.*

55. Jung, "Price Variations," 1959, 1960; Fenimore, "6 Ways"; "Smart Way"; Merle E. Dowd, "How to Bargain," *Popular Mechanics*, November 1968, 77; Groves, *How to Buy Automobiles*, 1, 99; Peter Frey, "Can You Get a Deal?" *Motor Trend*, September 1978, 48–49; Adams, "Tenderfoot's," 118; Sandra Hinson, "Buying a Car? Ex-Dealer Remar Sutton Tells How Not to Get Taken for a Ride," *People*, 6 June 1983, 91–92; Willingham, *Dealer Strategies*, 12, 21; McManus, *Consumer's Edge*, 20–21; Kurt Allen Weiss, *Have I Got a Deal for You! How to Buy or Lease any Car Without Getting Run Over* (Franklin Lakes, NJ: Career Press, 1997).

56. Reilly, *How to Outnegotiate Anyone.*

57. Duane L. Gregg, "How to Get the Best Deal on Your Next New Car," *Better Homes and Gardens*, September 1971, 30; Paula Sullivan, "Getting a Good Deal on a New Car," *Essence*, November 1982, 120; Jerry Edgerton, "Driving a Hard Bargain," *Money*, January 1982, 95–96; Ken Zino, "The Right Way to Buy a Car," *Home Mechanix*, September 1989, 29–31; Mel Bloom, "Tales Out of Car-Salesman School," *Readers Digest*, January 1990, 105–108; Jeff Guitierrez, "Insider's Car-Buying Tips," *Consumers Digest*, January–February 1994, 71–73.

58. "Automobiles at Your Own Prices" [Display Ad], *New York Times*, 20 February 1910, 5.

59. Jenny L. King, "Buyers Called Brainwashed, Want New Car Giveaways," *Automotive News*, 8 September 1980, 20–21; Jenny L. King, "Curbside Transactions Grow in Lusty Used Car Market," *Automotive News*, 7 September 1981, 46.

60. "F. Turner Automobile Broker" [Display Ad], *New York Times*, 29 November 1908, 3.

61. "Any Make New Automobile" [Classified Ad], *New York Times*, 3 May 1914, 5.

62. "Auto Broker Seized on Larceny Charge," *New York Times*, 6 March 1947, 26.

63. "Trust Suit Filed Against Nissan for Alleged Pricing Conspiracy," *New York Times*, 1 July 1972, 27; Jake Kelderman, "Court Bans Auto Brokers in Maryland," *Automotive News*, 24 December 1984, 7.

64. "The Cheapest Way to Buy a Car," *Good Housekeeping*, May 1981, 260; Julie Candler, "New Car Buying—Everything You Need to Know," *Ms.*, November 1984, 32; Melinda Grenier Guiles, "Car Buying Services Can Save Money Especially for Those Who Hate Haggling," *Wall Street Journal*, 23 April 1985, 33; "Something New: Car Buyer for Hire," *Nation's Business*, December 1982, 78–79.

65. Douglas Lavin and Krystal Miller, "Goodby to Haggling: Savvy Customers Are Buying Their Cars Like Refrigerators," *Wall Street Journal*, 20 August 1993, 1.

66. Charles A. Jaffe, "Joining the Club," *Automotive Executive*, February 1993, 26–28.

67. Joseph J. Corn, "Work and Vehicles: A Comment and Note," in Martin Wachs and Margaret Crawford, eds., *The Car and the City: The Automobile and the Built Environment* (Ann Arbor, MI: University of Michigan Press, 1992), 25.

68. John Keats, *The Insolent Chariots* (Greenwich, CT: Fawcett Publications, 1958), 9–11.

69. Quoted in Carroll Pursell, "The Construction of Masculinity and Technology," *Svenska National Kommittaen Feor Teknikhistoria* 11 (1993): 208.

70. Robert Slofs, "Buying an Automobile," *Outing*, December 1909, 345.

71. Gordon Grant, "The New Ritual," *Puck*, 16 October 1912, 7.

72. Paul H. Nystrom, *Automobile Selling: A Manual for Dealers* (New York: Motor, the National Magazine of Motoring, 1919), 77.

73. John Reed Scott, "Mrs. Randolph's Nerve," *Lippincott's Magazine*, December 1910, 708–18.

74. Louise Closser Hale, *A Motor Car Divorce* (New York: Dodd, Mead, 1906), 158.

75. "Advice to the First Car Pest," *Puck*, 2 January 1915, 19."

76. Virginia Scharff, "Gender, Electricity, and Automobility," in *The Car and the City*, ed. Wachs and Crawford, 84–85; see also Cindy Donatelli, "Driving the Suburbs: Mini-vans, Gender, and Family Values," *Material History Review* 54 (Fall 2001).

77. Paula D. Hodges, "Ford's Designs on Women," *Automotive Industries*, November 1981, 43.

78. Day Allen Willey, "Who Can Afford an Automobile?" *Good Housekeeping*, May 1909, 476.

79. Kevin F. McCrohan and Jay M. Finkelman, "Social Character and the New Automobile Industry," *California Management Review* (Fall 1981): 58–67.

80. Ken Gross, "The Name Game," *Automotive Executive*, February 1994, 40–43.

81. "Psychology of a Sale," *Current Opinion*, February 1920, 213.

82. "The Used Car Shopper: He Leaves Wife at Home, and Generally Doesn't Haggle," *Business Week*, 19 December 1959, 79.

83. C. L. Edholm, "Selling the Second-Hand Car," *Lippincott's Monthly Magazine*, August 1914, 211–14.

84. Gregory Hill, *Over the Curb* (Rosemead, CA: Gregory Publications, 1973), 36.

85. Helene M. Lawson, "Service Values–Profit Goals: The Divided Selves of Car Sales Women" (Ph.D. diss., Loyola University of Chicago, 1991), 6.

86. Benjamin Cheever, "How to Sell Cars," *New Yorker*, 1 May 2000, 136-55.

87. Ted Orme, "Top Guns," *Automotive Executive*, April 1989, 19; see also Ed Henry, "Confessions of a Car Salesman," *Kiplinger's Personal Finance Magazine*, March 1992, 48–53.

88. Parrish, *Car Buyer's Art*, 2–3.

89. Hill, *Over the Curb*, 80.

90. Marc Baldwin, "Discourse of the Deal: The Car Salesman as Symbol," in *Dominant Symbols in Popular Culture*, ed. Ray B. Browne, Marshall W. Fishwick, and Kevin O. Browne (Bowling Green, OH: Bowling Green State University, 1990), 167.

91. Browne, *Used-Car Game*, 49, 60.

92. Hale, *A Motor Car Divorce*, 117.

93. "The Winton Sixteen-Six" [Display Ad], *New York Times*, 3 November 1907, 11.

94. "We Want You to See This Latest Chalmers Model" [Display Ad], *New York Times*, 31 March 1911, 12.

95. "Automobile Training: A Pacific Coast School of Instruction," *Overland Monthly and Out West Magazine*, March 1909, 28.

96. Curt McConnell, *A Reliable Car and a Woman Who Knows It: The First Coast-to-Coast Auto Trips by Women, 1899–1916* (Jefferson, NC: McFarland, 2000).

97. Martin Wachs, "Men, Women and Wheels: The Historical Basis of Gender Dif-

ferences in Travel Patterns," in *The Changing Population: Impacts of Working Women and the Aging on Travel Patterns and Transportation*, 66th Annual Meeting of the Transportation Research Board, Washington, DC, January 1987, 7.

98. Virginia Scharff, *Taking the Wheel: Women and the Coming of the Motor Age* (New York: Free Press, 1991); Georgine Clarsen, "The Dainty Toe and the Brawny Male Arm: Conceptions of Bodies and Power in Automobile Technology," *Australian Feminist Studies* 15, no. 32 (2000): 153–63.

99. Jacob H. Newmark, *Automobile Salesmanship* (Detroit, MI: Automobile Publishing Co., 1915), 103–204; see also Eric Dregni and Karl Hagstrom Miller, *Ads That Put America on Wheels* (Osceola, WI: Motorbooks International, 1996), 103.

100. "Announcing Series Eight Cole" [Display Ad], *New York Times*, 23 September 1912, 9.

101. "Look for the Man in the Moon Car" [Display Ad], *New York Times*, 14 May 1916, 4; James H. Collins, "Putting the Motor on the Counter," *McClure's*, October 1916, 21; Charles L. Sanford, "Woman's Place in American Car Culture," in *The Automobile and American Culture*, ed. David L. Lewis and Laurence Goldstein (Ann Arbor: University of Michigan Press, 1983), 137–51.

102. Charles Coolidge Parlin and Fred Bremier, *The Passenger Car Industry: Report of a Survey* (Philadelphia: Curtis Publishing Company, 1932), 90.

103. Homer McKee, "What Salesmanship Means," *Harper's Weekly*, 11 January 1913, 15.

104. George H. Brown, "The Automobile Buying Decision within the Family," in Nelson N. Foote, ed., *Household Decision-Making* (New York: New York University Press, 1961), 193–99; Lloyd Wendt and Herman Kogan, *Give the Lady What She Wants: The Story of Marshall Field & Company* (Chicago: Rand McNally, 1952), 276.

105. Jacob H. Newmark, *Automobile Salesmanship* (Detroit, MI: Automobile Publishing Co., 1915), 73; James H. Collins, "Putting the Motor on the Counter," *McClure's*, October 1916, 21.

106. Collins, "Putting the Motor on the Counter," 23; *Ford Sales Manual*, 1926, Ford Research Center, record group 175.

107. *Selling Chevrolets: A Book of Information for Chevrolet Retail Salesmen* (Detroit, MI: Chevrolet Motor Co., 1930), 85, 155; see also Walter A. Friedman, *Birth of a Salesman: The Transformation of Selling in America* (Cambridge, MA: Harvard University Press, 2004), 222.

108. Sam E. Polson, "Dress Right! for Sales Success," *Cars and Trucks*, May 1979, 22–23; Gary James, "Ford Targets Women's Market," *Automotive Executive*, July 1985, 41–42; George P. Blumberg, "To Sell a Car That Women Love, It Helps If Women Sell It," *New York Times*, 26 October 2005, 12; Newmark, *Automobile Salesmanship*, 74, 80; *How to Run a Retail Automobile Business at a Profit* (Chicago: A. W. Shaw Co., 1917), 43; Nystrom, *Automobile Selling*, 70–71; Helen Bruno, "Why the Emphasis on Women," *NADA Magazine*, July 1955, 46; Sam H. White, "What Makes a Good Salesman?" *NADA Magazine*, April 1956, 41.

109. *Ford Sales Manual*, 41.

110. Alexander Johnston, "A Check List for Him Who Buys," *Country Life*, May 1917, 108.

111. "Oh, of Course!" [Cartoon], *Puck*, 2 January 1915, 10.

112. Bruno, "Why The Emphasis on Women."

113. Charlotte Huber, "Wanna Buy a Car, Lady?" *Retail Executive*, 19 July 1939, 13.

114. Sherman Chatzky, "Protest with Your Feet," *Money*, February 1999, 190.

115. Patricia Hinsberg, "DOT Tackles Showroom Chauvinism," *Automotive News*, 9 October 1978, 49; "Women Important to Car Business," *Automotive News*, 10 July 1978, 29.

116. Steve Huntley, "Selling Cars: A Vanishing American Art," *U.S. News & World Report*, 29 August 1983, 59; Joan Mooney, "Dealers Tune Approach to Meet Women's Market," *Automotive Executive*, August 1986, 71–75; Marc H. Stertz, "I've Got News for You," *Automotive Executive*, April 1991, 4; Mary Anne Shreve, "It's a Woman's World," *Automotive Executive*, November 1993, 18–20.

117. Marc H. Stertz, "Media Meanderings," *Automotive Executive*, August 1996, 2.

118. Patience Eden, "Business of Buying a Car," *Country Life*, September 1930, 50.

119. Loren Dunton, "How to Sell (Cars) to Women," *Ford Dealer Magazine*, May–June, 1966, 35–41; Nowland and Company, "Automobile Bootlegging: Pilot Study of Consumer Motives," ca. 1956, Ford Research Center, record group 695, box 6.

120. Paula Ganzi Licata, "She's Not What Dealers Bargain For," *Newsday* (New York), 13 October 2003, k: 81.

121. Louis J. Haugh, "Auto Promo Efforts to Women Not Carried to Dealer Level," *Advertising Age*, 23 January 1978, 56.

122. "More Women Buy Their Own Cars," *Wall Street Journal*, 18 June 1978, 1.

123. David W. Harless and George E. Hoffer, "Do Women Pay More for New Vehicles? Evidence from Transaction Price Data," *American Economic Review* 92, no. 1 (March 2002): 270–79.

124. Denise McCluggage, "How to Buy a Used Car," *American Home*, April 1971, 52–58; "Car Buying Without Fear," *U.S. News and World Report*, 12 October 1987, 76.

125. Meg Greenfield, "Nightfight with the Nicest Guy in Town," *The Reporter*, 14 July 1966, 35–37; Mike Knepper, "How to Get the Best New Car Deal," *Better Homes and Gardens*, May 1986, 91; Amy Lumet, "What's the Deal?" *Seventeen*, October 1993, 80; Laura Flynn McCarthy, "How to Buy a Used Car," *Seventeen*, May 1987, 90.

126. "Women Important to Car Business," *Automotive News*, 10 July 1978.

127. Gerald D. Bell, "Self-Confidence and Persuasion in Car Buying," *Journal of Marketing Research*, February 1967, 6–52.

128. Carr, *How to Outsmart*, 22; Parrish, *Car Buyer's Art*, 20.

129. "Women Have Become Car-Buying Force," *American International Automobile Dealers*, 6 June 2006, Detroit News, retrieved 21/06/2004 from www.aiada.org/id=42458.

130. "Survey Finds 77 Percent of Women Car Buyers Continue to Bring Man Along to Dealership," *The Auto Channel*, 1 June 2006, retrieved 21/7/2006 from www.theauto channel.com/news/2006/06/01/009311.

131. Helene M. Lawson, "Attacking Nicely: Care Saleswomen Adapt to an Incompatible Role," *Sociological Viewpoints* 10 (Fall 1994): 7.

132. Laurel Leff, "Rough Tough Males Who Sell Autos Fall for Feminine Touch," *Wall Street Journal*, 5 August 1977, 1.

133. For an alternative view, see S. Vernon Fuller, "Personal Difficulties Experienced by Automobile Sales Persons" (Ph.D. diss., Colorado State Teachers College, 1932), 4.

134. Margaret Jacques, "From Music to Motors," *Everybody's Magazine*, September 1914, 118.

135. Ginny Painter, "I Was Born Talking: Lois Koontz Nypl on Selling Cars," *Goldenseal* (Summer 2003): 45–49.

136. "Women Invade the Automobile Sales Room," *Wall Street Journal*, 6 November 1973, 1.

137. "Big Auto Agency Invites the Ladies to Make a Career of Selling His Wares," *Business Week*, 20 April 1957, 83; William D. Smith, "Saleswomen Can Boost Profits," *NADA Magazine*, July 1961, 66–67; John A. Russell, "No-Showroom Dealership Ranks as a Top Saab Outlet," *Automotive News*, 24 October 1977, 32.

138. Helene M. Lawson, *Ladies on the Lot: Women, Car Sales, and the Pursuit of the American Dream* (Lanham, MD: Rowman & Littlefield, 2000), 2; Mary Connelly, "From Vehicle Design to Retail, Ford Wants to Be Female Friendly," *Automotive News*, 17 March 1997, 3; Maureen McDonald, "Spreading the Word on Selling to and by Women," *Automotive News*, 8 February 1988, 54.

139. John Bentley, "Salespeople: Know Thy Product," July 1985, 39, 41; Raymond Serafin, "Special Showroom Deals in Different Attitudes," *Advertising Age*, 15 September 1986, 16; Patricia Kelsey, "Distaff Staff," *Automotive News*, 18 August 1986, E4; Lawson, *Ladies on the Lot*, 73–75.

140. Bob Girling, "Where "Fair" Rates Excellent," *Dealer World* [Ford], November–December 1986, 12–13; Lawson, "Attacking Nicely."

E P I L O G U E : Still Horse Trading in the Internet Age

1. "Facts for Motor Car Buyers" [Display Ad], *New York Times*, 1 October 1916, 12.

2. Doron P. Levin, "Car Buyers Caught in the Middle of GM's Battle with Discounters," *Wall Street Journal*, 21 June 1985, 29; Marc H. Stertz, "Margins Ain't Marginal," *Automotive Executive*, September 1994, 2.

3. "Everything Goes in Autos—Almost," *Business Week*, 29 March 1958, 26.

4. Kurt Allen Weiss, *Have I Got a Deal for You! How to Buy or Lease any Car Without Getting Run Over* (Franklin Lakes, NJ: Career Press, 1997), 81–82.

5. Ann Arnott, "The Really Shrewd Way to Buy a Car," *McCall's*, June 1989, 116.

6. Helene M. Lawson, *Ladies on the Lot: Women, Car Sales, and the Pursuit of the American Dream* (Lanham, MD: Rowman & Littlefield, 2000), 61–63.

7. Marc H. Stertz, "Divine Right," *Automotive Executive*, January 1994.

8. Ronald G. Shafer, "It's a Deal," *Wall Street Journal*, 13 June 1966, 1.

9. "Prices, a Starting Point for Bargaining," *Consumer Reports*, April 1963, 162–63; Merle E. Dowd, "How to Bargain," *Popular Mechanics*, November 1968, 76–81; D. L. Gregg, "How to Get the Most from Your Car at Trade-in Time," *Better Homes and Gardens*, September 1970, 12; "How to Buy a New Car and Sell Your Old One," *Motor Trend*, May 1975, 44; Douglas M. Lidster, "Buying a New Car? Here's How to Get the Best Deal," *Better Homes and Gardens*, September 1976, 39; "How to Drive a Hard Bargain Buying a New Car," *Business Week*, 26 January 1981, 121–22.

10. "Its Print Efforts Rejected, Car/Puter Turns to TV, Radio," *Advertising Age*, 12 June 1972, 12; Pat Fenton, "How to Buy a New Car Without Feeling You Bought the Brooklyn Bridge," *Retirement Living*, March 1973, 58; Robert J. Cole, "Personal Finance," *New York Times*, 29 October 1973, 55.

11. "Car Buyers Are Offered List of Dealer Prices," *Wall Street Journal*, 31 March 1983, 4.

12. Gerry Donohue, "Good Salesmanship," *Automotive Executive*, May 1987, 33–38; Linda Marsa, "Wheeling and Dealing: Savvy Shoppers Are Spending Less for Their New Cars," *Omni*, June 1994, 18.

13. "A Machine That Sells Automobiles," *Business Week*, 17 April 1954, 62.

14. "Would You Buy a Car from This Computer?" *Business Week*, 17 December 1984, 94.

15. Arthur Flax, "Net Results," *Automotive Executive*, October 1995, 18–19.

16. Ed Henry, "The Virtual Car Buyer," *Kiplinger's Personal Finance Magazine*, September 1995, 145–50.

17. Paul Solman, "Virtual Showroom," *Online Focus/Online NewsHour*, 29 December 1997, PBS, retrieved 24/6/2006 from www.pbs.org/newshour/bb/cyberspace/july-dec97/cars.

18. Robert L. Simison, "Auto Dealers Drop Their Old Tactics to Fight New Rivals," *Wall Street Journal*, 12 February 1996, 2.

19. Alex Taylor, "How to Buy a Car on the Internet and Other New Ways to Make the Second Biggest Purchase of a Lifetime," *Fortune*, 4 March 1996, 165; see also John Greenwald, "Buying a Car Without the Old Hassles," *Time*, 18 March 1996.

20. For example, see Michelle Slatalla, "Cruising the Great Car Lot of the Web," *New York Times*, 27 July 2006, 6.

21. James A. Willingham, "Internetworking," *Automotive Executive*, December 1999, 9; Mary Anne Shreve, "From Retail to e-Tail," *Automotive Executive*, December 1999, 28–29.

22. Saul Hansell, "G.M. Proposes an Online Site for Car Sales," *New York Times*, 12 August 2000, 1.

23. Amy Dunkin, "Buying a Car? Take a Spin on the Net," *Business Week*, 28 July 1997, 106–107.

24. Helen Kahn, "Mastering the Web," *Automotive Executive*, February 1999, 25; "Selling to 'Road Scholars,'" *Automotive Executive*, November 1998, 33.

25. Larry Armstrong, "Downloading Their Dream Cars," *Business Week*, 9 March 1998, 93–94; Matt Nauman, "Ford, Dealers Will Go Online," *San Jose Mercury News*, 26 August 2000, C1.

26. Mary Anne Shreve, "Third-Party Problems," *AutoExec*, December 2000, 34–37.

27. Shreve, "Third-Party Problems."

28. Solman, "Virtual Showroom."

29. David Stipp and Henry Goldblatt, "The Birth of Digital Commerce," *Fortune*, 9 December 1996, 159–64; Edward O. Welles, "Burning Down the House," *Inc.*, August 1997, 66–72.

30. Welles, "Burning Down the House"; see also Frank S. Washington, "Consumers in Command with Internet," *Automotive News*, 19 January 1998.

31. Laurie Freeman, "Auto-by-Tel," *Advertising Age*, 26 June 1998, 16; Welles, "Burning Down the House"; Steve Kichen, "Cruising the Internet," *Forbes*, 24 March 1997, 198–99.

32. Edward Harris, "Web Car Shopping Puts Buyers in Driver's Seat," *Wall Street Journal*, 15 April 1999, 10.

33. Fara Warner, "Racing for Slice of a $350–Billion Pie," *Wall Street Journal*, 24 January 2000, 1; idem, "Car Race in Cyberspace," *Wall Street Journal*, 18 February 1999, 1; Ripley Hotch, "Netting Rewards," *Automotive Executive*, October 1999, 22–24.

34. Shreve, "Third-Party Problems"; David F. Hyatt, *Franchise Laws in the Age of the*

Internet (McClean, VA: National Automobile Dealers Association, 2001); Mary Anne Shreve, "Net Gain," *AutoExec*, April 2001, 30–33; Tara Baukus Mello, "10 Tips to Igniting Online Sales," *AutoExec*, July 2002, 24–29.

35. Eric Young, "Who's in the Driver's Seat?" *Newsweek*, 19 March 2001, 62.

36. Shreve, "Third-Party Problems"; Keith Naughton and Joan Raymond, "Click Here for a New Sedan! (Not Yet, Alas)," *Newsweek*, 11 November 2002, 10–12.

37. Jeff Bennett, "Dealerships Still Key for Online Car Shopping," *San Jose Mercury News*, 23 October 2000, E12; Matt Nauman, "Automakers, Dealers See Web Car-Buying Sites in Retreat," *San Jose Mercury News*, 1 December 2000, c: 4; Bob Tedeschi, "Online Sites Grow up as Buyers and Sellers Become Beneficiaries," *New York Times*, 26 October 2005, 13.

38. Catherine Greenman, "Female Car Buyers Turn to Low-Key Web," *San Jose Mercury News*, 10 January 2001, business: 3; Florian Zettelmeyer, Fiona Scott Morton, and Jorge Silva-Risso, "How the Internet Lowers Prices: Evidence from Matched Survey and Automobile Transaction Data," *Journal of Marketing Research* 43 (May 2006): 168–81.

39. "Deals on Wheels"; see also Michelle Slatalla, "Why Kick the Tires? Just Click the Mouse," *New York Times*, 4 April 2002, 4.

40. Shreve, "Third-Party Problems"; Peter Bohr, "Kicking the Tires Virtually," *Road and Track*, May 1998, 98–103; Stefan Theil, "George Jetson's Car Lot," *Newsweek*, 30 October 2000, 90; Chandler Phillips, "Confessions of a Car Salesman," 2004, part 8: parting shots, Edmunds.Com, retrieved 12/9/2004 from www.edmunds.com/advice/buying/articles/42962/.

41. Guy Kawasaki, "Why Newspapers Are in Trouble," *Forbes*, February 1998, 102; Tara Baukus Mello, "Used to the Net," *Automotive Executive*, September 1999, 26–27; Matt Nauman, "A Click That Might Stick," *San Jose Mercury News*, 18 May 2001, D1; Gregory Jordan, "The Internet; Online Used Car Lots That Cover the Nation," *New York Times*, 22 October 2003, 13; Lisa Kalis and Dana White, "Kicking the Tires from Afar and Online," *New York Times*, 13 August 2004, 10.

42. Janet Adamy, "E-Tailers Can Peg Prices Depending on Who's Buying," *San Jose Mercury News*, 24 September 2000, F1; Walter Kirn, "The End of Shopping," *New York Times Magazine*, 4 December 2005, 17.

Index

Abbott and Costello, 130
Abelson, Elaine, 37
advertising, automobile, 98, 100; bait-and-switch, 102, 103, 127; blitz, 102, 104, 105; classified, 43, 68, 82; code of ethics for, 103–5; critics of, 105; deception in, 93, 102–5; lifestyle promotion as basis for, 1–2; list prices as part of, 56–62; for used cars, 81–82
advertising: and branding, 40; for carriages, 30; aimed at women, 40
African Americans: as car buyers, 144–45; and retailing, 38
Akerlof, George, 112
American Motors, 51
Ansonia Motor Car Company, 68
antitrust laws, 47
Armstrong, Denny, 146–47
Autobytel, 170
Automobile Information Disclosure Act (Monroney Act), 106–7, 108
automotive exceptionalism, 2–3, 15
AutoNation, 66–67
Avis, 65–66
Ayres, Ian, 145

Bacon, Les, 130
Baker, Russell, 113–14
barefoot pilgrims, 119, 168
bargaining, 2–3, 164; advice on, 145–48; by African Americans, 144–45; as applied to horse trading, 6–7; between car salesmen and prospective buyers, 118, 127–28, 138–48, 163, 173–74; persistence of, 173–74; as psychological game,

139–48; by women, 144, 159–60. See also pricing
Barlow, Uncle Ike, 17
barn traders, 11, 64
bartering, 6–7
Bean, Jonathan, 55
Better Business Bureau (BBB), 103–5, 143
bicycles, 30–33; as trade-ins, 68; and women, 32–33
bird dogging, 120–21
bishoping, 20
blitz advertising, 102–5
blue book values, 74–75
Bon Marché, 37, 39
Boone, W. J., 80
boot, 14
bootlegging. See gray market
Boucicaut, Aristide, 39
Brandeis, Louis D., 53
branding, 40
Browne, Joy, 79
Brun, L. J., 147

Calder, Lendol, 96
car brokers, 148–50
car buying: advice on, 143, 145–48; and car brokers, 148–50; chauffeur's role in, 43–44; as compared with horse trading, 43, 48, 51; by ethnic minorities, 144–45; history of, 3, 48–51; on the Internet, 61–62, 66, 166–72; negotiations involved in, 2–3, 41–42, 53–54; retail model applied to, 44–48; and single-pricing, 41–42; and women, 154–63. See also bargaining; used cars

car dealers: and car manufacturers, 42,
46–48, 98–101; codes of ethics for,
132–33; as compared with horse traders,
42–43, 48, 172, 174; during the Depression, 54; driving lessons offered by, 46;
and fair trade laws, 51–53, 55–56; fees
tacked on by, 57; government regulation
of, 51–53, 54–56, 97, 106–7, 108, 111;
and the Internet, 61–62; perceptions of,
48–49, 99, 114, 129–36; price-cutting by,
51–56, 100
Carfax, 86
car manufacturers: antitrust laws as applied
to, 47; and car dealers, 42, 46–48, 98–101;
list prices set by, 49–51, 52
CarMax, 66
Car/Puter, 166
Carr, Gary, 141
carriages, 29–31
cars: additional dealer markup on, 58; electric, 155–56; financing of, 95–98; list
prices for, 56–62; gray market for, 56, 90,
100–101, 172; maintenance of, 46; male
identification with, 150–54; marketing of,
1–2, 42; mass production of, 45; posted
pricing for, 94, 106–9, 123, 165–66;
retailing of, 44–48; shortage of during
World War II, 78, 89; single-pricing for,
41–42, 52, 59–60, 173; technical aspects
of, 157–58; value pricing for, 60–61; warranties for, 109–14; wholesale prices of,
165–66. *See also* advertising, automobile;
price pack; used cars
car sellers: career path of, 115–19, 135–36;
certification for, 133, 135; compensation
for, 115–16, 125–26; deceptions practiced
by, 134–35; expectations of, 119–20; and
Hull-Dobbs system, 126–27, 128, 142,
145; inside report on, 136–37; jargon
used by, 136; as male-dominated field,
135–36; manufacturers' courses for, 117;
reputation of, 129–36; robots as, 132,
167; tactics and strategies of, 119–29;
training for, 117–18, 136; for used cars,
129–31. *See also* car dealers
Caruso, H. J., 127

catalog sales of bicycles, 33
caveat emptor, 26–28; and used-car sales,
111–12
Chalmers Torpedo, 155
Chamberlain Associates, 74
chauffeurs, 43–44
Cheever, Benjamin, 127
Chrysler, 109; and price packing, 93; war-
ranty offered by, 111
Cicero, 8
Circuit City, 66
Clarsen, Georgine, 155
classified advertising: for new cars, 43; for
used cars, 68, 82
Consumer Reports, 145, 146, 166
contracts, 27
copers, 21
Corn, Joseph, 150
Curtice, Harlow, 56, 57, 93
Curtis Publishing Company, 69
customers. *See* car buying

Dahl, Roald, 129
David Harum (Westcott), 17, 18, 28
David, Paul A., 3
Davis, Deane C., 18
department stores, 39–40; pricing at, 37
Depression: impact of, on car dealers, 54;
and used-car loss control, 72
Dickens, Charles, 5
disintermediation, 168
Dobbs, James, 126
Driver's Mart, 66
driving lessons, 46, 155

Eagal, John, 46, 138–39
Earl, Harley J., 98
Eden, Patience, 159
Edmonds.com, 136–37
Edsel, 150–51
Eisenhower, Dwight, 99
Ellis, Peter, 170
Emdee, Florence, 161

Fabulous Sam, 130–31
fair trade laws, 51–53, 55–56

Federal Trade Commission (FTC), 55, 57, 70, 85, 106; and blue book values, 75; and used-car price controls, 76, 77; and used-car sales, 113–14
financing, automobile, 95–98
Flink, James, 99
Ford, Henry, 91, 96
Ford Model A, 91
Ford Model T, 42, 45, 91
Ford Motor Company, 45–46, 101; and blitz advertising, 104; and car dealers, 47–48, 50–51; and price-cutting, 53; and price packing, 91–92; rebates offered by, 51; and trade-ins, 70, 112
Forester, Frank, 8
Fox, George, 34, 100
fragmentation, 42
Friedman, Walter, 42, 116

Ganzi Licata, Paula, 159
Garvey, Ellen Gruber, 40
gender: as aspect of horse trading, 4, 6–7, 11–12, 23, 174; as factor in car buying, 149, 150–63, 174. *See also* male culture; women
General Motors, 42, 56; financing subsidiary of, 96; and price-cutting, 53–54; and price packing, 93; and trade-ins, 70–71. *See also* Saturn
Gillette, King Camp, 94
Girard, Joe, 117
glanders, 21
Glengarry, Glen Ross (Mamet), 116
Goldsmith, Vic, 123
government regulation: of the automobile industry, 51–53, 54–56, 97, 106–7, 108; of used-car sales, 113–14
gray market (bootlegging), 56, 90, 100–101, 172
guaranty policies, 39–40
Gypsies, 10, 82

Hale, Louise Closser, 152, 154–55
Hall, O. Z., 165
Hamilton, Walton, 27
Heald College, 155

heaves, 7
Henry, Ed, 167–68
Herbert, William Henry, 8
Hertz, 65–66
highball, as sales technique, 121–22, 127
Holzer, Tony, 130
Honda, 132
horses: soundness of, 21, 22–23; as symbols of masculinity, 5–6; teeth as indicator of age, 20; as trade-in for cars, 138–39; trade-ins of, 64; and women, 5–6
horse traders: compared with car dealers, 42–43, 48, 174; reputation of, 8–10, 16–17; urban, 11
horse trading, 2, 25; advertising for, 19; as a business, 4, 10–11, 23–24; deceptions used in, 14–16, 18–21; folkways of, 22; as a game, 11–15; gendered aspects of, 4, 6–7, 11–12, 23; and Gypsies, 10; legal issues involving, 18, 22–23; morality of, 9–10, 15; popular culture of, 10–11; and religion, 9, 17; rules of, 15–18, 21–23; urban, 11; and used-car sales, 64, 71, 81, 86–87; warranties offered in, 21–23, 110; and whiskey, 12; with women, 7
Horwitz, Morton, 27
Huizenga, H. Wayne, 66–67
Hull, Horace, 126
Hull-Dobbs system, 126–27, 128, 142, 145
Hyater, John, 169
Hylton, John, 14

implied warranty, 25–26, 112
Internet, as medium for car sales, 61–62, 66, 166–72

Jefferson, Thomas, 14
Jenkins, "Po Boy," 11, 16
Jordan, Ned, 1, 156
Jung, Allen, 144

Keats, John, 98, 150
Kelley, Les, 74, 78
Kelley Blue Book, 74
Kennedy, John F., 129
Korean War, 99

Lallement, Pierre, 31
Lawson, Helene, 153, 161
Leach, William, 37
legal principles: and caveat emptor, 26–27;
    and horse trading, 18, 22–23; and implied
    warranty, 25–26
lemon laws, 111
lemons, 81–82
Light, Lois, 161–63
Lincoln, Abraham, 8, 13, 129
Longstreet, Augustus, 16
lowball, as sales technique, 121, 122, 127

Macy's, 37, 39
Main, Sailor, 102
male culture: car as symbolic of masculinity,
    150–54; horse trading as manifestation
    of, 11–13, 23
Mamet, David, 116
manufacturer's suggested retail price
    (MSRP), 2, 58, 79; as regulated by federal
    law, 106–7, 108–9
Marryat, Frederick, 6
Martin, Judith, 158
Mayer, Milton, 112
McIntyre, Stephen, 43–44
McKay, Douglas, 99–100
McNamara, Robert S., 104
merchantability, 27–28
Miller-Tydings Act of 1937, 55, 56
Monod, David, 36
Monroney, A. S. Mike, 103, 104, 106,
    140
Monroney Act, 106–7, 108, 172
Montgomery Ward, 33
MSRP. *See* manufacturer's suggested retail
    price
Muntz, Earl "Madman," 78, 102, 130

National Automobile Chamber of Com-
    merce, 72
National Automobile Dealers Association
    (NADA), 48, 54–55, 99, 118–19; and
    advertising code of ethics, 103, 132–33;
    and used-car sales, 69, 73, 74, 75, 76;
    Web site for, 169

National Independent Automobile Dealers
    Association (NIADA), 113, 131
National Industrial Recovery Act, 72
National Recovery Administration (NRA),
    price regulation by, 54–55, 72, 75, 76–77
National Used Car Dealers Association,
    131
Nixon, Richard, 129

odometer tampering, 84–86
Office of Price Administration (OPA), 58,
    78–79, 89
Official Used Car Guide (NADA), 76
over-allowances for used cars, 64–65, 70–73,
    87, 89; efforts to control, 73–79

Packard Motor Car Company, 68, 70
Palmer, Potter, 39
path dependence, 3
peddlers, 34–36
Peerless, 109
Penn Yan, PA, 9
Phillips, Chandler, 136–37, 141
Playboy (automobile), 1, 156
Pontiac, 91
Popular Science, 146
Power, J. D., III, 168
price packing, 88, 107–8, 168; and after-
    market add-ons, 94–98; attempts to
    regulate, 106–9; financing as part of,
    95–98; as price padding, 91–94
pricing: for cars, 46–62; at department
    stores, 37; negotiated, 34–36; single,
    25–26, 36–38. *See also* over-allowances

Quakers: as horse traders, 8–9; as retailers,
    37, 38

Ranney, Elliott, 50
Rayport, Jeffrey, 168
Reader's Digest, 145–46
rebates, 51
refund policies, 25–26, 39
religion, and horse trading, 9, 17
rental car firms, used-car sales by, 65
retail exceptionalism, 15

retailing: of bicycles, 32–33; of cars, 44–48; as distinguished from horse trading, 24; and refundability, 25–26, 39; and satisfaction guaranteed, 39–40; single-price, 25–26; and women, 36–37. *See also* car dealers
return policies, 39–40
Richberg, Donald, 55
roadsters, 1
road traders, 10–11, 64
Robinson-Patman Act of 1936, 55
robots, 132, 167
Rogers, Will, 28
Romney, George, 57, 141
Roosevelt, Franklin D., 54, 75
Royce, Michael, 147
Rubenstein, James, 42

Sahl, Mort, 150–51
salesmen. *See* car sellers
satisfaction, culture of, 26
Saturn, 65; single-pricing for, 41–42, 59–60
Scharff, Virginia, 152, 155
Sears Motor Buggy, 44–45
Sears Roebuck, 33; as car retailer, 44–45
segmentation, 42
Shore, Mike, 130
Siegelman, Peter, 145
Sloan, Alfred, 42
Slofs, Robert, 151
Smith, A. O., 73
Smith, Betty, 38
"snide" double-cross, 14–15
speedometers. *See* odometer tampering
spinners, 86
Stearns, Peter, 3
Stertz, Marc, 166
Stewart, Alexander T., 37
Stieglitz, Alfred, 6
Strasser, Susan, 26
Studebaker Company, 110, 164–65
Sutton, Remar, 147
Swiencicki, Mark, 37

Tappan, Arthur, 37
Tappan, Lewis, 37

Tedlow, Richard, 42
Testa, Trebatius, 8
Times Square Automobile Company, 43, 50
trade-ins. *See* over-allowances; under-allowances; used cars
Travelers, 10
Truth in Lending Act, 97
turn-overs (TOs), as sales technique, 122–25

under-allowances for used cars, 89, 90, 92
unification, 42
used-car dealers, 64–67
used cars, 62; advertising for, 81–82; classified ads for, 68, 82; clearinghouse proposed for, 69; as compared with horse trading, 64, 71, 81, 86–87; deceptive buyers and sellers of, 79–86; government regulation of, 113–14; on the Internet, 66, 171–72; junking of, 72–73; and male culture, 153; market for, 67–69; new-car dealers' concerns about, 67–69; and odometer tampering, 84–86; over-allowances for, 64–65, 70–79, 87; pricing of, 65–66, 74–79, 86–87; salesmen of, 129–31; as trade-ins, 63–64, 68–69, 70–73, 80–81; under-allowances for, 89, 90, 92; warranties for, 111–12; in the West, 78

Vallery, Clarence, 46
Veblen, Thorstein, 5–6

Wachs, Martin, 155
wagons, 29–30
Wanamaker, John, 37, 44
Wanamaker's, 37
warranties: for cars, 109–14; for horses, 21–23, 110; implied, 25–26, 112
Weith, Warren, 83
Wendt, Lloyd, 37
Westcott, Edward Noyes, 28
Wharton, Edith, 30, 155
whiskey, 12
wholesale prices, 166
Wilkie Buick, 102

Willys-Overland, 65

Wisconsin, business regulation in, 55

Wisconsin Automotive Trade Association, 78

women: advertising aimed at, 40; advice for, 160; bargaining by, 144; and bicycling, 32–33; and car brokers, 149; as car buyers, 154–61, 171; and carriages, 30; as car sellers, 161–62; and horses, 5–6; horse trading with, 7; and Internet car buying, 171; and retailing, 36–37; stereotypes of, 158–60

Woods, Allen, 130

World War II, car shortage during and after, 78, 89

World Wide Web. *See* Internet